D1507267

Level 2

STUDENT
BOOK

Units 1-8

LANGUAGE!® Live

VOYAGER SOPRIS
LEARNING®

Louisa Moats, Ed.D., Author

For a complete listing of copyright permission acknowledgements, please see p. 376.

Copyright 2015 Voyager Sopris Learning, Inc.
All rights reserved.

3 4 5 6 7   HPS   19 18 17 16

978-1-4916-9011-6
1-4916-9011-9
333358

No portion of this work may be reproduced or transmitted
by any means, electronic or mechanical, including photocopying
or recording, or by any information storage and retrieval system,
without the express written permission of the publisher.

Printed in the United States of America
Published and Distributed by

VOYAGER SOPRIS
LEARNING®

17855 Dallas Parkway, Suite 400 • Dallas, TX 75287 • 800-547-6747
www.voyagersopris.com

Table of Contents

Unit 1

Lesson 1 1
Lesson 2 7
Lesson 3 11
Lesson 4 12
Lesson 5 16
Lesson 6 17
Lesson 7 22
Lesson 8 26
Lesson 9 27
Lesson 10 30

Unit 2

Lesson 1 35
Lesson 2 42
Lesson 3 49
Lesson 4 50
Lesson 5 55
Lesson 6 57
Lesson 7 63
Lesson 8 66
Lesson 9 68
Lesson 10 70

Unit 3

Lesson 1 71
Lesson 2 82
Lesson 3 89
Lesson 4 90
Lesson 5 97
Lesson 6 99
Lesson 7 119
Lesson 8 124
Lesson 9 126
Lesson 10 140

Unit 4

Lesson 1 145
Lesson 2 154
Lesson 3 159
Lesson 4 161
Lesson 5 166
Lesson 6 167
Lesson 7 174
Lesson 8 177
Lesson 9 179
Lesson 10 184

Unit 5

Lesson 1 189
Lesson 2 197
Lesson 3 201
Lesson 4 203
Lesson 5 209
Lesson 6 210
Lesson 7 216
Lesson 8 218
Lesson 9 221
Lesson 10 225

Unit 6

Lesson 1 229
Lesson 2 235
Lesson 3 243
Lesson 4 246
Lesson 5 251
Lesson 6 252
Lesson 7 267
Lesson 8 269
Lesson 9 273
Lesson 10 280

Let's Focus: Excerpt from *Holes*

Content Focus
crime and punishment

Type of Text
literature

Author's Name _____

Author's Purpose _____

Big Ideas
Consider the following Big Idea questions. Write your answer for each question.

To what degree is our destiny within our control? Explain your answer.

_____

_____

Is punishment a pathway to rehabilitation and reformation? Explain your answer.

_____

_____

Narrative Preview Checklist: the excerpt from *Holes* on pages 3–6.

☐ Title: What clue does it provide about the passage?

☐ Pictures: What additional information is added here?

☐ Margin Information: What vocabulary is important to understand this story?

Enduring Understandings
After reading the text . . .

_____

_____

_____

_____

_____

Key Passage Vocabulary: Excerpt from *Holes*

Read each word. Write the word in column 3. Then, circle a number to rate your knowledge of the word.

Vocabulary	Part of Speech	Write the Word	Knowledge Rating
commit	(v)		0 1 2 3
dazed	(adj)		0 1 2 3
barren	(adj)		0 1 2 3
juvenile	(adj)		0 1 2 3
declare	(v)		0 1 2 3
premises	(n)		0 1 2 3
aware	(adj)		0 1 2 3
consist	(v)		0 1 2 3
avoid	(v)		0 1 2 3
vast	(adj)		0 1 2 3

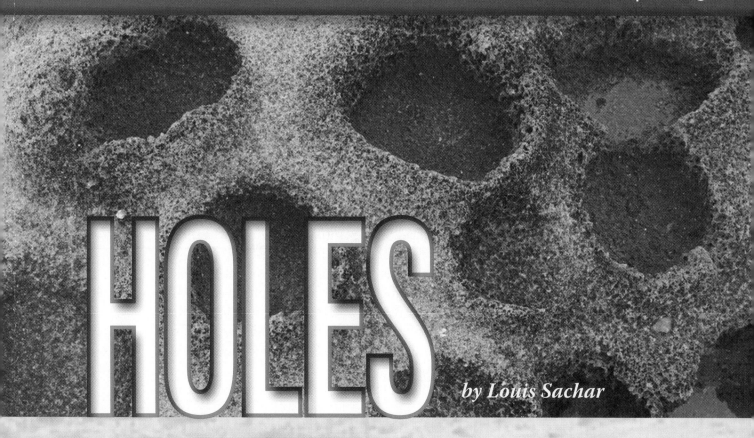

HOLES

by Louis Sachar

*Stanley Yelnats is an overweight kid from a poor family. And he's being punished for a crime he didn't **commit**. The judge gave him an option: Either go to jail or go to Camp Green Lake. So Stanley chose Camp*
5 *Green Lake. After a long, lonely ride on a bus with no air-conditioning, Stanley has arrived at camp. What he finds is nothing like what he expected.*

Stanley felt somewhat **dazed** as the guard unlocked his handcuffs and led him off the bus. He'd been on the
10 bus for over eight hours.

"Be careful," the bus driver said as Stanley walked down the steps.

Stanley wasn't sure if the bus driver meant for him to be careful going down the steps, or if he was telling
15 him to be careful at Camp Green Lake. "Thanks for the ride," he said. His mouth was dry and his throat hurt. He stepped onto the hard, dry dirt. There was a band of sweat around his wrist where the handcuff had been.

The land was **barren** and desolate. He could see a
20 few run-down buildings and some tents. Farther away there was a cabin beneath two tall trees. Those two trees were the only plant life he could see. There weren't even weeds. **1**

commit
to do something that is against the law or harmful

dazed
very confused and unable to think clearly

barren
without plant or animal life

1 What did Camp Green Lake look like?

juvenile

related to a person under 18 years of age

declare

to state something in a firm or official way

premises

the land and buildings owned by a person or company

aware

knowing something exists or is happening

2 Why is Stanley happy to enter the building?

3 Who do you think the new character is?

4 Why did the guard laugh?

5 Why does Stanley feel sorry for the guard and bus driver?

25 The guard led Stanley to a small building. A sign in front said, YOU ARE ENTERING CAMP GREEN LAKE **JUVENILE** CORRECTIONAL FACILITY. Next to it was another sign which **declared** that it was a violation of the Texas Penal Code to bring guns, explosives, weapons, drugs, or alcohol onto the **premises**.

30 As Stanley read the sign he couldn't help but think, *Well, duh!*

The guard led Stanley into the building, where he felt the welcome relief of air-conditioning. **2**

A man was sitting with his feet up on a desk. He
35 turned his head when Stanley and the guard entered, but otherwise didn't move. Even though he was inside, he wore sunglasses and a cowboy hat. He also held a can of soda, and the sight of it made Stanley even more **aware** of his own thirst.

40 He waited while the bus guard gave the man some papers to sign. **3**

"That's a lot of sunflower seeds," the bus guard said.

Stanley noticed a burlap sack filled with sunflower seeds on the floor next to the desk.

45 "I quit smoking last month," said the man in the cowboy hat. He had a tattoo of a rattlesnake on his arm, and as he signed his name, the snake's rattle seemed to wiggle. "I used to smoke a pack a day. Now I eat a sack of these every week."

50 The guard laughed. **4**

There must have been a small refrigerator behind his desk, because the man in the cowboy hat produced two more cans of soda. For a second Stanley hoped that one might be for him, but the man gave one to the guard and
55 said the other was for the driver.

"Nine hours here, and now nine hours back," the guard grumbled. "What a day."

Stanley thought about the long, miserable bus ride and felt a little sorry for the guard and the bus driver. **5**

60 The man in the cowboy hat spit sunflower seed shells into a wastepaper basket. Then he walked around the desk to Stanley. "My name is Mr. Sir," he said. "Whenever you speak to me you must call me by my name, is that clear?"

65 Stanley hesitated. "Uh, yes, Mr. Sir," he said, though he couldn't imagine that was really the man's name.

"You're not in the Girl Scouts anymore," Mr. Sir said. **6**

❖

Stanley had to remove his clothes in front of Mr. Sir, who made sure he wasn't hiding anything. He was then 70 given two sets of clothes and a towel. Each set **consisted** of a long-sleeve orange jumpsuit, an orange T-shirt, and yellow socks. Stanley wasn't sure if the socks had been yellow originally.

He was also given white sneakers, an orange cap, and 75 a canteen made of heavy plastic, which unfortunately was empty. The cap had a piece of cloth sewn on the back of it, for neck protection.

Stanley got dressed. The clothes smelled like soap.

Mr. Sir told him he should wear one set to work in 80 and one set for relaxation. Laundry was done every three days. On that day his work clothes would be washed. Then the other set would become his work clothes, and he would get clean clothes to wear while resting.

"You are to dig one hole each day, including Saturdays 85 and Sundays. Each hole must be five feet deep and five feet across in every direction. Your shovel is your measuring stick. Breakfast is served at 4:30." **7**

Stanley must have looked surprised, because Mr. Sir went on to explain that they started early to **avoid** the 90 hottest part of the day. "No one is going to baby-sit you," he added. "The longer it takes you to dig, the longer you will be out in the sun. If you dig up anything interesting, you are to report it to me or any other counselor. When you finish, the rest of the day is yours."

95 Stanley nodded to show he understood.

"This isn't a Girl Scout camp," said Mr. Sir.

He checked Stanley's backpack and allowed him to keep it. Then he led Stanley outside into the blazing heat.

"Take a good look around you," Mr. Sir said. "What 100 do you see?"

Stanley looked out across the **vast** wasteland. The air seemed thick with heat and dirt. "Not much," he said, then hastily added, "Mr. Sir."

Mr. Sir laughed. "You see any guard towers?"

105 "No."

consist
to be made up of

avoid
to stay away from something or someone

vast
extremely large

6 What kind of comment is this?

7 Predict the purpose of digging the holes.

"How about an electric fence?"

"No, Mr. Sir."

"There's no fence at all, is there?"

"No, Mr. Sir."

8 Why does Mr. Sir ask these questions?

110 "You want to run away?" Mr. Sir asked him. **8**

Stanley looked back at him, unsure what he meant.

"If you want to run away, go ahead, start running. I'm not going to stop you."

Stanley didn't know what kind of game Mr. Sir was

115 playing.

"I see you're looking at my gun. Don't worry. I'm not going to shoot you." He tapped his holster. "This is for yellow-spotted lizards. I wouldn't waste a bullet on you." **9**

9 How is Mr. Sir making Stanley feel?

120 "I'm not going to run away," Stanley said.

"Good thinking," said Mr. Sir. "Nobody runs away from here. We don't need a fence. Know why? Because we've got the only water for a hundred miles. You want to run away? You'll be buzzard food in three days."

125 Stanley could see some kids dressed in orange and carrying shovels dragging themselves toward the tents.

"You thirsty?" asked Mr. Sir.

"Yes, Mr. Sir," Stanley said gratefully.

"Well, you better get used to it. You're going

130 to be thirsty for the next eighteen months."

Louis Sachar says that while he usually starts a book by thinking about the characters, he wrote *Holes* by thinking about the setting first. "The story began with the place, and the characters and plot grew out of it," says Sachar. "At the time I began the book, we had just returned from the relative coolness of a vacation in Maine to the Texas summer. Anybody who has ever tried to do yard work in Texas in July can easily imagine Hell to be a place where you are required to dig a hole five feet deep and five feet across day after day under the brutal Texas sun." Into this searing landscape Sachar introduced Stanley Yelnats. "He's a kind of pathetic kid who feels like he has no friends, feels like his life is cursed. And I think everyone can identify with that in one way or another." Sachar was born in East Meadow, New York, in 1954. He now lives in Austin, Texas.

Nouns and Pronouns

Part A. Nouns

Read the following paragraph and circle all of the nouns. Write the proper nouns and plural noun below.

> Stanley wasn't sure if the bus driver meant for him to be careful going down the steps, or if he was telling him to be careful at Camp Green Lake. "Thanks for the ride," he said. His mouth was dry and his throat hurt. He stepped onto the hard, dry dirt. There was a band of sweat around his wrist where the handcuff had been.

Proper nouns: _____

Plural noun: _____

Part B. Pronouns

Pronouns take the place of nouns and can be found in different parts of sentences.

Pronouns							
Subject	I	you	he	she	it	we	they
Object	me	you	him	her	it	us	them

Read the following sentences and circle the pronouns.

1. He stepped onto the hard, dry dirt.

2. Stanley wasn't sure if the bus driver meant for him to be careful going down the steps, or if he was telling him to be careful at Camp Green Lake.

3. "I quit smoking last month," said the man in the cowboy hat.

4. Mr. Sir told him he should wear one set to work in and one set for relaxation.

5. "The longer it takes you to dig, the longer you will be out in the sun."

Action Verbs and Linking Verbs

Part A. Action Verbs

Read the following sentences and underline the action verb in each sentence.

1. He stepped onto the hard, dry dirt.

2. He checked Stanley's backpack and allowed him to keep it.

3. Then he led Stanley outside into the blazing heat.

4. Stanley looked out across the vast wasteland.

5. Nobody runs away from here.

Part B. Linking Verbs

| am | is | are | was | were |

Read the following sentences and underline the linking verb in each sentence.

1. His mouth was dry and his throat hurt.

2. The land was barren and desolate.

3. Farther away there was a cabin beneath two tall trees.

4. Those two trees were the only plant life he could see.

5. "You are to dig one hole each day, including Saturdays and Sundays."

Masterpiece Sentences: A Six-Stage Process

Stage	Process	Questions to Answer	Examples
Stage 1: Prepare Your Canvas	Choose a noun for the subject. Choose a verb for the predicate.	**Subject:** Who or what did it? **Predicate:** What did the subject do? What did the subject do it to?	The man chewed sunflower seeds
Stage 2: Paint Your Predicate	Tell more about what happened.	When? Where? How?	instead of smoking in his office constantly
Stage 3: Move Your Predicate Painters	Move the predicate painters to create a different sentence structure.		Instead of smoking, the man constantly chewed sunflower seeds in his office.
Stage 4: Paint Your Subject	Tell more about the subject.	Which one? What kind? How many?	mean-looking grouchy lone
Stage 5: Paint Your Words	Select words or phrases in your sentence and replace them with more descriptive words or phrases.		Instead of smoking, the lone, ~~grouchy~~, ~~mean-looking~~ man constantly chewed sunflower seeds in his office.
Stage 6: Finishing Touches	Finalize sentence structure; check spelling and punctuation.		Instead of smoking, the lone irritable man who had an icy stare constantly chewed sunflower seeds in his office.

Stage 1

Use the following questions to create simple sentences about the characters in *Holes*.

Who did it?	What did they do?	Sentence

Who did it?	What did they do?	What did they do it to?	Sentence

Capitalization and Punctuation

Sentences begin with capital letters and end with a period, an exclamation point, or a question mark. Read the following paragraph and correct all capitalization and punctuation errors. Use the editing marks to make your corrections.

Editing Marks	
Capitalization	≡
Lowercase	/
Insert period	⊙

Example:

"be careful," the Bus driver said as stanley walked down the steps⊙

The Guard led stanley into the building, where he felt the welcome relief

of air-conditioning

A man was sitting with his feet up on a desk he turned his head when

stanley and the guard entered, but otherwise didn't move. Even though

he was inside, He wore sunglasses and a Cowboy hat. he also held a can

of soda, and the sight of it made stanley even more aware of his own

thirst

Critical Understandings: Question Words

How to Answer Questions

Question Words	How to Answer
If the question asks . . .	Your answer must include . . .
Who	information about a person or group
What	an action or name of a thing
When	a specific time, date, or event
Where	a general location or specific place

Respond to each question using complete sentences. Refer to the chart above to determine how to respond to each question.

1. Who is the juvenile camp resident?

_____

_____

_____

_____

2. What is Camp Green Lake Juvenile Correctional Facility?

_____

_____

_____

_____

3. Where is Camp Green Lake?

_____

_____

_____

_____

4. When does Stanley get to leave the Camp Green Lake premises?

_____

_____

_____

_____

Close Reading

Read the text.

Excerpt from *Holes*

Stanley Yelnats is an overweight kid from a poor family. And he's being punished for a crime he didn't **commit**. *The judge gave him an option: Either go to jail or go to Camp Green Lake. So Stanley chose Camp Green Lake. After a long, lonely ride on a bus with no air-conditioning, Stanley*
5 *has arrived at camp. What he finds is nothing like what he expected.*

Stanley felt somewhat **dazed** as the guard unlocked his handcuffs and led him off the bus. He'd been on the bus for over eight hours.

"Be careful," the bus driver said as Stanley walked down the steps.

Stanley wasn't sure if the bus driver meant for him to be careful going
10 down the steps, or if he was telling him to be careful at Camp Green Lake. "Thanks for the ride," he said. His mouth was dry and his throat hurt. He stepped onto the hard, dry dirt. There was a band of sweat around his wrist where the handcuff had been.

The land was **barren** and desolate. He could see a few run-down buildings
15 and some tents. Farther away there was a cabin beneath two tall trees. Those two trees were the only plant life he could see. There weren't even weeds.

Close Reading (*cont.*)

The guard led Stanley to a small building. A sign in front said, YOU ARE ENTERING CAMP GREEN LAKE **JUVENILE** CORRECTIONAL

20 FACILITY. Next to it was another sign which **declared** that it was a violation of the Texas Penal Code to bring guns, explosives, weapons, drugs, or alcohol onto the **premises**.

As Stanley read the sign he couldn't help but think, *Well, duh!*

The guard led Stanley into the building, where he felt the welcome relief

25 of air-conditioning.

A man was sitting with his feet up on a desk. He turned his head when Stanley and the guard entered, but otherwise didn't move. Even though he was inside, he wore sunglasses and a cowboy hat. He also held a can of soda, and the sight of it made Stanley even more **aware** of his own thirst.

30 He waited while the bus guard gave the man some papers to sign.

"That's a lot of sunflower seeds," the bus guard said.

Stanley noticed a burlap sack filled with sunflower seeds on the floor next to the desk.

"I quit smoking last month," said the man in the cowboy hat. He had a

35 tattoo of a rattlesnake on his arm, and as he signed his name, the snake's rattle seemed to wiggle. "I used to smoke a pack a day. Now I eat a sack of these every week."

The guard laughed.

There must have been a small refrigerator behind his desk, because the

40 man in the cowboy hat produced two more cans of soda. For a second Stanley hoped that one might be for him, but the man gave one to the guard and said the other was for the driver.

"Nine hours here, and now nine hours back," the guard grumbled. "What a day."

45 Stanley thought about the long, miserable bus ride and felt a little sorry for the guard and the bus driver.

The man in the cowboy hat spit sunflower seed shells into a wastepaper basket. Then he walked around the desk to Stanley. "My name is Mr. Sir," he said. "Whenever you speak to me you must call me by my name, is

50 that clear?"

Close Reading (*cont.*)

Stanley hesitated. "Uh, yes, Mr. Sir," he said, though he couldn't imagine that was really the man's name.

"You're not in the Girl Scouts anymore," Mr. Sir said.

Stanley had to remove his clothes in front of Mr. Sir, who made sure
55 he wasn't hiding anything. He was then given two sets of clothes and a towel. Each set **consisted** of a long-sleeve orange jumpsuit, an orange T-shirt, and yellow socks. Stanley wasn't sure if the socks had been yellow originally.

He was also given white sneakers, an orange cap, and a canteen made
60 of heavy plastic, which unfortunately was empty. The cap had a piece of cloth sewn on the back of it, for neck protection.

Stanley got dressed. The clothes smelled like soap.

Mr. Sir told him he should wear one set to work in and one set for relaxation. Laundry was done every three days. On that day his work
65 clothes would be washed. Then the other set would become his work clothes, and he would get clean clothes to wear while resting.

"You are to dig one hole each day, including Saturdays and Sundays. Each hole must be five feet deep and five feet across in every direction. Your shovel is your measuring stick. Breakfast is served at 4:30."

70 Stanley must have looked surprised, because Mr. Sir went on to explain that they started early to **avoid** the hottest part of the day. "No one is going to baby-sit you," he added. "The longer it takes you to dig, the longer you will be out in the sun. If you dig up anything interesting, you are to report it to me or any other counselor. When you finish, the rest of the
75 day is yours."

Stanley nodded to show he understood.

"This isn't a Girl Scout camp," said Mr. Sir.

He checked Stanley's backpack and allowed him to keep it. Then he led Stanley outside into the blazing heat.

Close Reading (*cont.*)

80 "Take a good look around you," Mr. Sir said. "What do you see?"

Stanley looked out across the **vast** wasteland. The air seemed thick with heat and dirt. "Not much," he said, then hastily added, "Mr. Sir."

Mr. Sir laughed. "You see any guard towers?"

"No."

85 "How about an electric fence?"

"No, Mr. Sir."

"There's no fence at all, is there?"

"No, Mr. Sir."

"You want to run away?" Mr. Sir asked him.

90 Stanley looked back at him, unsure what he meant.

"If you want to run away, go ahead, start running. I'm not going to stop you."

Stanley didn't know what kind of game Mr. Sir was playing.

"I see you're looking at my gun. Don't worry. I'm not going to shoot you."
95 He tapped his holster. "This is for yellow-spotted lizards. I wouldn't waste a bullet on you."

"I'm not going to run away," Stanley said.

"Good thinking," said Mr. Sir. "Nobody runs away from here. We don't need a fence. Know why? Because we've got the only water for a hundred
100 miles. You want to run away? You'll be buzzard food in three days."

Stanley could see some kids dressed in orange and carrying shovels dragging themselves toward the tents.

"You thirsty?" asked Mr. Sir.

"Yes, Mr. Sir," Stanley said gratefully.

105 "Well, you better get used to it. You're going to be thirsty for the next eighteen months."

Quick Write in Response to Reading

Imagine you are Stanley Yelnats and you are writing a letter to your parents about your first day at Camp Green Lake. First, describe the camp. Then, explain the daily routine. Finally, express your feelings about the camp. The greeting and closing have been provided. Remember to use first person (I, me) as you write the letter.

Dear Mom and Dad,

_____

_____

_____

_____

_____

_____

_____

_____

_____

_____

_____

_____

_____

_____

_____

_____

_____

_____

_____

_____

Love,
Stanley

Let's Focus: "The Science of Catching Criminals"

Content Focus
crime and punishment

Type of Text
informational

Author's Name _____

Author's Purpose _____

Big Ideas
Consider the following Big Idea questions. Write your answer for each question.

Is punishment always just?

_____

_____

How does science influence crime and punishment?

_____

_____

Informational Preview Checklist: "The Science of Catching Criminals" on pages 19 and 20.

☐ Title: What clue does it provide about the passage?

☐ Pictures and Captions: What additional information is added here?

☐ Headings: What topics will this text include?

☐ Margin Information: What vocabulary is important to understand this text?

☐ Maps, Charts, and Graphs: Are additional visuals present that will help me understand?

Enduring Understandings
After reading the text . . .

_____

_____

_____

_____

_____

_____

Key Passage Vocabulary: "The Science of Catching Criminals"

Read each word. Write the word in column 3. Then, circle a number to rate your knowledge of the word.

Vocabulary	Part of Speech	Write the Word	Knowledge Rating
evidence	(n)		0 1 2 3
fiber	(n)		0 1 2 3
innocence	(n)		0 1 2 3
convict	(v)		0 1 2 3
trace	(n)		0 1 2 3
preserve	(v)		0 1 2 3
identify	(v)		0 1 2 3
unique	(adj)		0 1 2 3
suspect	(n)		0 1 2 3
witness	(n)		0 1 2 3

The Science of Catching Criminals

In courts of law, the tiniest piece of **evidence** can bring a criminal to justice. Something as small as a **fiber** can connect a thief to a burglary. The science used to show a person's guilt or **innocence** is called forensics.

5 A forensic team is made up of different people. Some work at the crime scene itself. Others work in labs to study the evidence. All of them have the same goal: to use evidence to catch and **convict** a criminal.

At the Crime Scene

Anyone who commits a crime leaves evidence behind.
10 He or she may try to clean up, but usually some **trace** remains. It could be a fingerprint or a shoe print. It might be a bit of blood or skin. It may be a hair or thread. **1**

For this reason, a forensic investigation starts at the crime scene. First, police investigators **preserve** the scene.
15 They seal it off to make sure nobody changes it. Then, they gather evidence. Because evidence can be very small, the investigators must be very careful. They use special tools to scan every inch. They place tiny samples in clean containers. Even dust, pollen, or seeds can help break a
20 case. The examiners try not to overlook anything.

evidence
something that shows another thing happened or is true

fiber
a thin thread

innocence
the state of not being guilty

convict
to find someone guilty in a court of law

trace
a small sign that someone or something was present

preserve
to keep something the way it is

1 How can trace evidence lead to conviction of a criminal?

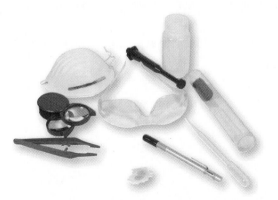

identify

to recognize; to match with a person or name

unique

one of a kind; different from all others

suspect

a person who police think may be guilty of a crime

witness

a person who saw something happen

2 Where can DNA be found?

3 What trace evidence was used to convict Buell?

4 The Ford Heights Four spent many years in prison and thought they were going to be killed. How would you feel if you were wrongly convicted of a terrible crime?

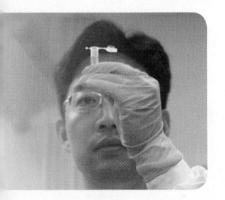

Back at the Lab

Once collected, the evidence is sent to a special lab. There, forensic scientists study it closely. They put it under microscopes. They run tests on it. They learn what it is made of and where it came from. If a piece
25 of evidence is from a human body, the scientists can **identify** its DNA.

All living things have DNA. It is in every cell of a person's body. It tells the cells how to grow. When blood, skin, or hair is left at a crime scene, the person's DNA is
30 left there too. Each person's DNA is **unique**, just like a fingerprint. If the DNA in a piece of evidence matches the DNA in a blood sample from a **suspect**, it can be evidence of guilt. If it doesn't, it can be evidence of innocence. **2**

The Power of Forensic Science

35 Whether it's a speck of fuzz or human blood, forensic evidence can make or break a case. Here are a couple of examples.

In 1982, orange fibers were found on the body of a murder victim in Ohio. Forensic scientists concluded that
40 they were carpet fibers from a van. Later, a woman was kidnapped by a man named Robert Anthony Buell, but she escaped and reported him to the police. Investigators learned that Buell had a van with orange carpeting. They took samples of the fibers for analysis. The fibers from
45 the van carpet matched the fibers on the victim. Buell was proven guilty. **3**

In another famous case, four men were convicted of a murder in Illinois. This crime happened before DNA testing could be done. The ruling was based on the
50 report of a **witness** who said she had seen the crime. The men were sentenced to a very long time in prison. Two were put on Death Row. Later, the witness confessed that her report had been a lie. By this time, DNA testing had been developed. It was used to show that the Ford
55 Heights Four were innocent and that another man was guilty.

Thanks to forensic science, justice was served. **4**

Summarize with IVF Topic Sentences

Write an IVF Topic Sentence for each section of the text and the text as a whole.

I (Identify the item)	V (select Verb)	F (Finish your thought)

Verb Bank

explains	tells	shows	provides	presents
describes	gives	compares	lists	teaches

Possessive Nouns

Singular possessive noun: add **'s** to show ownership or possession

> **Example:** The **man's** name was Mr. Sir.

Plural possessive noun: add **s'** to show ownership or possession

> **Example:** The **boys'** shovels served as measuring sticks.

Part A

Read the sentences and underline the possessive nouns. Write an S above the singular possessive nouns and a P above the plural possessive nouns.

1. As he signed his name, the snake's rattle on his tattoo seemed to wiggle.

2. He checked Stanley's backpack and allowed him to keep it.

3. Science is often used in courts of law to help prove a person's guilt or innocence.

4. The killers' DNA led to their convictions.

5. Each person's DNA is unique.

Part B

Rewrite the sentence, changing the underlined phrase to include a possessive noun.

> **Example:** The <u>sunglasses that belonged to the guard</u> were dark and shiny.
> The guard's sunglasses were dark and shiny.

1. <u>The jumpsuit that belonged to Stanley</u> was orange.

   _____

2. <u>The testimony of the eyewitness</u> was false.

   _____

3. Investigators often find <u>fingerprints that belong to criminals</u> at the scene of a crime.

   _____

4. <u>The attention of police investigators</u> to detail can often lead to solving a crime.

   _____

5. Fibers from <u>the carpet in the van</u> were used to catch a murderer.

   _____

Present and Past Tense Verbs

Read the following sentences and underline the verbs. Use the chart below the sentences to sort the verbs according to their tense: present or past.

Example: Forensic science <u>was</u> essential in solving the crime.

1. Investigators carefully preserve the crime scene.

2. They take samples of the evidence.

3. She is a victim of a crime.

4. Forensic scientists matched a man's fingerprint with the one from the crime scene.

5. The jury believed the false testimony.

Present Tense Verbs	Past Tense Verbs
	was

Masterpiece Sentences: Stage 1

Write a Stage 1 Masterpiece Sentence next to each picture. Answer three questions: Who or what? Did what? To what? Remember to capitalize and punctuate each sentence.

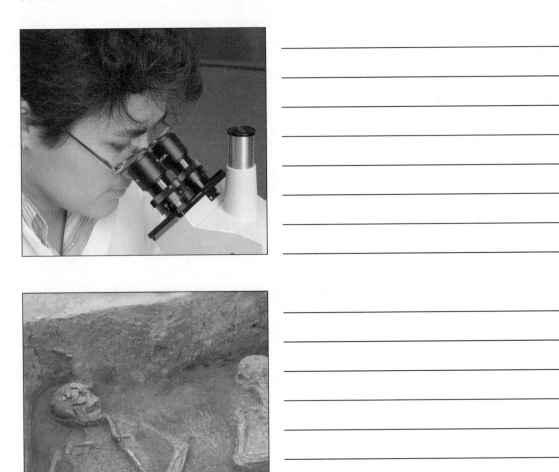

Sentence Structure

Part A. Simple Subject and Simple Predicate

Read the following sentences and underline the simple subject (who or what) once. Underline the simple predicate (did what) twice.

1. The tiniest bit of evidence may bring a criminal to justice.

2. Because such small bits of evidence can be important, police investigators are very attentive.

3. Investigators carefully preserve the crime scene, looking for these things.

4. Forensic scientists matched a man's fingerprint with the one found at the crime scene.

5. The fibers from the van carpet matched the fibers on the victim.

Part B. Subject-Verb Agreement

Singular subject nouns require a singular verb. Plural subject nouns require a plural verb. Look at the following examples.

> **Examples:**
> **Singular subject noun:** The **investigator** *takes* samples.
> **Plural subject noun:** The **investigators** *take* samples.

Tip: If the noun is singular, the verb needs an -s. If the noun is plural, the verb doesn't need an -s. You only need one -s in each sentence!

For each sentence, rewrite the subject noun and verb. If it is a singular noun, make it plural. If it is a plural noun, make it singular.

> **Examples:**
> The **investigators** *look* for evidence.   The **investigator** *looks* for evidence.
> The **scientist** *examines* the blood.   The **scientists** *examine* the blood.

1. The fiber matches the victim. _____

2. Policemen discover a van. _____

3. The boy claims to be an eyewitness. _____

4. The tests prove their innocence. _____

5. Criminals leave evidence at a crime scene. _____

Passage Comprehension

How to Answer Questions

Question Words	How to Answer
If the question asks . . .	Your answer must include . . .
Who	information about a person or group
What	an action or name of a thing
When	a specific time, date, or event
Where	a general location or specific place

Respond to each question using complete sentences. Refer to the chart above to determine how to respond to each question.

1. What examples of trace evidence are used to solve crimes?

_____

_____

_____

_____

2. When is DNA better evidence than an eyewitness?

_____

_____

_____

_____

3. Who is similar to Stanley Yelnats? Why?

_____

_____

_____

_____

4. When did the Ford Heights Four become different from Stanley Yelnats?

_____

_____

_____

_____

Close Reading

Read the text.

"The Science of Catching Criminals"

In courts of law, the tiniest piece of **evidence** can bring a criminal to justice. Something as small as a **fiber** can connect a thief to a burglary. The science used to show a person's guilt or **innocence** is called forensics. A forensic team is made up of different people. Some work at the crime scene itself. Others work in labs
5 to study the evidence. All of them have the same goal: to use evidence to catch and **convict** a criminal.

At the Crime Scene

Anyone who commits a crime leaves evidence behind. He or she may try to clean up, but usually some **trace** remains. It could be a fingerprint or a shoe print. It might be a bit of blood or skin. It may be a hair or thread.

10 For this reason, a forensic investigation starts at the crime scene. First, police investigators **preserve** the scene. They seal it off to make sure nobody changes it. Then, they gather evidence. Because evidence can be very small, the investigators must be very careful. They use special tools to scan every inch. They place tiny samples in clean containers. Even dust, pollen, or seeds can help break a case.
15 The examiners try not to overlook anything.

Close Reading (*cont.*)

Back at the Lab

Once collected, the evidence is sent to a special lab. There, forensic scientists study it closely. They put it under microscopes. They run tests on it. They learn what it is made of and where it came from. If a piece of evidence is from a human body, the scientists can **identify** its DNA.

20 All living things have DNA. It is in every cell of a person's body. It tells the cells how to grow. When blood, skin, or hair is left at a crime scene, the person's DNA is left there too. Each person's DNA is **unique**, just like a fingerprint. If the DNA in a piece of evidence matches the DNA in a blood sample from a **suspect**, it can be evidence of guilt. If it doesn't, it can be evidence of innocence.

- Define DNA: _____

_____

_____

_____

_____

_____

- Examples of evidence that include DNA: _____

_____

_____

Close Reading (*cont.*)

The Power of Forensic Science

25 Whether it's a speck of fuzz or human blood, forensic evidence can make or break a case. Here are a couple of examples.

In 1982, orange fibers were found on the body of a murder victim in Ohio. Forensic scientists concluded that they were carpet fibers from a van. Later, a woman was kidnapped by a man named Robert Anthony Buell, but she escaped
30 and reported him to the police. Investigators learned that Buell had a van with orange carpeting. They took samples of the fibers for analysis. The fibers from the van carpet matched the fibers on the victim. Buell was proven guilty.

In another famous case, four men were convicted of a murder in Illinois. This crime happened before DNA testing could be done. The ruling was based on the
35 report of a **witness** who said she had seen the crime. The men were sentenced to a very long time in prison. Two were put on Death Row. Later, the witness confessed that her report had been a lie. By this time, DNA testing had been developed. It was used to show that the Ford Heights Four were innocent and that another man was guilty.

40 Thanks to forensic science, justice was served.

Six Traits of Effective Writing

Trait	What does this mean?	Comments
Ideas and Content	Focus on the main ideas or story line. Supporting details (expository) or images/events (narrative) build understanding.	
Organization	Order of ideas and supporting details (expository) or clear beginning, middle, and end (narrative) make sense. Introduction, transitions, and conclusion help keep the reader hooked on the writing.	
Voice and Audience Awareness	Style suits both the audience and purpose of the writing.	
Word Choice	"Just right" words for the topic and audience	
Sentence Fluency	Varied sentence use; no run-on sentences and sentence fragments	
Conventions	Spelling, punctuation, grammar and usage, capitalization, and indenting paragraphs	

Editor's Marks

∧ add or change text
⊇ delete text
∽ move text
¶ new paragraph
≡ capitalize
/ lowercase
⊙ insert period
◯ check spelling or spell out word

Prepare to Write: Summary Paragraph

Part A. Study the Prompt

Read the prompt and circle the topic. Underline the instructions.

Write a paragraph that summarizes the text "The Science of Catching Criminals." Make sure to include examples in your paragraph.

Part B. Write the Topic Sentence

Write an IVF topic sentence for your summary paragraph.

_____

_____

_____

_____

_____

_____

Prepare to Write (*cont.*)

Part C. Two-Column Notes

Topic: _____	
Heading	**Important Facts**
At the Crime Scene	— —
Back at the Lab	— — —
The Power of Forensic Science	— —

Part D. Write the Concluding Sentence

Use the Number Topic Sentence pattern to write a concluding sentence for your summary paragraph. Answer the question *why* is it important?

_____

_____

_____

Topic Sentence Patterns

Write a topic sentence based on the content of "The Science of Catching Criminals" using each of the following patterns.

IVF Topic Sentence

Follow the three-step process for writing a topic sentence. Choose a verb that matches the purpose of the writing. Consider one of these verbs: explains, provides, reveals, exposes, describes.

I (Identify)	V (Choose a strong verb)	F (Finish the thought–big idea)
An article in the newspaper	explained	the suspicious circumstances surrounding the actor's death.

Sample topic sentence: An article in the newspaper explained the suspicious circumstances surrounding the actor's death.

New topic sentence: _____

_____

Number Topic Sentence

Use this kind of sentence if the written response can be quantified. Consider using specific number words, like *two* or *three*, or more general number words, like *several*, *some*, or *many*.

Number Word	Topic (what the paragraph will be about)
Several	suspicious circumstances surrounded the actor's death.

Sample topic sentence: Several suspicious circumstances surrounded the actor's death.

New topic sentence: _____

_____

The Writer's Checklist

Trait	Yes	No	Did the writer . . .?
Ideas and Content			focus all sentences on the topic
			provide supporting details for the topic sentence
Organization			write a topic sentence
			tell things in an order that makes sense
			write a concluding sentence
Voice and Audience Awareness			think about the audience and purpose for writing
Word Choice			try to find a unique way to say things
Sentence Fluency			write complete sentences
Conventions			capitalize words correctly:
			capitalize the first word of each sentence
			capitalize proper nouns, including people's names
			punctuate correctly:
			put a period or question mark at the end of each sentence
			use grammar correctly:
			use the correct verb tense
			make sure the verb agrees with the subject in number
			use correct spelling

Let's Focus: "Thank You, M'am"

Content Focus
forgiveness; empowerment

Type of Text
literature—short story

Author's Name _____ Author's Purpose _____

Big Ideas
Consider the following Big Idea questions. Write your answer for each question.

Can a brief, chance encounter make a lasting impact?

_____

_____

Do people always need to be punished for their crimes?

_____

_____

Narrative Preview Checklist: "Thank You, M'am" on pages 37–41.

☐ Title: What clue does it provide about the passage?

☐ Pictures: What additional information is added here?

☐ Margin Information: What vocabulary is important to understand this story?

Enduring Understandings
After reading the text . . .

_____

_____

_____

_____

_____

Key Passage Vocabulary: "Thank You, M'am"

Read each word. Write the word in column 3. Then, circle a number to rate your knowledge of the word.

Vocabulary	Part of Speech	Write the Word	Knowledge Rating
balance	(n)		0 1 2 3
permit	(v)		0 1 2 3
release	(v)		0 1 2 3
frail	(adj)		0 1 2 3
furnished	(adj)		0 1 2 3
suede	(n)		0 1 2 3
presentable	(adj)		0 1 2 3
embarrass	(v)		0 1 2 3
latch	(v)		0 1 2 3
stoop	(n)		0 1 2 3

Thank You, M'am

by Langston Hughes

She was a large woman with a large purse that had everything in it but a hammer and nails. It had a long strap, and she carried it slung across her shoulder. It was about eleven o'clock at night, dark, and she was walking
5 alone, when a boy ran up behind her and tried to snatch her purse. The strap broke with the single tug the boy gave it from behind. But the boy's weight and the weight of the purse combined caused him to lose his **balance**. Instead of taking off full blast as he had hoped, the boy
10 fell on his back on the sidewalk, and his legs flew up. The large woman simply turned around and kicked him right square in his blue-jeaned sitter. Then she reached down, picked the boy up by his shirtfront, and shook him until his teeth rattled. **1**

15 After that the woman said, "Pick up my pocketbook, boy, and give it here."

She still held him tightly. But she bent down enough to **permit** him to stoop and pick up her purse. Then she said, "Now ain't you ashamed of yourself?"

20 Firmly gripped by his shirtfront, the boy said, "Yes'm."

The woman said, "What did you want to do it for?"

The boy said, "I didn't aim to."

She said, "You a lie!"

balance
the ability to stay steady and not fall

permit
to allow

1 What do you think the lady will do next?

release
to let go of; to set free

frail
weak and easily broken

furnished
having furniture, appliances, or basic supplies

2 Where is the lady taking the boy?

3 Why does Mrs. Jones want the boy to remember her?

25   By that time two or three people passed, stopped, turned to look, and some stood watching.

"If I turn you loose, will you run?" asked the woman.

"Yes'm," said the boy.

"Then I won't turn you loose," said the woman. She 30 did not **release** him.

"Lady, I'm sorry," whispered the boy.

"Um-hum! Your face is dirty. I got a great mind to wash your face for you. Ain't you got nobody home to tell you to wash your face?"

35   "No'm," said the boy.

"Then it will get washed this evening," said the large woman, starting up the street, dragging the frightened boy behind her. **2**

He looked as if he were fourteen or fifteen, **frail** and 40 willow-wild, in tennis shoes and blue jeans.

The woman said, "You ought to be my son. I would teach you right from wrong. Least I can do right now is to wash your face. Are you hungry?"

"No'm," said the being-dragged boy. "I just want you 45 to turn me loose."

"Was I bothering *you* when I turned that corner?" asked the woman.

"No'm."

"But you put yourself in contact with *me*," said the 50 woman. "If you think that that contact is not going to last awhile, you got another thought coming. When I get through with you, sir, you are going to remember Mrs. Luella Bates Washington Jones." **3**

Sweat popped out on the boy's face and he began to 55 struggle. Mrs. Jones stopped, jerked him around in front of her, put a half-nelson about his neck, and continued to drag him up the street. When she got to her door, she dragged the boy inside, down a hall, and into a large kitchenette-**furnished** room at the rear of the house. She 60 switched on the light and left the door open. The boy could hear other roomers laughing and talking in the large house. Some of their doors were open, too, so he knew he and the woman were not alone. The woman still had him by the neck in the middle of her room.

65   She said, "What is your name?"

"Roger," answered the boy.

"Then, Roger, you go to that sink and wash your face," said the woman, whereupon she turned him loose—at last. Roger looked at the door—looked at the woman—
70   looked at the door—*and went to the sink.* **4**

"Let the water run until it gets warm," she said. "Here's a clean towel."

"You gonna take me to jail?" asked the boy, bending over the sink.

75   "Not with that face, I would not take you nowhere," said the woman. "Here I am trying to get home to cook me a bite to eat, and you snatch my pocketbook! Maybe you ain't been to your supper either, late as it be. Have you?"

80   "There's nobody home at my house," said the boy.

"Then we'll eat," said the woman, "I believe you're hungry—or been hungry—to try to snatch my pocketbook!"

"I wanted a pair of blue **suede** shoes," said the boy. **5**

85   "Well, you didn't have to snatch *my* pocketbook to get some suede shoes," said Mrs. Luella Bates Washington Jones. "You could of asked me."

"M'am?"

The water dripping from his face, the boy looked at
90   her. There was a long pause. A very long pause. After he had dried his face and not knowing what else to do dried it again, the boy turned around, wondering what next. The door was open. He could make a dash for it down the hall. He could run, run, run, run, *run*!

95   The woman was sitting on the daybed. After a while she said, "I were young once and I wanted things I could not get." **6**

There was another long pause. The boy's mouth opened. Then he frowned, not knowing he frowned.

100   The woman said, "Um-hum! You thought I was going to say *but*, didn't you? You thought I was going to say, *but I didn't snatch people's pocketbooks.* Well, I wasn't going to say that." Pause. Silence. "I have done things, too, which I would not tell you, son—neither tell God,
105   if He didn't already know. Everybody's got something in common. So you set down while I fix us something to eat. You might run that comb through your hair so you will look **presentable**."

suede
soft, velvety leather

presentable
fit to appear in public

4 Why didn't Roger run?

5 Was Roger stealing to get something he wants or something he needs?

6 What is Mrs. Jones trying to do?

embarrass
to make someone uncomfortable or ashamed

latch
to grip; to fasten onto

stoop
a small porch

7 Reread the last two sentences. What does this mean?

8 Why is Mrs. Jones being so nice to someone who tried to steal from her?

9 Is this how the story should have ended?

110 In another corner of the room behind a screen was a gas plate and an icebox. Mrs. Jones got up and went behind the screen. The woman did not watch the boy to see if he was going to run now, nor did she watch her purse, which she left behind her on the daybed. But the
115 boy took care to sit on the far side of the room, away from the purse, where he thought she could easily see him out of the corner of her eye if she wanted to. He did not trust the woman *not* to trust him. And he did not want to be mistrusted now. **7**

"Do you need somebody to go to the store," asked the
120 boy, "maybe to get some milk or something?"

"Don't believe I do," said the woman, "unless you just want sweet milk yourself. I was going to make cocoa out of this canned milk I got here."

"That will be fine," said the boy.

125 She heated some lima beans and ham she had in the icebox, made the cocoa, and set the table. The woman did not ask the boy anything about where he lived, or his folks, or anything else that would **embarrass** him. Instead, as they ate, she told him about her job in a
130 hotel beauty shop that stayed open late, what the work was like, and how all kinds of women came in and out, blondes, red-heads, and Spanish. Then she cut him a half of her ten-cent cake.

"Eat some more, son," she said. **8**

135 When they were finished eating, she got up and said, "Now, here, take this ten dollars and buy yourself some blue suede shoes. And next time, do not make the mistake of **latching** onto *my* pocketbook *nor nobody else's*—because shoes come by devilish like that will burn
140 your feet. I got to get my rest now. But from here on in, son, I hope you will behave yourself."

She led him down the hall to the front door and opened it. "Goodnight! Behave yourself, boy!" she said, looking out into the street as he went down the steps.

145 The boy wanted to say something else other than "Thank you, m'am" to Mrs. Luella Bates Washington Jones, but although his lips moved, he couldn't even say that as he turned at the foot of the barren **stoop** and looked up at the large woman in the door. Then she shut
150 the door. **9**

As a young child in the early 1900s, **James Mercer Langston Hughes** was sent to live with his grandmother in Kansas while his mother searched for work. It was a volatile time where nonwhite people like Hughes, who was mixed race and identified as black, were judged harshly for their skin color. He sought refuge from his poor living conditions in books and writing. ". . . it was that books began to happen to me, and I began to believe in nothing but books and the wonderful world in books—where if people suffered, they suffered in beautiful language, not in monosyllables, as we did in Kansas." It is most likely that "Thank You, M'am" was written as a tribute to those who helped him along the way with friendship and kindness. Hughes went on to be a great American writer and social activist for the black community in the United States. He often helped young writers of color with their work, giving advice and guiding them toward the right people in the publishing world.

Langston Hughes

Nouns

Job: Naming words that answer the *who* or *what* questions

Types of Nouns			
Concrete	**Abstract**	**Common**	**Proper**
stoop	balance	justice	Federal Bureau of Investigation
beans	goodness	beans	Alabama
purse	intelligence	purse	Nike

		Inflectional Ending	**Examples**
Singular	one	**none**	• book • table • chair • glass • patch • fox • child • goose • woman
Plural	more than one	**-s**	• books • tables • chairs
		-es	• glasses • patches • foxes
		irregular	• children • geese • women
Possessive	ownership	**'s** (singular)	• book's page • glass's edge • table's leg • patch's pattern • chair's cushion • fox's den
		' (plural)	• books' pages • glasses' edges • tables' legs • patches' patterns • chairs' cushions • foxes' tails
		's (plural irregular)	• children's toys • women's clothes • geese's feathers

Pronouns

Job: Take the place of nouns

Identify the type of pronouns in each section and label them in the chart. Then, write the plural forms of each pronoun type.

Types of Pronouns		
Person	**Singular**	**Plural**
First Person	I	
Second Person	you	
Third Person	he, she, it	
First Person	me	
Second Person	you	
Third Person	him, her, it	
First Person	my	
Second Person	your	
Third Person	his, her, its	

Tracking Pronouns

Read the paragraph and underline the subject, object, and possessive pronouns. In the parentheses under each pronoun, write the noun it replaced.

She was a large woman with a large purse that had everything in it but a
(   )   (   )

hammer and nails. It had a long strap, and she carried it slung across her
            (   )   (   )(   )

shoulder. It was about eleven o'clock at night, dark, and she was walking
          (   )   (   )

alone, when a boy ran up behind her and tried to snatch her purse. The
                            (   ) (   )

strap broke with the single tug the boy gave it from behind. But the boy's
                              (   )

weight and the weight of the purse combined caused him to lose
                                                    (   )

his balance. Instead of taking off full blast as he had hoped, the boy
(   )   (   )

fell on his back on the sidewalk, and his legs flew up. The large woman
(   )   (   )

simply turned around and kicked him right square in his blue-jeaned
                              (   ) (   )

sitter. Then she reached down, picked the boy up by his shirtfront, and
        (   )   (   )

shook him until his teeth rattled.
      (   )(   )

Verbs

Action Verbs: Describe actions that we can see and some that we cannot see
Linking Verbs: Connect or link the subject to a word or group of words in the predicate
Verb Tense: Signals time

Verbs	Yesterday	Today	Tomorrow
	Past	Present	Future
regular verbs	walked	walk(s)	
	matched	match(es)	
irregular verbs	sat	sit(s)	
linking verbs	was/were	am/is/are	

Underline the verb in each of the following sentences. Place check marks in the chart to identify each verb as action or linking and present or past tense.

Sentence	Type		Tense	
	Action	Linking	Present	Past
Ex: She <u>is</u> a large woman.		✓	✓	
She <u>heated</u> lima beans and ham on her stove.	✓			✓
1. There was another long pause.				
2. The boy's mouth opened.				
3. Then he frowned.				
4. Mrs. Jones got up and went behind the screen.				
5. "Now, here, take this ten dollars and buy yourself some blue suede shoes."				

Adverbs

Adverbs describe verbs by answering *when*, *where*, or *how* questions.

Read the following sentences and answer the questions about the underlined verbs. Then, write the adverbs in the chart below.

1. The boy's legs <u>flew</u> up. Flew where? _____

2. The boy <u>fell</u> back on the sidewalk. Fell how? _____

3. Then it <u>will get washed</u> soon. Will get washed when? _____

4. Roger <u>looked</u> down. Looked where? _____

5. There<u>'s</u> nobody there. Is where? _____

6. You gonna <u>hurt</u> me now? Hurt when? _____

7. The woman <u>was sitting</u> quietly. Was sitting how? _____

8. He barely <u>managed</u> to say "Thank you" before she shut the door. Managed how?

   _____

9. Sweat immediately <u>popped out</u> on the boy's face and he began to struggle. Popped out how?

   _____

10. Mrs. Jones stopped, <u>jerked</u> him forward, <u>put</u> a half-nelson about his neck tightly, and <u>dragged</u> him inside.

    Jerked where? _____

    Put how? _____

    Dragged where? _____

Adverbs			

Prepositions and Prepositional Phrases

A **preposition** is a connecting word that shows the position or relationship between two words in a sentence.

Common Prepositions		
at	by	for
from	in	of
on	to	with

Circle the prepositions and underline the prepositional phrase. Draw an arrow between the two words connected by the preposition.

Example: Sweat appeared (on) the boy's **face**.

1. **He** turned at the barren **stoop**.

2. The **water** dripped from his **face.**

3. **He** frowned for a **minute**.

4. **He** stood by the **door**.

5. She heated **food** on the hot **plate**.

Masterpiece Sentences: Predicate Painters

Use the predicate painter questions to expand the simple predicate in the following sentences.

1. The woman sat.

    Sat where? _____

    Sat when? _____

    Sat how? _____

    New sentence: _____

    _____

2. The boy lingered.

    Lingered where? _____

    Lingered when? _____

    Lingered how? _____

    New sentence: _____

    _____

3. The woman and the boy talk.

    Talk where? _____

    Talk when? _____

    Talk how? _____

    New sentence: _____

    _____

Critical Understandings: Question Words

How to Answer Questions

Question Words	How to Answer
If the question asks . . .	**Your answer must include . . .**
Why	a reason or explanation
How	the way something is done

Respond using complete sentences. Use the chart above to help you.

1. Why does Roger make contact with Mrs. Jones?

   _____

   _____

   _____

2. Why does Mrs. Jones feed Roger and have him clean himself up?

   _____

   _____

   _____

3. How does Mrs. Jones feel about stealing? Use the following quote to inform your answer: "shoes come by devilish like that will burn your feet."

   _____

   _____

   _____

   _____

4. How did Roger's character change over time? Provide evidence for your answer.

   _____

   _____

   _____

   _____

   _____

Close Reading

Read the text.

"Thank You, M'am"

She was a large woman with a large purse that had everything in it but a hammer and nails. It had a long strap, and she carried it slung across her shoulder. It was about eleven o'clock at night, dark, and she was walking alone, when a boy ran up behind her and tried to snatch her
5   purse. The strap broke with the single tug the boy gave it from behind. But the boy's weight and the weight of the purse combined caused him to lose his **balance**. Instead of taking off full blast as he had hoped, the boy fell on his back on the sidewalk, and his legs flew up. The large woman simply turned around and kicked him right square in his blue-jeaned
10 sitter. Then she reached down, picked the boy up by his shirtfront, and shook him until his teeth rattled.

After that the woman said, "Pick up my pocketbook, boy, and give it here."

She still held him tightly. But she bent down enough to **permit** him to stoop and pick up her purse. Then she said, "Now ain't you ashamed
15 of yourself?"

Firmly gripped by his shirtfront, the boy said, "Yes'm."

The woman said, "What did you want to do it for?"

The boy said, "I didn't aim to."

She said, "You a lie!"

Close Reading (*cont.*)

20 By that time two or three people passed, stopped, turned to look, and some stood watching.

"If I turn you loose, will you run?" asked the woman.

"Yes'm," said the boy.

"Then I won't turn you loose," said the woman. She did not **release** him.

25 "Lady, I'm sorry," whispered the boy.

"Um-hum! Your face is dirty. I got a great mind to wash your face for you. Ain't you got nobody home to tell you to wash your face?"

"No'm," said the boy.

"Then it will get washed this evening," said the large woman, starting up
30 the street, dragging the frightened boy behind her.

He looked as if he were fourteen or fifteen, **frail** and willow-wild, in tennis shoes and blue jeans.

The woman said, "You ought to be my son. I would teach you right from wrong. Least I can do right now is to wash your face. Are you hungry?"

35 "No'm," said the being-dragged boy. "I just want you to turn me loose."

"Was I bothering *you* when I turned that corner?" asked the woman.

"No'm."

"But you put yourself in contact with *me*," said the woman. "If you think that that contact is not going to last awhile, you got another thought
40 coming. When I get through with you, sir, you are going to remember Mrs. Luella Bates Washington Jones."

Close Reading (*cont.*)

Sweat popped out on the boy's face and he began to struggle. Mrs. Jones stopped, jerked him around in front of her, put a half-nelson about his neck, and continued to drag him up the street. When she got to her door,

45 she dragged the boy inside, down a hall, and into a large kitchenette-**furnished** room at the rear of the house. She switched on the light and left the door open. The boy could hear other roomers laughing and talking in the large house. Some of their doors were open, too, so he knew he and the woman were not alone. The woman still had him by the neck

50 in the middle of her room.

She said, "What is your name?"

"Roger," answered the boy.

"Then, Roger, you go to that sink and wash your face," said the woman, whereupon she turned him loose—at last. Roger looked at the door—

55 looked at the woman—looked at the door—*and went to the sink*.

"Let the water run until it gets warm," she said. "Here's a clean towel."

"You gonna take me to jail?" asked the boy, bending over the sink.

"Not with that face, I would not take you nowhere," said the woman. "Here I am trying to get home to cook me a bite to eat, and you snatch

60 my pocketbook! Maybe you ain't been to your supper either, late as it be. Have you?"

"There's nobody home at my house," said the boy.

"Then we'll eat," said the woman, "I believe you're hungry—or been hungry—to try to snatch my pocketbook!"

65 "I wanted a pair of blue **suede** shoes," said the boy.

"Well, you didn't have to snatch *my* pocketbook to get some suede shoes," said Mrs. Luella Bates Washington Jones. "You could of asked me."

"M'am?"

The water dripping from his face, the boy looked at her. There was a long

70 pause. A very long pause. After he had dried his face and not knowing what else to do, dried it again, the boy turned around, wondering what next. The door was open. He could make a dash for it down the hall. He could run, run, run, run, *run*!

Close Reading (*cont.*)

The woman was sitting on the daybed. After a while she said, "I were young
75 once and I wanted things I could not get."

There was another long pause. The boy's mouth opened. Then he frowned,
not knowing he frowned.

The woman said, "Um-hum! You thought I was going to say *but*, didn't you?
You thought I was going to say, *but I didn't snatch people's pocketbooks.*
80 Well, I wasn't going to say that." Pause. Silence. "I have done things, too,
which I would not tell you, son—neither tell God, if He didn't already know.
Everybody's got something in common. So you set down while I fix us
something to eat. You might run that comb through your hair so you will
look **presentable**."

85 In another corner of the room behind a screen was a gas plate and an
icebox. Mrs. Jones got up and went behind the screen. The woman did
not watch the boy to see if he was going to run now, nor did she watch
her purse, which she left behind her on the daybed. But the boy took care
to sit on the far side of the room, away from the purse, where he thought
90 she could easily see him out of the corner of her eye if she wanted to.
He did not trust the woman *not* to trust him. And he did not want to be
mistrusted now.

"Do you need somebody to go to the store," asked the boy, "maybe to get
some milk or something?"

95 "Don't believe I do," said the woman, "unless you just want sweet milk
yourself. I was going to make cocoa out of this canned milk I got here."

"That will be fine," said the boy.

She heated some lima beans and ham she had in the icebox, made the
cocoa, and set the table. The woman did not ask the boy anything about
100 where he lived, or his folks, or anything else that would **embarrass** him.
Instead, as they ate, she told him about her job in a hotel beauty shop that
stayed open late, what the work was like, and how all kinds of women came
in and out, blondes, red-heads, and Spanish. Then she cut him a half of her
ten-cent cake.

Close Reading (*cont.*)

105 "Eat some more, son," she said.

When they were finished eating, she got up and said, "Now, here, take this ten dollars and buy yourself some blue suede shoes. And next time, do not make the mistake of **latching** onto *my* pocketbook *nor nobody else's*—because shoes come by devilish like that will burn your feet. I

110 got to get my rest now. But from here on in, son, I hope you will behave yourself."

She led him down the hall to the front door and opened it. "Goodnight! Behave yourself, boy!" she said, looking out into the street as he went down the steps.

115 The boy wanted to say something else other than "Thank you, m'am" to Mrs. Luella Bates Washington Jones, but although his lips moved, he couldn't even say that as he turned at the foot of the barren **stoop** and looked up at the large woman in the door. Then she shut the door.

Quick Write Preparation

Part A. Paint the Subject

Generate a list of words that describe Mrs. Luella Bates Washington Jones.

_____

_____

Circle three traits that you can describe and include examples.

Part B. Write a Number Topic Sentence

Use the choices provided in the chart and develop a number topic sentence.

Number Word	Topic (what the paragraph will be about)
several	Describe Mrs. Luella Bates Washington Jones's character.
three	

Reminder: Do not start your sentence with "There are."

Topic Sentence:

_____

_____

Part C. Write an IVF Concluding Sentence

Rewrite your number topic sentence as an IVF sentence.

I (Identify the item.)	V (Select a verb.)	F (Finish your thought.)
Mrs. Luella Bates Washington Jones		(Rename the traits.)

Possible verb choices: embodies, embraces, illustrates, personifies, exemplifies, incorporates, combines

_____

_____

_____

Quick Write in Response to Reading

Write a paragraph that describes Mrs. Luella Bates Washington Jones. Focus on the kind of person she was as opposed to her physical features. Use the Number Topic sentence from page 55 and the IVF sentence as your concluding sentence. For each identified trait, provide an example from the text to illustrate it.

_____

_____

_____

_____

_____

_____

_____

_____

_____

_____

_____

_____

_____

_____

_____

_____

_____

_____

_____

_____

Let's Focus: "If I Were in Charge of the World"/"We Real Cool"

Content Focus
empowerment

Type of Text
literature—poetry

Authors' Names _____

Authors' Purposes _____

Big Ideas
Consider the following Big Idea questions. Write your answer for each question.

Are we in control of our lives? Why or why not?

_____

_____

To what degree do the choices we make as teens affect our futures? Explain.

_____

_____

Poetry Preview Checklist: "If I Were in Charge of the World" and "We Real Cool" on pages 59 and 60.

☐ Title: What clue does it provide about the poem?

☐ Pictures: What additional information is added here?

☐ Margin Information: What vocabulary is important to understand this poem?

☐ Form: What do you notice about the poem's length, shape, layout, punctuation?

Enduring Understandings
After reading the poems . . .

_____

_____

_____

_____

_____

Key Passage Vocabulary: "If I Were in Charge of the World" and "We Real Cool"

Read each word. Write the word in column 3. Then, circle a number to rate your knowledge of the word.

Vocabulary	Part of Speech	Write the Word	Knowledge Rating
charge	(n)		0 1 2 3
cancel	(v)		0 1 2 3
allergy	(n)		0 1 2 3
healthy	(adj)		0 1 2 3
lonely	(adj)		0 1 2 3
punch	(v)		0 1 2 3
allow	(v)		0 1 2 3
lurk	(v)		0 1 2 3
straight	(adv)		0 1 2 3
sin	(n)		0 1 2 3

If I Were In Charge of the World

by Judith Viorst

If I were in **charge** of the world
I'd **cancel** oatmeal,
Monday mornings,
Allergy shots, and also
5 Sara Steinberg.

If I were in charge of the world
There'd be brighter night lights,
Healthier hamsters, and
Basketball baskets forty-eight inches lower.

10 If I were in charge of the world
You wouldn't have **lonely**.
You wouldn't have clean.
You wouldn't have bedtimes.
Or "Don't **punch** your sister."
15 You wouldn't even have sisters.

If I were in charge of the world
A chocolate sundae with whipped cream and nuts
    would be a vegetable.
All 007 movies would be G.
20 And a person who sometimes forgot to brush,
And sometimes forgot to flush,
Would still be **allowed** to be
In charge of the world.

charge
the responsibility of managing or controlling something

cancel
to stop something from happening or existing

allergy
an illness from eating, breathing, or touching something

healthy
in a good state or condition

lonely
sad from being without the company of others

punch
to hit hard with a fist

allow
to let something happen

We Real Cool

by Gwendolyn Brooks

THE POOL PLAYERS. SEVEN AT THE GOLDEN SHOVEL.

lurk
to wait in secret; to hang out where you shouldn't be

straight
in a firm and direct way

sin
an offense against religious or moral law

We real cool. We
Left school. We

Lurk late. We
Strike straight. We

Sing sin. We
Thin gin. We

Jazz June. We
Die soon.

poetic justice

Judith Viorst is an accomplished author for adults and children alike. Her poetry for children and their parents, like *If I Were in Charge of the World*, is meant to make a deep connection to both age groups, even if it is a picture book. "Don't limit your vocabulary," Viorst says when asked what is something crucial children's authors ought to know. "Don't offer a bunch of goody-goody sentiments. And to the best of your ability, find the kid in you, the one who is speaking out of your own experience." This is perhaps why her writing is so relatable to people of all ages. In 2011, Viorst received the Foremother Award for Lifetime Achievement from the National Research Center for Women & Families.

Gwendolyn Brooks was a creative child, publishing her first poem when she was just thirteen years old. She used several forms of poetry, including sonnet and free verse. Brooks was conscious of the inequality of black authors and poets in the writing community and set out to be a social activist for her people through her creativity. "I don't want to stop a concern with words doing good jobs, which has always been a concern of mine, but I want to write poems that will be meaningful . . . things that will touch them." She didn't want her works to be seen as a solution to a problem, but instead something that makes the reader think about the problems people are facing and cause them to take action. Brooks became the first black woman to be appointed as the poetry consultant to the Library of Congress and the first black author to win the Pulitzer Prize.

Summarize with IVF Topic Sentences

Read "If I Were in Charge of the World" and "We Real Cool" on pages 59 and 60 with your partner. Write an IVF Topic Sentence for each poem.

I (Identify the item.)	V (Select a verb.)	F (Finish your thought.)

Verb Bank

explains	tells	shows	provides	presents
describes	gives	compares	lists	teaches

Masterpiece Sentences and Commas

Use your answers to the following questions to create sentences. Answer the predicate painter questions with prepositional phrases or adverbs. When the sentence begins with a prepositional phrase, it is followed by a comma.

Prepositional Phrase or Adverb When?	Subject Who?	Action Verb (past tense) Did what?	Direct Object To what?	Prepositional Phrase or Adverb Where?
After school	athletes	played	soccer	in the park
After school, athletes played soccer in the park.				

Prepositional Phrase or Adverb Where?	Subject What?	Action Verb (past tense) Did what?	Direct Object To what?	Prepositional Phrase or Adverb How?

Prepositional Phrase or Adverb Where?	Subject Who?	Action Verb (past tense) Did what?	Direct Object To what?	Prepositional Phrase or Adverb How?

Prepositional Phrase or Adverb When?	Subject What?	Action Verb (past tense) Did what?	Direct Object To what?	Prepositional Phrase or Adverb How?

Prepositional Phrase or Adverb When?	Subject Who?	Action Verb (present tense) Do what?	Direct Object To what?	Prepositional Phrase or Adverb Where?

Pronouns and Point of View

The position of the narrator in relation to other people and events in the story is called point of view. The point of view is often described in terms of first person, second person, or third person.

Person	Pronoun forms				Used when the narrator is . . .
First Person	I me my mine	we us our ours			Writing about him- or herself
Second Person	you your yours				Writing to explain something to someone
Third Person	she her hers	he him his	it it its	they them their theirs	Writing about a person, place, thing, or idea

"Thank You, M'am"

Point of View _____

Pronouns to Prove It: _____

"If I Were in Charge of the World"

Point of View _____

Pronouns to Prove It: _____

"We Real Cool"

Point of View _____

Pronouns to Prove It: _____

Elements of Poetry

Thought	Thought is the element that contains the poem's message. One component of thought is the theme, which is often stated as a universal truth—unlimited by time and space.
Imagery	Imagery refers to the poem's creation of mental pictures, or images, for the reader. Metaphor, simile, and personification are examples of techniques that poets use to create imagery.
Mood	Poems evoke emotions and set an atmosphere or a tone for the reader. This element is called mood.
Melody	Melody is the element created by a poet's use of sound. Alliteration, rhyme, assonance, consonance, and onomatopoeia are examples of devices used to create melody in poetry.
Meter	Patterns of stressed and unstressed syllables in a poem create meter or poetic rhythm.
Form	Form is the element that defines the poem's actual structure. Examples of poetic forms include quatrain, sonnet, blank verse, limerick, ballad, and free (open) verse.

Complete the chart below based on the poem "If I Were in Charge of the World."

"If I Were in Charge of the World"	
Thought	
Imagery	
Mood	
Melody	

Critical Understandings: Direction Words

Prompt	How to Respond	Model
If the prompt asks you to . . .	**The response requires you to . . .**	**For example . . .**
Analyze	break down and evaluate or draw conclusions about the information	**Analyze** the development of the text's central idea.
Assess	decide on the value, impact, or accuracy	**Assess** the level of pressure in an arranged marriage.
Compare	state the similarities between two or more things	**Compare** novels and dramas.
Contrast	state the difference between two or more things	**Contrast** a biography with an autobiography.
Create	make or produce something	**Create** a timeline of events.
Define	tell or write the meaning or definition	**Define** the unknown word using context clues.
Delineate	show or list evidence, claims, ideas, reasons, or events	**Delineate** the evidence in the text.
Describe	state detailed information about a topic	**Describe** the relationship between the plot and character development.
Determine	find out, verify, decide	**Determine** the main idea.
Distinguish	recognize or explain the differences	**Distinguish** between facts and opinions.
Evaluate	think carefully to make a judgment; form a critical opinion of	**Evaluate** the ANC's plan for change.
Explain	express understanding of an idea or concept	**Explain** how the author develops the narrator's point of view.
Identify	say or write what it is	**Identify** the character's motive.
Infer	provide a logical answer using evidence and prior knowledge	Use information from the text to **infer** the value of education.
Interpret	make sense of or assign meaning to something	**Interpret** the quote to confirm your understanding.
Paraphrase	say or write it using different words	**Paraphrase** the main idea.
Report	Tell or write about a topic	**Report** the main events of the setting.
Summarize	tell the most important ideas or concepts	**Summarize** the key details of the passage.
Tell	say or write specific information	**Tell** the date that the poem was written.
Use	apply information or a procedure	**Use** text features to identify the topic.

Passage Comprehension

Read the prompts and respond using complete sentences. Use the chart on page 66 to determine how to respond.

1. Use context to determine who the poems are about.

   _____

   _____

   _____

   _____

   _____

2. Empowerment and hopelessness are antonyms. Explain how these terms relate to each poem as well as the short story "Thank You, M'am."

   _____

   _____

   _____

   _____

   _____

   _____

   _____

   _____

   _____

3. Describe the setting in the poem "We Real Cool."

   _____

   _____

4. Explain how the choices that the pool players make will affect their lives.

   _____

   _____

   _____

5. Tell the things the author of "If I Were in Charge of the World" dislikes.

   _____

   _____

   _____

Close Reading

Read the text.

"If I Were in Charge of the World"

If I were in **charge** of the world
I'd **cancel** oatmeal,
Monday mornings,
Allergy shots, and also
5 Sara Steinberg.

If I were in charge of the world
There'd be brighter night lights,
Healthier hamsters, and
Basketball baskets forty-eight inches lower.

10 If I were in charge of the world
You wouldn't have **lonely**.
You wouldn't have clean.
You wouldn't have bedtimes.
Or "Don't **punch** your sister."
15 You wouldn't even have sisters.

If I were in charge of the world
A chocolate sundae with whipped cream and nuts
    would be a vegetable.
All 007 movies would be G.
20 And a person who sometimes forgot to brush,
And sometimes forgot to flush,
Would still be **allowed** to be
In charge of the world.

Close Reading (*cont.*)

> ### "We Real Cool"
>
> THE POOL PLAYERS. SEVEN AT THE GOLDEN SHOVEL.
>
> We real cool. We
> Left school. We
>
> **Lurk** late. We
> 5 Strike **straight**. We
>
> Sing **sin**. We
> Thin gin. We
>
> Jazz June. We
> Die soon.

Prepare to Write: Poetry

Part A. Study the Prompt

Read the prompt. Identify the directions and purpose for writing.

Imagine you are in charge of the world, and rewrite the poem "If I Were in Charge of the World" to reflect the changes you would make.

Directions: _____

Purpose for writing: _____

Part B. Analyze the Stanzas and Develop Ideas

First Stanza Focus
If I were in charge of the world
I'd cancel _____,
_____,
_____, and also _____.

Second Stanza Focus
If I were in charge of the world
There'd be _____,
_____, and
_____.

Third Stanza Focus
If I were in charge of the world
You wouldn't have _____.
You wouldn't have _____.
You wouldn't have _____.
Or "_____."
You wouldn't even have _____.

Fourth Stanza Focus
If I were in charge of the world
_____ would be a vegetable.
All _____.
And a person who sometimes _____,
And sometimes _____,
Would still be allowed to be
In charge of the world.

Let's Focus: Excerpt from *The Outsiders*

Content Focus
friendship; belonging

Type of Text
literature—novel

Author's Name _____   **Author's Purpose** _____

Big Ideas
Consider the following Big Idea questions. Write your answer for each question.

Do people have an innate need to fit in? Why or why not?

_____

_____

What is the effect of hatred between social groups?

_____

_____

Narrative Preview Checklist: the excerpt from *The Outsiders* on pages 74–81.

☐ Title: What clue does it provide about the passage?

☐ Pictures: What additional information is added here?

☐ Margin Information: What vocabulary is important to understand this story?

Enduring Understandings
After reading the text . . .

_____

_____

_____

_____

Key Passage Vocabulary: Excerpt from *The Outsiders*

Read each word. Write the word in column 3. Then, circle a number to rate your knowledge of the word.

Vocabulary	Part of Speech	Write the Word	Rate the Word
falter	(v)		0 1 2 3
abruptly	(adv)		0 1 2 3
resemblance	(n)		0 1 2 3
deserve	(v)		0 1 2 3
ornery	(adj)		0 1 2 3
casual	(adj)		0 1 2 3
possession	(n)		0 1 2 3
hesitation	(n)		0 1 2 3
strict	(adj)		0 1 2 3
deny	(v)		0 1 2 3

Story Map

Story Title *The Outsiders*

Introduction

Setting

_____

_____

_____

Characters

_____

_____

_____

Conflict (rising action)

Climax!

_____

_____

_____

_____

_____

_____

Dally goes to visit Johnny and Ponyboy at the church. Johnny is seriously injured and burned when he tries to save children from the church fire.

Johnny and Ponyboy hide out in an abandoned church.

Johnny kills one of the Socs because he was trying to drown Ponyboy.

The Socs go looking for Johnny and Ponyboy for being with their girls.

Johnny and Ponyboy, members of the greasers' gang, meet Socs' girlfriends at the movies.

Initiating Event _____

The Socs (short for Socials) attacked Johnny when he was sixteen. His friend Ponyboy is jumped by the Socs while walking home from the movies.

_____

_____

_____

Resolution

_____

_____

_____

_____

_____

Conclusion

_____

_____

_____

_____

_____

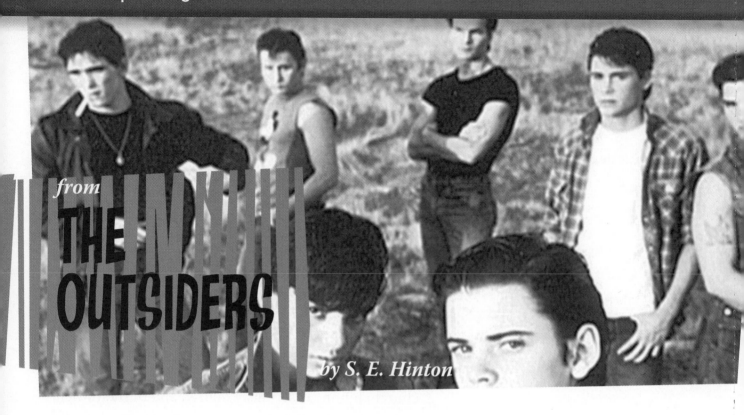

from

THE OUTSIDERS

by S. E. Hinton

*Clockwise, starting at top left:
Dallas, Two-Bit, Darry, Sodapop,
Steve, Ponyboy, and Johnny*

No one ever said life was easy. But Ponyboy is pretty sure that he's got things figured out. He knows that he can count on his brothers, Darry and Sodapop. And he knows that he can count on his friends—true friends
5 who would do anything for him, like Johnny and Two-Bit. And when it comes to the Socs—a vicious gang of rich kids who enjoy beating up on the "greasers" like him and his friends—he knows that he can count on them for trouble. But one night someone takes things too far, and
10 Ponyboy's world is turned upside down . . . **1**

1 What do you
think will
happen to
Ponyboy?

The nurses wouldn't let us see Johnny. He was in critical condition. No visitors. But Two-Bit wouldn't take no for an answer. That was his buddy in there and he aimed to see him. We both begged and pleaded, but we
15 were getting nowhere until the doctor found out what was going on.

"Let them go in," he said to the nurse. "He's been asking for them. It can't hurt now."

Two-Bit didn't notice the expression in his voice.
20 It's true, I thought numbly, he is dying. We went in, practically on tiptoe, because the quietness of the hospital scared us. Johnny was lying still, with his eyes

closed, but when Two-Bit said, "Hey, Johnnykid," he opened them and looked at us, trying to grin. "Hey, y'all."

25 The nurse, who was pulling the shades open, smiled and said, "So he can talk after all."

Two-Bit looked around. "They treatin' you okay, kid?"

"Don't . . ."—Johnny gasped—"don't let me put enough grease on my hair."

30 "Don't talk," Two-Bit said, pulling up a chair, "just listen. We'll bring you some hair grease next time. We're havin' the big rumble tonight."

Johnny's huge black eyes widened a little, but he didn't say anything.

35 "It's too bad you and Dally can't be in it. It's the first big rumble we've had—not countin' the time we whipped Shepard's outfit." **2**

"He came by," Johnny said.

"Tim Shepard?"

40 Johnny nodded. "Came to see Dally."

Tim and Dallas had always been buddies.

"Did you know you got your name in the paper for being a hero?"

Johnny almost grinned as he nodded. "Tuff

45 enough," he managed, and by the way his eyes were glowing, I figured Southern gentlemen had nothing on Johnny Cade.

I could see that even a few words were tiring him out; he was as pale as the pillow and looked awful. Two-Bit

50 pretended not to notice.

"You want anything besides hair grease, kid?"

Johnny barely nodded. "The book"—he looked at me—"can you get another one?"

Two-Bit looked at me too. I hadn't told him about

55 *Gone with the Wind*.

"He wants a copy of *Gone with the Wind* so I can read it to him," I explained. "You want to run down to the drugstore and get one?" **3**

"Okay," Two-Bit said cheerfully. "Don't y'all run off."

60 I sat down in Two-Bit's chair and tried to think of something to say. "Dally's gonna be okay," I said finally. "And Darry and me, we're okay now."

I knew Johnny understood what I meant. We had always been close buddies, and those lonely days in the

2 Why can't Johnny and Dally be in the rumble?

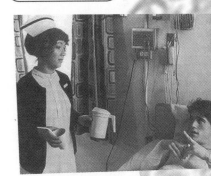

S. E. Hinton appeared as the nurse in the 1983 film version.

3 Why does Johnny want Ponyboy to read to him?

falter

to fade off or stumble; to lose confidence

65 church strengthened our friendship. He tried to smile again, and then suddenly went white and closed his eyes tight.

"Johnny!" I said, alarmed. "Are you okay?"

He nodded, keeping his eyes closed. "Yeah, it just

70 hurts sometimes. It usually don't... I can't feel anything below the middle of my back . . ."

He lay breathing heavily for a moment. "I'm pretty bad off, ain't I, Pony?"

"You'll be okay," I said with fake cheerfulness. "You

75 gotta be. We couldn't get along without you."

The truth of that last statement hit me. We couldn't get along without him. We needed Johnny as much as he needed the gang. And for the same reason.

"I won't be able to walk again," Johnny started, then

80 **faltered**. "Not even on crutches. Busted my back."

"You'll be okay," I repeated firmly. Don't start crying, I commanded myself, don't start crying, you'll scare Johnny.

"You want to know something, Ponyboy? I'm scared

85 stiff. I used to talk about killing myself . . ." He drew a quivering breath. "I don't want to die now. It ain't long enough. Sixteen years ain't long enough. I wouldn't mind it so much if there wasn't so much stuff I ain't done yet and so many things I ain't seen. It's not fair. You know

90 what? That time we were in Windrixville was the only time I've been away from our neighborhood." **4**

4 | Why does Johnny want to live?

"You ain't gonna die," I said, trying to hold my voice down. "And don't get juiced up, because the doc won't let us see you no more if you do."

95 Sixteen years on the streets and you can learn a lot. But all the wrong things, not the things you want to learn. Sixteen years on the streets and you see a lot. But all the wrong sights, not the sights you want to see.

Johnny closed his eyes and rested quietly for a

100 minute. Years of living on the East Side teaches you how to shut off your emotions. If you didn't, you would explode. You learn to cool it. **5**

5 | What likely happens on the East Side that makes them have to shut off their emotions?

A nurse appeared in the doorway. "Johnny," she said quietly, "your mother's here to see you."

105 Johnny opened his eyes. At first they were wide with surprise, then they darkened. "I don't want to see her," he said firmly. **6**

"She's your mother."

"I said I don't want to see her." His voice was rising.

110 "She's probably come to tell me about all the trouble I'm causing her and about how glad her and the old man'll be when I'm dead. Well, tell her to leave me alone. For once"—his voice broke—"for once just to leave me alone." He was struggling to sit up, but he suddenly gasped, went

115 whiter than the pillowcase, and passed out cold.

The nurse hurried me out the door. "I was afraid of something like this if he saw anyone."

I ran into Two-Bit, who was coming in.

"You can't see him now," the nurse said, so Two-Bit

120 handed her the book. "Make sure he can see it when he comes around." She took it and closed the door behind her. Two-Bit stood and looked at the door a long time. "I wish it was any one of us except Johnny," he said, and his voice was serious for once. "We could get along without

125 anyone but Johnny."

Turning **abruptly**, he said, "Let's go see Dallas."

As we walked out into the hall, we saw Johnny's mother. I knew her. She was a little woman, with straight black hair and big black eyes like Johnny's. But that was

130 as far as the **resemblance** went. Johnnycake's eyes were fearful and sensitive; hers were cheap and hard. As we passed her she was saying, "But I have a right to see him. He's my son. After all the trouble his father and I've gone to raise him, this is our reward! He'd rather see

135 those no-count hoodlums than his own folks . . ." She saw us and gave us such a look of hatred that I almost backed up. "It was your fault. Always running around in the middle of the night getting jailed and heaven knows what else . . ." I thought she was going to cuss us out. I

140 really did. **7**

abruptly
in a sudden or unexpected way

resemblance
a similarity, or likeness, between two things

6 What kind of relationship does Johnny have with his mother?

7 Who does Johnny's mom blame for his condition?

deserve

to earn something by your words or actions

ornery

grouchy and bad-tempered

8 What can you speculate about Ponyboy's mother?

Two-Bit's eyes got narrow and I was afraid he was going to start something. I don't like to hear women get sworn at, even if they **deserve** it. "No wonder he hates your guts," Two-Bit snapped. He was going to tell her off
145 real good, but I shoved him along. I felt sick. No wonder Johnny didn't want to see her. No wonder he stayed overnight at Two-Bit's or at our house, and slept in the vacant lot in good weather. I remembered my mother . . . beautiful and golden, like Soda, and wise and firm,
150 like Darry. **8**

"Oh, lordy!" There was a catch in Two-Bit's voice and he was closer to tears than I'd ever seen him. "He has to live with that."

We hurried to the elevator to get to the next floor.
155 I hoped the nurse would have enough sense not to let Johnny's mother see him. It would kill him.

Dally was arguing with one of the nurses when we came in. He grinned at us. "Man, am I glad to see you! These —— hospital people won't let me smoke, and I
160 want out!"

We sat down, grinning at each other. Dally was his usual mean, **ornery** self. He was okay.

"Shepard came by to see me a while ago."

"That's what Johnny said. What'd he want?"
165 "Said he saw my picture in the paper and couldn't believe it didn't have 'Wanted Dead or Alive' under it. He mostly came to rub it in about the rumble. Man, I hate not bein' in that."

Only last week Tim Shepard had cracked three of
170 Dally's ribs. But Dally and Tim Shepard had always been buddies; no matter how they fought, they were two of a kind, and they knew it.

Dally was grinning at me. "Kid, you scared the devil outa me the other day. I thought I'd killed you."
175 "Me?" I said, puzzled. "Why?"

"When you jumped out of the church. I meant to hit you just hard enough to knock you down and put out the fire, but when you dropped like a ton of lead I thought I'd aimed too high and broke your neck." He thought for a
180 minute. "I'm glad I didn't, though." **9**

9 What happened at the church?

"I'll bet," I said with a grin. I'd never liked Dally—but then, for the first time, I felt like he was my buddy. And all because he was glad he hadn't killed me.

Dally looked out the window. "Uh . . ."—he sounded
185 very **casual**—"how's the kid?"

"We just left him," Two-Bit said, and I could tell that he was debating whether to tell Dally the truth or not. "I don't know about stuff like this . . . but . . . well, he seemed pretty bad to me. He passed out cold before we
190 left him."

Dally's jaw line went white as he swore between clenched teeth. **10**

"Two-Bit, you still got that fancy black-handled switch?"
195 "Yeah."

"Give it here."

Two-Bit reached into his back pocket for his prize **possession**. It was a jet-handled switchblade, ten inches long, that would flash open at a mere breath. It was
200 the reward of two hours of walking aimlessly around a hardware store to divert suspicion. He kept it razor sharp. As far as I knew, he had never pulled it on anyone; he used his plain pocketknife when he needed a blade. But it was his showpiece, his pride and joy—every time he
205 ran into a new hood he pulled it out and showed off with it. Dally knew how much that knife meant to Two-Bit, and if he needed a blade bad enough to ask for it, well, he needed a blade. That was all there was to it. Two-Bit handed it over to Dally without a moment's **hesitation**. **11**

210 "We gotta win that fight tonight," Dally said. His voice was hard. "We gotta get even with the Socs. For Johnny."

He put the switch under his pillow and lay back, staring at the ceiling. We left. We knew better than to
215 talk to Dally when his eyes were blazing and he was in a mood like that.

We decided to catch a bus home. I just didn't feel much like walking or trying to hitch a ride. Two-Bit left me sitting on the bench at the bus stop while he went to
220 a gas station to buy some cigarettes. I was kind of sick to my stomach and sort of groggy. I was nearly asleep

casual
relaxed; laid back

possession
something owned

hestitation
a delay or a pause

10 How does Dally feel about Johnny's condition?

11 Speculate why Dally wanted the knife.

strict

firm; having many rules and expecting to be obeyed

deny

to say something isn't true

12 Who does Ponyboy live with?

13 What does Ponyboy think about the rumble?

when I felt someone's hand on my forehead. I almost jumped out of my skin. Two-Bit was looking down at me worriedly. "You feel okay? You're awful hot."

225   "I'm all right," I said, and when he looked at me as if he didn't believe me, I got a little panicky. "Don't tell Darry, okay? Come on, Two-Bit, be a buddy. I'll be well by tonight. I'll take a bunch of aspirins."

     "All right," Two-Bit said reluctantly. "But Darry'll kill

230 me if you're really sick and go ahead and fight anyway."

     "I'm okay," I said, getting a little angry. "And if you keep your mouth shut, Darry won't know a thing."

     "You know somethin'?" Two-Bit said as we were riding home on the bus. "You'd think you could get away

235 with murder, living with your big brother and all, but Darry's **stricter** with you than your folks were, ain't he?" **12**

     "Yeah," I said, "but they'd raised two boys before me. Darry hasn't."

     "You know, the only thing that keeps Darry from

240 bein' a Soc is us."

     "I know," I said. I had known it for a long time. In spite of not having much money, the only reason Darry couldn't be a Soc was us. The gang. Me and Soda. Darry was too smart to be a greaser. I don't know how I knew, I

245 just did. And I was kind of sorry.

     I was silent most of the way home. I was thinking about the rumble. I had a sick feeling in my stomach and it wasn't from being ill. It was the same kind of helplessness I'd felt that night Darry yelled at me for

250 going to sleep in the lot. I had the same deathly fear that something was going to happen that none of us could stop. As we got off the bus I finally said it. "Tonight— I don't like it one bit." **13**

     Two-Bit pretended not to understand. "I never knew

255 you to play chicken in a rumble before. Not even when you was a little kid."

     I knew he was trying to make me mad, but I took the bait anyway. "I ain't chicken, Two-Bit Mathews, and you know it," I said angrily. "Ain't I a Curtis, same as Soda

260 and Darry?"

     Two-Bit couldn't **deny** this, so I went on: "I mean, I got an awful feeling something's gonna happen."

"Somethin' is gonna happen. We're gonna stomp the Socs' guts, that's what."

265   Two-Bit knew what I meant, but doggedly pretended not to. He seemed to feel that if you said something was all right, it immediately was, no matter what. He's been that way all his life, and I don't expect he'll change. Sodapop would have understood, and we would have

270 tried to figure it out together, but Two-Bit just ain't Soda. Not by a long shot.

S. E. Hinton

Susan Eloise Hinton was inspired to write her first novel, *The Outsiders*, when she was fifteen and just starting high school. Like many female authors, she shortened her name to S. E. Hinton so male readers and reviewers would not dismiss her work simply because she was a woman. There were two rival gangs at Hinton's school. She always felt sympathy toward the "greasers," which influenced her to write from their point of view. Because of the violence and illegal activities, such as underage drinking and smoking, *The Outsiders* was banned in a lot of schools. However, it's becoming more popular in school curriculums now due to how relatable such events can be in young kids' lives. Hinton wanted to show something she saw every day in hopes of connecting with others who share the same experiences. Hinton has won many awards for her novels, including being inducted into the Oklahoma Writers Hall of Fame.

Compound Words

Read the excerpt. Underline the compound words in the excerpt and write them on the lines. Draw a line between the two smaller words and write a definition.

> Two-Bit reached into his back pocket for his prize possession. It was a jet-handled switchblade, ten inches long, that would flash open at a mere breath. It was the reward of two hours of walking aimlessly around a hardware store to divert suspicion. He kept it razor sharp. As far as I knew, he had never pulled it on anyone; he used his plain pocketknife when he needed a blade. But it was his showpiece, his pride and joy—every time he ran into a new hood he pulled it out and showed off with it.

1. _____

   _____

2. _____

   _____

3. _____

   _____

4. _____

   _____

Adjectives

Read the sentences and underline the adjectives in each sentence. Look for the words that answer the *which one*, *what kind*, or *how many* question. Some sentences will have more than one adjective.

> **Examples:**
> And he knows that he can count on his friends—<u>true</u> friends who would do anything for him.
>
> He was as <u>pale</u> as the pillow.
>
> I figured <u>Southern</u> gentlemen had nothing on Johnny Cade.

1. And when it comes to the Socs—a vicious gang of rich kids who enjoy beating up on the "greasers" like him and his friends—he knows that he can count on them for trouble.

2. We had always been close buddies, and those lonely days in the church strengthened our friendship.

3. Sixteen years on the streets and you can learn a lot.

4. Dally's jaw line went white as he swore between clenched teeth.

5. Two-Bit reached into his back pocket for his prize possession.

6. In spite of not having much money, the only reason Darry couldn't be a Soc was us.

7. "I mean, I got an awful feeling something's gonna happen."

8. Johnnycake's eyes were fearful and sensitive; hers were cheap and hard.

9. She was a little woman, with straight black hair and big black eyes like Johnny's.

10. Dally was his usual mean, ornery self.

Adjectives that Compare

Adjectives' endings signal a comparison between nouns or pronouns.

Comparative: When comparing two nouns or pronouns, add -**er**.

Superlative: When comparing three or more nouns or pronouns, add -**est** to the one that is "the most."

> **Adjective:** She is **tall**.
> **Comparative:** She is **taller** *than* I am.
> **Superlative:** She is *the* **tallest** person on the team.

Part A

Read the sentences and circle the correct form of the adjective.

> **Examples:**
> She is the (sweeter, sweetest) person I have ever met.
> This test is (harder, hardest) than the previous test.

1. He is (smarter, smartest) than his brother.

2. That stray cat is the (meaner, meanest) cat I have ever seen.

3. You seem (happier, happiest) today than you were yesterday.

4. His voice is (louder, loudest) than mine.

5. The book has the (smaller, smallest) print I have ever read.

Part B

Read Ponyboy's poem and underline the adjectives that compare.

Johnny needs his friends
to face the Grim Reaper and know he's "tuffer" than him.

But, Johnny's all alone
to rumble with death; the harshest warrior ever known.

Johnny don't go
you're my best friend and I love you like a bro.

Johnny don't stay
your life gets harder every day.

Johnny don't die
you're the gentlest of the greasers; not afraid to cry.

Johnny don't survive
Leave this place for heaven—where those richer than the Socs reside.

Masterpiece Sentences: Stage 4—Painting the Subject

Answer the questions below each picture to expand or paint the subject.

Friends posed for a picture.

What kind? _____

Which ones? _____

How many? _____

New sentence: _____

_____

_____

_____

A teenager needed a friend.

What kind? _____

Which ones? _____

How many? _____

New sentence: _____

_____

_____

_____

Warriors battled.

What kind? _____

Which ones? _____

How many? _____

New sentence: _____

_____

_____

_____

Masterpiece Sentences: Stages 1–4

Use the picture to create a base sentence. Then, answer the questions in the Masterpiece Sentences chart to create a Stage 4 sentence.

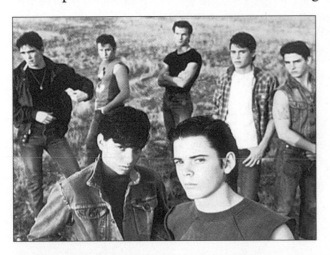

Stage	Process	Questions to Answer	Answers
Stage 1: Prepare Your Canvas	Choose a noun for the subject. Choose a verb for the predicate.	Who did it? Did what? To what?	
Stage 2: Paint Your Predicate	Tell more about what happened.	When? Where? How?	
Stage 3: Move the Predicate Painters	Improve sentence structure by moving painters.		
Stage 4: Paint Your Subject	Tell more about the subject.	Which one? What kind? How many?	
New Sentence			

Spotlight on Punctuation: Dialogue

Part A

Underline the words spoken by a character and circle the quotation marks and commas that separate the dialogue from the rest of the text.

A nurse appeared in the doorway. "Johnny," she said quietly, "your mother's here to see you."

Johnny opened his eyes. At first they were wide with surprise, then they darkened. "I don't want to see her," he said firmly.

"She's your mother."

"I said I don't want to see her." His voice was rising. "She's probably come to tell me about all the trouble I'm causing her and about how glad her and the old man'll be when I'm dead. Well, tell her to leave me alone. For once"—his voice broke—"for once just to leave me alone." He was struggling to sit up, but he suddenly gasped, went whiter than the pillowcase, and passed out cold.

The nurse hurried me out the door. "I was afraid of something like this if he saw anyone."

I ran into Two-Bit, who was coming in.

"You can't see him now," the nurse said, so Two-Bit handed her the book. "Make sure he can see it when he comes around." She took it and closed the door behind her. Two-Bit stood and looked at the door a long time. "I wish it was any one of us except Johnny," he said, and his voice was serious for once. "We could get along without anyone but Johnny."

Spotlight on Punctuation: Dialogue (*cont.*)

Part B

Identify the speaker of each piece of dialogue on the previous page. Copy the complete sentences in the chart under the correct character.

Johnny	Nurse	Ponyboy	Two-Bit

Passage Comprehension

Read the prompts and respond using complete sentences. Refer to the chart on page 66 to determine how to respond.

1. Describe Ponyboy's family.

   _____

   _____

   _____

2. Tell the names of the greasers.

   _____

   _____

3. Use context to determine the meaning of this quote: "We couldn't get along without him. We needed Johnny as much as he needed the gang. And for the same reason."

   _____

   _____

   _____

   _____

4. Explain Johnny's reaction to his mother's visit.

   _____

   _____

   _____

5. Describe how Johnny fits the stereotype of gang members.

   _____

   _____

   _____

   _____

6. Explain how greasers and Socs are different and alike.

   _____

   _____

   _____

   _____

Close Reading

Read the text.

Excerpt from *The Outsiders*

No one ever said life was easy. But Ponyboy is pretty sure that he's got things figured out. He knows that he can count on his brothers, Darry and Sodapop. And he knows that he can count on his friends—true friends who would do anything for him, like Johnny and Two-Bit. And when it comes to the Socs—a
5 *vicious gang of rich kids who enjoy beating up on the "greasers" like him and his friends—he knows that he can count on them for trouble. But one night someone takes things too far, and Ponyboy's world is turned upside down . . .*

The nurses wouldn't let us see Johnny. He was in critical condition. No visitors. But Two-Bit wouldn't take no for an answer. That was his buddy in
10 there and he aimed to see him. We both begged and pleaded, but we were getting nowhere until the doctor found out what was going on.

"Let them go in," he said to the nurse. "He's been asking for them. It can't hurt now."

Two-Bit didn't notice the expression in his voice. It's true, I thought numbly,
15 he is dying. We went in, practically on tiptoe, because the quietness of the hospital scared us. Johnny was lying still, with his eyes closed, but when Two-Bit said, "Hey, Johnnykid," he opened them and looked at us, trying to grin. "Hey, y'all."

The nurse, who was pulling the shades open, smiled and said, "So he can
20 talk after all."

Close Reading (*cont.*)

Two-Bit looked around. "They treatin' you okay, kid?"

"Don't . . ."—Johnny gasped—"don't let me put enough grease on my hair."

"Don't talk," Two-Bit said, pulling up a chair, "just listen. We'll bring you some hair grease next time. We're havin' the big rumble tonight."

25 Johnny's huge black eyes widened a little, but he didn't say anything.

"It's too bad you and Dally can't be in it. It's the first big rumble we've had—not countin' the time we whipped Shepard's outfit."

"He came by," Johnny said.

"Tim Shepard?"

30 Johnny nodded. "Came to see Dally."

Tim and Dallas had always been buddies.

"Did you know you got your name in the paper for being a hero?"

Johnny almost grinned as he nodded. "Tuff enough," he managed, and by the way his eyes were glowing, I figured Southern gentlemen had nothing on 35 Johnny Cade.

I could see that even a few words were tiring him out; he was as pale as the pillow and looked awful. Two-Bit pretended not to notice.

"You want anything besides hair grease, kid?"

Johnny barely nodded. "The book"—he looked at me—"can you get another 40 one?"

Two-Bit looked at me too. I hadn't told him about *Gone with the Wind*.

"He wants a copy of *Gone with the Wind* so I can read it to him," I explained. "You want to run down to the drugstore and get one?"

"Okay," Two-Bit said cheerfully. "Don't y'all run off."

45 I sat down in Two-Bit's chair and tried to think of something to say. "Dally's gonna be okay," I said finally. "And Darry and me, we're okay now."

I knew Johnny understood what I meant. We had always been close buddies, and those lonely days in the church strengthened our friendship. He tried to smile again, and then suddenly went white and closed his eyes tight.

50 "Johnny!" I said, alarmed. "Are you okay?"

He nodded, keeping his eyes closed. "Yeah, it just hurts sometimes. It usually don't . . . I can't feel anything below the middle of my back . . ."

He lay breathing heavily for a moment. "I'm pretty bad off, ain't I, Pony?"

"You'll be okay," I said with fake cheerfulness. "You gotta be. We couldn't get 55 along without you."

The truth of that last statement hit me. We couldn't get along without him. We needed Johnny as much as he needed the gang. And for the same reason.

Close Reading (*cont.*)

"I won't be able to walk again," Johnny started, then **faltered**. "Not even on crutches. Busted my back."

60 "You'll be okay," I repeated firmly. Don't start crying, I commanded myself, don't start crying, you'll scare Johnny.

"You want to know something, Ponyboy? I'm scared stiff. I used to talk about killing myself . . ." He drew a quivering breath. "I don't want to die now. It ain't long enough. Sixteen years ain't long enough. I wouldn't mind it so much if there 65 wasn't so much stuff I ain't done yet and so many things I ain't seen. It's not fair. You know what? That time we were in Windrixville was the only time I've been away from our neighborhood."

"You ain't gonna die," I said, trying to hold my voice down. "And don't get juiced up, because the doc won't let us see you no more if you do."

70 Sixteen years on the streets and you can learn a lot. But all the wrong things, not the things you want to learn. Sixteen years on the streets and you see a lot. But all the wrong sights, not the sights you want to see.

Johnny closed his eyes and rested quietly for a minute. Years of living on the East Side teaches you how to shut off your emotions. If you didn't, you would 75 explode. You learn to cool it.

Close Reading (*cont.*)

A nurse appeared in the doorway. "Johnny," she said quietly, "your mother's here to see you."

Johnny opened his eyes. At first they were wide with surprise, then they darkened. "I don't want to see her," he said firmly.

80 "She's your mother."

"I said I don't want to see her." His voice was rising. "She's probably come to tell me about all the trouble I'm causing her and about how glad her and the old man'll be when I'm dead. Well, tell her to leave me alone. For once"—his voice broke—"for once just to leave me alone." He was struggling to sit up, but he

85 suddenly gasped, went whiter than the pillowcase, and passed out cold.

The nurse hurried me out the door. "I was afraid of something like this if he saw anyone."

I ran into Two-Bit, who was coming in.

"You can't see him now," the nurse said, so Two-Bit handed her the book.

90 "Make sure he can see it when he comes around." She took it and closed the door behind her. Two-Bit stood and looked at the door a long time. "I wish it was any one of us except Johnny," he said, and his voice was serious for once. "We could get along without anyone but Johnny."

Turning **abruptly**, he said, "Let's go see Dallas."

95 As we walked out into the hall, we saw Johnny's mother. I knew her. She was a little woman, with straight black hair and big black eyes like Johnny's. But that was as far as the **resemblance** went. Johnnycake's eyes were fearful and sensitive; hers were cheap and hard. As we passed her she was saying, "But I have a right to see him. He's my son. After all the trouble his father and I've gone to raise

100 him, this is our reward! He'd rather see those no-count hoodlums than his own folks . . ." She saw us and gave us such a look of hatred that I almost backed up. "It was your fault. Always running around in the middle of the night getting jailed and heaven knows what else . . ." I thought she was going to cuss us out. I really did.

105 Two-Bit's eyes got narrow and I was afraid he was going to start something. I don't like to hear women get sworn at, even if they **deserve** it. "No wonder he hates your guts," Two-Bit snapped. He was going to tell her off real good, but I shoved him along. I felt sick. No wonder Johnny didn't want to see her. No wonder he stayed overnight at Two-Bit's or at our house, and slept in the vacant

110 lot in good weather. I remembered my mother . . . beautiful and golden, like Soda, and wise and firm, like Darry.

"Oh, lordy!" There was a catch in Two-Bit's voice and he was closer to tears than I'd ever seen him. "He has to live with that."

Close Reading (*cont.*)

115 We hurried to the elevator to get to the next floor. I hoped the nurse would have enough sense not to let Johnny's mother see him. It would kill him.

Dally was arguing with one of the nurses when we came in. He grinned at us. "Man, am I glad to see you! These —— hospital people won't let me smoke, and I want out!"

We sat down, grinning at each other. Dally was his usual mean, **ornery** self.
120 He was okay.

"Shepard came by to see me a while ago."

"That's what Johnny said. What'd he want?"

"Said he saw my picture in the paper and couldn't believe it didn't have 'Wanted Dead or Alive' under it. He mostly came to rub it in about the rumble.
125 Man, I hate not bein' in that."

Only last week Tim Shepard had cracked three of Dally's ribs. But Dally and Tim Shepard had always been buddies; no matter how they fought, they were two of a kind, and they knew it.

Dally was grinning at me. "Kid, you scared the devil outa me the other day.
130 I thought I'd killed you."

"Me?" I said, puzzled. "Why?"

"When you jumped out of the church. I meant to hit you just hard enough to knock you down and put out the fire, but when you dropped like a ton of lead I thought I'd aimed too high and broke your neck." He thought for a minute. "I'm
135 glad I didn't, though."

"I'll bet," I said with a grin. I'd never liked Dally—but then, for the first time, I felt like he was my buddy. And all because he was glad he hadn't killed me.

Close Reading (*cont.*)

Dally looked out the window. "Uh . . ."—he sounded very **casual**—"how's the kid?"

140 "We just left him," Two-Bit said, and I could tell that he was debating whether to tell Dally the truth or not. "I don't know about stuff like this . . . but . . . well, he seemed pretty bad to me. He passed out cold before we left him."

Dally's jaw line went white as he swore between clenched teeth.

"Two-Bit, you still got that fancy black-handled switch?"

145 "Yeah."

"Give it here."

Two-Bit reached into his back pocket for his prize **possession**. It was a jet-handled switchblade, ten inches long, that would flash open at a mere breath. It was the reward of two hours of walking aimlessly around a hardware store to

150 divert suspicion. He kept it razor sharp. As far as I knew, he had never pulled it on anyone; he used his plain pocketknife when he needed a blade. But it was his showpiece, his pride and joy—every time he ran into a new hood he pulled it out and showed off with it. Dally knew how much that knife meant to Two-Bit, and if he needed a blade bad enough to ask for it, well, he needed a blade. That was all

155 there was to it. Two-Bit handed it over to Dally without a moment's **hesitation**.

"We gotta win that fight tonight," Dally said. His voice was hard. "We gotta get even with the Socs. For Johnny."

He put the switch under his pillow and lay back, staring at the ceiling. We left. We knew better than to talk to Dally when his eyes were blazing and he was

160 in a mood like that.

We decided to catch a bus home. I just didn't feel much like walking or trying to hitch a ride. Two-Bit left me sitting on the bench at the bus stop while he went to a gas station to buy some cigarettes. I was kind of sick to my stomach and sort of groggy. I was nearly asleep when I felt someone's hand on my forehead. I

165 almost jumped out of my skin. Two-Bit was looking down at me worriedly. "You feel okay? You're awful hot."

"I'm all right," I said, and when he looked at me as if he didn't believe me, I got a little panicky. "Don't tell Darry, okay? Come on, Two-Bit, be a buddy. I'll be well by tonight. I'll take a bunch of aspirins."

170 "All right," Two-Bit said reluctantly. "But Darry'll kill me if you're really sick and go ahead and fight anyway."

"I'm okay," I said, getting a little angry. "And if you keep your mouth shut, Darry won't know a thing."

"You know somethin'?" Two-Bit said as we were riding home on the bus.

175 "You'd think you could get away with murder, living with your big brother and all, but Darry's **stricter** with you than your folks were, ain't he?"

"Yeah," I said, "but they'd raised two boys before me. Darry hasn't."

"You know, the only thing that keeps Darry from bein' a Soc is us."

Close Reading (*cont.*)

"I know," I said. I had known it for a long time. In spite of not having much
180 money, the only reason Darry couldn't be a Soc was us. The gang. Me and Soda.
Darry was too smart to be a greaser. I don't know how I knew, I just did. And I
was kind of sorry.

I was silent most of the way home. I was thinking about the rumble. I had
a sick feeling in my stomach and it wasn't from being ill. It was the same kind
185 of helplessness I'd felt that night Darry yelled at me for going to sleep in the
lot. I had the same deathly fear that something was going to happen that none
of us could stop. As we got off the bus I finally said it. "Tonight—I don't like it
one bit."

Two-Bit pretended not to understand. "I never knew you to play chicken in a
190 rumble before. Not even when you was a little kid."

I knew he was trying to make me mad, but I took the bait anyway. "I ain't
chicken, Two-Bit Mathews, and you know it," I said angrily. "Ain't I a Curtis,
same as Soda and Darry?"

Two-Bit couldn't **deny** this, so I went on: "I mean, I got an awful feeling
195 something's gonna happen."

"Somethin' is gonna happen. We're gonna stomp the Socs' guts, that's what."

Two-Bit knew what I meant, but doggedly pretended not to. He seemed to
feel that if you said something was all right, it immediately was, no matter what.
He's been that way all his life, and I don't expect he'll change. Sodapop would
200 have understood, and we would have tried to figure it out together, but Two-Bit
just ain't Soda. Not by a long shot.

Quick Write in Response to Reading

Character Sketch

Choose a character from *The Outsiders* and compare yourself to the character. Identify three character traits that you share with the character. Provide evidence from the text and your life to support your writing. Use the character sketch to organize your thoughts before you begin writing.

Character: _____   You

Trait #1	**Trait #1**
Text Evidence:	Life Evidence:

Trait #2	**Trait #2**
Text Evidence:	Life Evidence:

Trait #3	**Trait #3**
Text Evidence:	Life Evidence:

Quick Write in Response to Reading (*cont.*)

Let's Focus: Excerpt from *The Play of the Diary of Anne Frank*

Content Focus
family; ostracism

Type of Text
literature—drama (based on a true story)

Authors' Names _____

Authors' Purpose _____

Big Ideas
Consider the following Big Idea questions. Write your answer for each question.

Are all people really good at heart?

_____

_____

Are people a product of their beliefs or a product of their circumstances?

_____

_____

Drama Preview Checklist: the excerpt from *The Play of the Diary of Anne Frank* on pages 101–118.

☐ Title: What clue does it provide about the play?

☐ Pictures: What additional information is added here?

☐ Features: What other text features do you notice?

○ How many acts?

○ How many scenes?

○ How many characters?

Enduring Understandings
After reading the play . . .

_____

_____

_____

_____

Key Passage Vocabulary: Excerpt from *The Play of the Diary of Anne Frank*

Read each word. Write the word in column 3. Then, circle a number to rate your knowledge of the word.

Vocabulary	Part of Speech	Write the Word	Rate the Word
awkward	(adj)		0 1 2 3
conspicuous	(adj)		0 1 2 3
indicate	(v)		0 1 2 3
dependable	(adj)		0 1 2 3
leisure	(n)		0 1 2 3
regulations	(n)		0 1 2 3
interval	(n)		0 1 2 3
garment	(n)		0 1 2 3
concentrate	(v)		0 1 2 3
peculiar	(adj)		0 1 2 3

from The Play of
THE DIARY OF
Anne Frank

by Frances Goodrich and Albert Hackett

List of Characters
(in the order of their appearance)

MR. FRANK	*Pronunciation:*	Frahnk
MIEP GIES	*Pronunciation:*	Meep
MRS. VAN DAAN	*Pronunciation:*	*Petronella,* Pet-row-nell'-ah
MR. VAN DAAN	*Pronunciation:*	Fahn Dahn
PETER VAN DAAN	*Pronunciation:*	Pay'-ter
MRS. FRANK	*Pronunciation:*	*Edith,* Ae'-dith
MARGOT FRANK	*Pronunciation:*	Mar'-gott
ANNE FRANK	*Pronunciation:*	Ah'-nah
MR. KRALER	*Pronunciation:*	Krah'-ler

ACT ONE

Scene One
The top floors of a warehouse in Amsterdam, Holland. November 1945. Late afternoon.

5

10

15

MR FRANK enters. He is weak and ill and is making a supreme effort at self-control. His clothes are threadbare. He carries a small rucksack. A scarf catches his eye. He takes it down, puts it around his neck, then wanders towards the couch, but stops as he sees the glove. He picks it up. Suddenly all control is gone. He breaks down and weeps. MIEP GIES enters up the stairs. She is a Dutch girl of about twenty-two, pregnant now. She is compassionate and protective in her attitude towards MR FRANK. She has been a stenographer and secretary in his business. She has her coat and hat on, ready to go home. A small silver cross hangs at her throat. **1**

> **1** What does the cross tell you about Miep?

MIEP   Are you all right, Mr. Frank?

MR FRANK   *(quickly controlling himself)* Yes, Miep, yes.

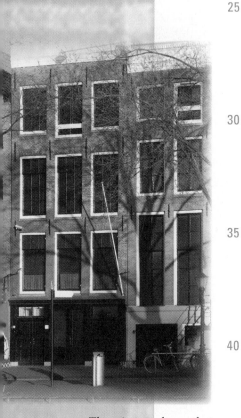

The spice warehouse that enclosed the secret annex

	MIEP	Everyone in the office has gone home—it's after six. Don't stay up here, Mr. Frank. What's the use of torturing yourself like this?
20		
	MR FRANK	I've come to say good-bye—I'm leaving here, Miep.
	MIEP	What do you mean? Where are you going? Where?
	MR FRANK	I don't know yet. I haven't decided.
	MIEP	Mr. Frank, you can't leave here. This is your home.
25		Amsterdam is your home. Your business is here, waiting for you. You're needed here. Now that the war is over, there are things that . . .
	MR FRANK	I can't stay in Amsterdam, Miep. It has too many memories for me. Everywhere there's something—
30		the house we lived in—the school—the street organ playing out there. I'm not the person you used to know, Miep. I'm a bitter old man. Forgive me. I shouldn't speak to you like this—after all that you did for us—the suffering . . .
35	**MIEP**	No. No. It wasn't suffering. You can't say we suffered.
	MR FRANK	I know what you went through, you and Mr. Kraler. I'll remember it as long as I live. Come, Miep. *(He remembers his rucksack, crosses below the table to*
40		*the couch and picks up his rucksack.)*
	MIEP	Mr. Frank, did you see? There are some of your papers here. *(She takes a bundle of papers from the shelves, then crosses below the table to* MR FRANK.*)*
45		We found them in a heap of rubbish on the floor after—after you left.
	MR FRANK	Burn them. *(He opens his rucksack and puts the glove in it.)*
	MIEP	But, Mr. Frank, there are letters, notes . . .
	MR FRANK	Burn them. All of them.
50	**MIEP**	Burn this? *(She hands him a worn, velour-covered book.)* **2**

2 What does Miep know that Mr. Frank does not?

MR FRANK   *(quietly)* Anne's diary. *(He opens the diary and reads.)* 'Monday, the sixth of July, nineteen hundred and forty-two.' *(To* MIEP.*)* Nineteen hundred and forty-two. Is it possible, Miep? Only three years ago. *(He reads.)* 'Dear Diary, since you and I are going to be great friends, I will start by telling you about myself. My name is Anne Frank. I am thirteen years old. I was born in Germany the twelfth of June, nineteen twenty-nine. As my family is Jewish, we emigrated to Holland when Hitler came to power.' **3**

3 Why did the Franks leave Germany when Hitler came to power?

MR FRANK **ANNE'S VOICE**   *(together)* 'My father started a business, importing spice and herbs. Things went well for us until nineteen forty. Then the War came and the Dutch—*(He turns the page.)* defeat, followed by the arrival of the Germans. Then things got very bad for the Jews.'

(MR FRANK'S voice dies out as ANNE'S VOICE *grows stronger.)* **4**

4 What is happening on stage here?

ANNE   You could not do this and you could not do that. They forced father out of his business. We had to wear yellow stars. I had to turn in my bike. I couldn't go to a Dutch school any more. I couldn't go to the cinema, or ride in an automobile, or even on a streetcar, and a million other things. But somehow we children still managed to have fun. Yesterday, father told me we were going into hiding. Where, he wouldn't say. At five o'clock this morning mother woke me and told me to hurry and get dressed. I was to put on as many clothes as I could. It would look too suspicious if we walked along carrying suitcases. It wasn't until we were on our way that I learned where we were going. Our hiding place was to be upstairs in the building where father used to have his business. Three other people were coming in with us—the Van Daans and their son Peter. Father knew the Van Daans but we had never met them.

(The sound of distant ships' sirens is heard.)

awkward
uncomfortable; not sure what to do or say

conspicuous
easily seen

indicate
to signal something with a movement or gesture

A replica of the bookcase that hid the door to the secret annex

5 Who does Mrs. Van Daan think has taken the Franks?

Scene Two
Early morning. July 1942.

The three members of the VAN DAAN *family are waiting for the* FRANKS *to arrive.* MR VAN DAAN *is smoking a cigarette and watching his wife with a nervous eye. His overcoat and suit are expensive and well-cut.* MRS VAN DAAN *is sitting on the couch. She is a pretty woman in her early forties and is clutching her possessions: a hat-box, a handbag and an attractive straw carry-all.* PETER VAN DAAN *is standing at the window in the room. He is a shy,* **awkward** *boy of sixteen. He wears a cap, a short overcoat, and long Dutch trousers, like 'plus fours'. All the* VAN DAANS *have the* **conspicuous** *yellow Star of David on the left breast of their clothing.*

95

100

105

MRS V.DAAN   Something's happened to them. I know it.

MR V.DAAN   Now, Kerli!

MRS V.DAAN   Mr. Frank said they'd be here at seven o'clock. He said . . .

110 **MR V.DAAN**   They have two miles to walk. You can't expect . . .

MRS V.DAAN   They've been picked up.

(The door below opens.)

That's what happened. They've been taken. **5**

(MR VAN DAAN **indicates** *that he hears someone coming.)*

115

MR V.DAAN   You see?

(MR FRANK comes up the stairwell from below.)

MR FRANK   Mrs. Van Daan, Mr. Van Daan. *(He shakes hands with them. He moves to* PETER *and shakes his hand.)* There were too many of the Green Police on the streets—we had to take the long way round.

120

dependable
trustworthy; able to be counted on or relied on

125

130

135

(MIEP, *not pregnant now,* MARGOT, MR KRALER, *and* MRS FRANK *come up the stairs.* MARGOT *is eighteen, beautiful, quiet and shy. She carries a leatherette hold-all and a large brown paper bag, which she puts on the table.* KRALER *is a Dutchman,* **dependable** *and kindly. He wears a hearing aid in his ear and carries two brief-cases.* MRS FRANK *is a young mother, gently bred and reserved. She, like* MR FRANK, *has a slight German accent. She carries a leatherette shopping bag and her handbag. We see the Star of David conspicuous on the* FRANKS' *clothing.* KRALER *acknowledges the* VAN DAANS, *moves to the shelves and checks their contents.* MIEP *empties her straw bag of the clothes it contains and piles them on the table.*)

MRS FRANK   Anne?

140

(ANNE FRANK *comes quickly up the stairs. She is thirteen, quick in her movements, interested in everything and mercurial in her emotions. She wears a cape, long wool socks and carries a school bag.*)

MR FRANK   My wife, Edith. Mr. and Mrs. Van Daan.

145

(MRS FRANK *shakes* MR VAN DAAN'S *hand, then hurries across to shake hands with* MRS VAN DAAN. *She then moves to the sink and inspects it.*)

Their son, Peter—my daughters, Margot and Anne. **6**

150

(ANNE *gives a polite little curtsy as she shakes* MR VAN DAAN'S *hand. She puts her bag on the left end of the table then immediately starts off on a tour of investigation of her new home, going upstairs to the attic room.*)

6 How many people will be living in the annex?

leisure

time when you are not working or busy with tasks

regulations

rules set by people in power to control how things are done

KRALER   I'm sorry there is still so much confusion.

MR FRANK   Please. Don't think of it. After all, we'll have plenty
155   of **leisure** to arrange everything ourselves.

MIEP   *(indicating the sink cupboard)* We put the stores of
food you sent in here. *(She crosses to the shelves.)*
Your drugs are here—soap, linen, here.

MRS FRANK   Thank you, Miep.

160   **MIEP**   I made up the beds—the way Mr. Frank and
Mr. Kraler said. Forgive me. I have to hurry. I've
got to go to the other side of town to get some ration
books for you.

MRS V.DAAN   Ration books? If they see our names on ration
165   books, they'll know we're here.

KRALER
MIEP   *(together)*   There isn't anything . . .
Don't worry. Your names won't be on them.
(As she hurries out.) I'll be up later.

7 Who is helping
the Franks hide?

MR FRANK   Thank you, Miep. **7**

170   *(MIEP exits down the stairwell.)*

MRS FRANK   It's illegal, then, the ration books? We've never done
anything illegal.

MR FRANK   We won't be living exactly according to **regulations**
here.

175   **KRALER**   This isn't the black market, Mrs. Frank. This is
what we call the white market—helping all of the
hundreds and hundreds who are hiding out in
Amsterdam.

*(The carillon is heard playing the quarter hour
180   before eight. KRALER looks at his watch. ANNE comes
down from the attic, stops at the window and looks
out through the curtains.)*

ANNE   It's the Westertoren.

185	KRALER	I must go. I must be out of here and downstairs in the office before the workmen get here. Miep or I, or both of us, will be up each day to bring you food and news and find out what your needs are. Tomorrow I'll get you a better bolt for the door at the foot of the stairs. It needs a bolt that you can throw yourself and open only at our signal. *(To MR FRANK.)* Oh—you'll tell them about the noise?
190		
	MR FRANK	I'll tell them.
	KRALER	Good-bye, then, for the moment. I'll come up again, after the workmen leave.
195	MR FRANK	*(shaking* KRALER'S *hand)* Good-bye, Mr. Kraler.
	MRS FRANK	*(shaking* KRALER'S *hand)* How can we thank you?
	KRALER	I never thought I'd live to see the day when a man like Mr. Frank would have to go into hiding. When you think . . .
200		*(KRALER breaks off and exits down the stairs. MR FRANK follows him down the stairs and bolts the door after him. In the **interval** before he returns, PETER goes to MARGOT, gives a stiff bow and shakes hands with her. ANNE watches, and as they complete their greeting, moves to PETER and holds out her hand. PETER does not see her and turns away. MR FRANK comes up the stairs.)*
205		
	MRS FRANK	What did he mean, about the noise?
	MR FRANK	First, let's take off some of these clothes. **8**
210		*(ANNE moves below the table, stands with her back to the audience, removes her cape and beret and puts them on the pile of clothes on the table. They all start to take off **garment** after garment. On each of their coats, sweaters, blouses, suits and dresses is another yellow Star of David. MR and MRS FRANK are under-dressed quite simply. The others wear several things, sweaters, extra dresses, bathrobes, aprons, etc. MRS FRANK takes off her gloves, carefully folding them before putting them away.)*
215		

interval
a period of time between two dates or events

garment
an item of clothing

8 Why do the Franks have so many clothes on?

220   **MR V.DAAN**   It's a wonder we weren't arrested, walking along the streets—Petronella with a fur coat in July—and that cat of Peter's crying all the way.

ANNE   *(removing a pair of panties)* A cat?

MRS FRANK   *(shocked)* Anne, please!

225   **ANNE**   It's all right. I've got on three more *(She removes two more pairs of panties. Finally, as they finish removing their surplus clothing, they settle down.)*

MR FRANK   Now. About the noise. While the men are in the building below, we must have complete quiet. Every
230   sound can be heard down there, not only in the workrooms, but in the offices, too. The men come about eight-thirty, and leave at about five-thirty. So, to be perfectly safe, from eight in the morning until six in the evening we must move only when it is
235   necessary and then in stockinged feet. We must not speak above a whisper. We must not run any water. We cannot use the sink, or even, forgive me, the WC. The pipes go down through the workrooms. It would be heard. No rubbish . . .

240   *(The sound of marching feet is heard.* MR FRANK, *followed by* ANNE, *peers out of the window. Satisfied that the marching feet are going away, he returns and continues.)*

No rubbish must ever be thrown out which might
245   reveal that someone is living here—not even a potato paring. We must burn everything in the stove at night. This is the way we must live until it is over, if we are to survive. **9**

(There is a pause. MARGOT *accidentally drops the nightgown she is taking off.* PETER *jumps to pick it up*
250   *for her.)*

9 What can't the Franks and Van Daans do from 8:00 to 6:00?

MRS FRANK	Until it is over.
MR FRANK	After six we can move about—we can talk and laugh and have our supper and read and play games—just as we would at home. *(He looks at his watch.)* And now I think it would be wise if we all went to our rooms, and were settled before eight o'clock. Mrs. Van Daan, you and your husband will go upstairs. I regret that there's no place up there for Peter. But he will be here, near us. This will be our common room, where we'll meet to talk and eat and read, like one family.
MRS V.DAAN	And where do you and Mrs. Frank sleep?
MR FRANK	This room is also our bedroom.
	(MRS VAN DAAN rises in protest.)
MRS V.DAAN} **MR V.DAAN}**	*(together)* That isn't right. We'll sleep here and you take the room upstairs. It's your place.
MR FRANK	Please. I've thought this out for weeks. It's the best arrangement. The only arrangement.
	(MR VAN DAAN starts to load his arms with the clothes he and his wife have taken off and thrown across the couch.)
MRS V.DAAN	*(shaking MR FRANK'S hand)* Never, never can we thank you. *(She moves to MRS FRANK and shakes her hand.)* I don't know what would have happened to us, if it hadn't been for Mr. Frank.
MR FRANK	You don't know how your husband helped me when I came to this country—knowing no-one—not able to speak the language. I can never repay him for that. May I help you with your things? **10**
MR V.DAAN	No. No. *(He picks up the carton and moves towards the attic stairs. To MRS VAN DAAN)* Come along, liefje.

10 Why does Mr. Frank offer to help hide the Van Daans?

	MRS V.DAAN	You'll be all right, Peter? You're not afraid?
285	**PETER**	*(embarrassed)* Please, Mother. *(He picks up his gear. MRS FRANK goes to the head of the stairwell and stares thoughtfully down. MR and MRS VAN DAAN go upstairs.)*
290	**MR FRANK**	You, too, must have some rest, Edith. You didn't close your eyes last night. Nor you, Margot.
	ANNE	I slept, Father. Wasn't that funny? I knew it was the last night in my own bed, and yet I slept soundly.
295	**MR FRANK**	I'm glad, Anne. Now you'll be able to help me straighten things in here. *(To MRS FRANK and MARGOT.)* Come with me—you and Margot rest in this room for the time being.
	MRS FRANK	You're sure? I could help, really. And Anne hasn't had her milk.
300	**MR FRANK**	I'll give it to her. *(He crosses to the table and picks up the piles of clothes.)* Anne, Peter—it's best that you take off your shoes now, before you forget. *(He leads the way to the room, goes in and switches on the pendant light. MARGOT goes into the room. ANNE and PETER remove their shoes.)*
305	**MRS FRANK**	You're sure you're not tired, Anne?
	ANNE	I feel fine. I'm going to help father.
	MRS FRANK	Peter, I'm glad you are to be with us.
	PETER	Yes, Mrs. Frank.
310		*(MRS FRANK goes into the room and closes the door. During the following scene MR FRANK helps MARGOT to hang up clothes. PETER takes his cat out of its case.)*

	ANNE	What's your cat's name?
	PETER	'Mouschi'.
315	ANNE	Mouschi! Mouschi! Mouschi! *(She picks up the cat.)* I love cats. I have one—a darling little cat. But they made me leave her behind. I left some food and a note for the neighbors to take care of her—I'm going to miss her terribly. What is yours? A him or a her?
320	PETER	He's a tom. He doesn't like strangers. *(He takes the cat from* ANNE, *and puts it back in its carrier.)* **11**
	ANNE	Then I'll have to stop being a stranger, won't I? Is he fixed?
	PETER	Huh?
325	ANNE	Did you have him altered?
	PETER	No.
	ANNE	Oh, you ought to—to keep him from fighting. Where did you go to school?
	PETER	Jewish Secondary.
330	ANNE	But that's where Margot and I go. I never saw you around.
	PETER	I used to see you—sometimes.
	ANNE	You did?
335	PETER	In the school yard. You were always in the middle of a bunch of kids. *(He takes a penknife from his pocket.)* **12**
	ANNE	Why didn't you ever come over?
	PETER	I'm sort of a lone wolf. *(He starts to rip off his Star of David.)*

11 How are Peter and his cat alike?

12 What do we know about Anne?

concentrate

to give all your attention to something

13 What does Peter realize that Anne doesn't quite understand?

340	ANNE	What are you doing?

PETER　Taking it off.

340　ANNE　What are you doing?

PETER　Taking it off.

ANNE　But you can't do that. *(She grabs his hands and stops him.)* They'll arrest you if you go out without your star.

345　PETER　*(pulling away)* Who's going out? *(He crosses to the stove, lifts the lid and throws the star into the stove.)* **13**

ANNE　Why, of course. You're right. Of course we don't need them any more. *(She takes* PETER'S *knife and removes her star.* PETER *waits for her star to throw it away.)*

350

I wonder what our friends will think when we don't show up today?

PETER　I didn't have any dates with anyone.

355　ANNE　*(concentrating on her star)* Oh, I did. I had a date with Jopie this afternoon to go and play ping-pong at her house. Do you know Jopie de Waal?

PETER　No.

ANNE　Jopie's my best friend. I wonder what she'll think
360　when she telephones and there's no answer? Probably she'll go over to the house—I wonder what she'll think—we left everything as if we'd suddenly been called away—breakfast dishes in the sink—beds not made . . . *(As she pulls off her star, the cloth
365　underneath shows clearly the colour and form of the star.)* Look! It's still there. What're you going to do with yours?

PETER　Burn it. *(He moves to the stove and holds out his hand for* ANNE'S *star.* ANNE *starts to give the star to
370　* PETER, *but cannot.)*

ANNE   It's funny. I can't throw it away. I don't know why.

PETER   You can't throw . . . ? Something they branded you
        with? That they made you wear so they could spit
        on you?

375   ANNE   I know. I know. But after all, it is the Star of David,
                isn't it? **14**

        (The VAN DAANS *have arranged their things, have
        put their clothes in the wardrobe and are sitting on
        the bed, fanning themselves.*)

380   PETER   Maybe it's different for a girl.

        (ANNE *puts her star in her school bag.*)

MR FRANK   Forgive me, Peter. Now, let me see. We must find
           a bed for your cat. I'm glad you brought your cat.
           Anne was feeling so badly about hers.

385   (*He sees a small worn wash-tub and pulls it from the
           top shelf.*)

           Here we are. Will it be comfortable in that?

PETER   Thanks.

MR FRANK   And here is your room. But I warn you, Peter, you
390   can't grow any more. Not at inch, or you'll have
           to sleep with your feet out of the skylight. Are
           you hungry?

PETER   No.

MR FRANK   We have some bread and butter.

395   PETER   No, thank you.

MR FRANK   (*with a friendly pat on* PETER'S *shoulder*) You can
           have it for luncheon, then. And tonight we will have
           a real supper—our first supper together.

> **14** Would you have
> been able to
> burn something
> that was a
> symbol of your
> faith?

peculiar
strange; odd

400 **PETER** Thanks. Thanks. (*He goes into his room.* MR FRANK *closes the door after* PETER, *then sits and removes his shoes.*)

MR FRANK That's a nice boy, Peter.

ANNE He's awfully shy, isn't he?

MR FRANK You'll like him, I know.

405 **ANNE** I certainly hope so, since he's the only boy I'm likely to see for months and months. **15**

15 How long does Anne think she will have to hide?

MR FRANK Anne, there's a box there. Will you open it?

(*The sound of children playing is heard from the street below.* MR FRANK *goes to the sink and pours a glass of milk from the thermos bottle.*)

410

ANNE You know the way I'm going to think of it here? I'm going to think of it as a boarding-house. A very **peculiar** Summer boarding-house, like the one that we . . . (*She breaks off as she looks in the box.*) Father! Father! My film stars. I was wondering where they were—and Queen Wilhelmina. How wonderful!

415

MR FRANK There's something more. Go on. Look further.

(ANNE *digs deeper into the box and brings out a velour-covered book. She examines it in delighted silence for a moment, then opens the cover slowly, and looks up at* MR FRANK *with shining eyes.*)

420

ANNE A diary! (*She throws her arms around him.*) I've never had a diary. And I've always longed for one. (*She rushes to the table and looks for a pencil.*) Pencil, pencil, pencil, pencil. (*She darts across to the stair-well and starts down the stairs.*) I'm going down to the office to get a pencil.

425

MR FRANK   Anne! No! *(He strides to* ANNE *and catches her arm.*
430   MRS FRANK *aware of the sudden movement and*
             sounds, sits up. After a moment she rises, goes to
             the window and looks out, then returns and sits on
             the bed.)

ANNE   *(startled)* But there's no-one in the building now.

435 MR FRANK   It doesn't matter. I don't want you ever to go beyond
             that door.

ANNE   *(sobered)* Never? Not even at night time, when
             everyone is gone? Or on Sundays? Can't I go down
             to listen to the radio?

440 MR FRANK   Never. I am sorry, Anneke. It isn't safe. No, you
             must never go beyond that door.

ANNE   I see. *(For the first time she realizes what 'going into*
             hiding' means.) **16**

MR FRANK   It'll be hard, I know. But always remember this,
445   Anneke. There are no walls, there are no bolts,
             no locks that anyone can put on your mind. Miep
             will bring us books. We will read history, poetry,
             mythology. *(He gives* ANNE *the glass of milk.)* Here's
             your milk.

450   *(MR FRANK puts his arm about* ANNE, *and crosses*
             with her to the couch, where they sit side by side.)

             As a matter of fact, between us, Annie, being here
             has certain advantages for you. For instance you
             remember the battle you had with your mother the
455   other day on the subject of goloshes? You said you'd
             rather die than wear goloshes. But in the end you
             had to wear them. Well now, you see for as long as
             we are here, you will never have to wear goloshes.
             Isn't that good? And the coat that you inherited from
460   Margot—

             (ANNE makes a wry face.)

             —you won't have to wear that. And the piano. You
             won't have to practice on the piano. I tell you, this is
             going to be a fine life for you. **17**

> **16** What does
> "going into
> hiding" actually
> mean?

> **17** How is Mr.
> Frank trying to
> ease Anne's
> panic?

465 (ANNE'S *panic is gone.* PETER *appears in the doorway of his room, with a saucer in one hand and the cat in the other.*)

PETER I—I—I thought I'd better get some water for Mouschi before . . .

470 **MR FRANK** Of course.

(*The carillon begins its melody and strikes eight. As it does so,* MR FRANK *motions for* PETER *and* ANNE *to be quiet, tiptoes to the window in the rear wall and peers down.* MR VAN DAAN *rises and moves*

475 *to the head of the attic stairs.* MR FRANK *puts his finger to his lips, indicating to* ANNE *and* PETER *that they must be silent, then steps down towards* PETER *indicating he can draw no water.* PETER *starts back to his room.* ANNE *rises and crosses below the table to* PETER. MR FRANK *crosses quietly towards the*

480 *girls' room. As* PETER *reaches the door of his room a board creaks under his foot. The three are frozen for a minute in fear.* ANNE *then continues over to* PETER *on tiptoe and pours some milk in the saucer.* PETER *squats on the floor, putting the milk down before the*

485 *cat and encouraging him to drink.* MR FRANK *crosses to them, gives* ANNE *his fountain pen, then crosses to the girls' room, goes inside, sits on the bed and puts a comforting arm around* MRS FRANK. ANNE *squats for a moment beside* PETER, *watching the*

490 *cat, then opens her diary and writes. All are silent and motionless, except* MR VAN DAAN *who returns to* MRS VAN DAAN *and fans her with a newspaper. The Westertoren finishes tolling the hour. As* ANNE *begins to write, her voice is heard faintly at first,*

495 *then with growing strength.*)

ANNE   I expect I should be describing what it feels like
to go into hiding. But I really don't know yet,
myself. I only know it's funny never to be able to
500   go outdoors—never to breathe fresh air—never
to run and shout and jump. It's the silence in the
night that frightens me most. Every time I hear a
creak in the house, or a step on the street outside,
I'm sure they're coming for us. The days aren't so
505   bad. At least we know that Miep and Mr. Kraler are
down there below us in the office. Our protectors,
we call them. I asked father what would happen to
them if the Nazis found out they were hiding us.
Pim said that they would suffer the same fate that
510   we would. Imagine! They know this and yet when
they come up here, they're always cheerful and
gay as if there were nothing in the world to bother
them. Friday, the twenty-first of August, nineteen
forty-two. Today I'm going to tell you our general
515   news. Mother is unbearable. She insists on treating
me like a baby, which I loathe. Otherwise things are
going better. The weather is . . . **18**

> **18** Why is Anne amazed by Miep and Mr. Kraler?

Frances Goodrich, Albert Hackett

In the 1920s, screenwriters Albert Hackett and Frances Goodrich traveled to Hollywood to follow their passion, shortly after marrying one another. Only a handful of years after the end of World War II, Hackett and Goodrich wrote an original play, *The Diary of Anne Frank,* based on the book *The Diary of a Young Girl* by Anne Frank. The play opened on Broadway in 1955 to much success and has been widely performed since then. Hackett and Goodrich received several awards for this play, including a Pulitzer Prize for Drama in 1956 and Best Written Drama from the Writers Guild of America in 1960.

SCREENPLAY
It's A Wonderful Life

SCREENPLAY
Father of the Bride

SCREENPLAY
Seven Brides for Seven Brothers

Parts of a Paragraph

Topic sentence tells what the paragraph is about.

Supporting details give facts or reasons about the topic.

Transition words link one supporting detail to the next.

Elaborations add interest for the reader. **Elaborations (Es)** are **e**xplanations, **e**xamples, and **e**vidence.

Conclusion restates the topic sentence or big idea.

Part A

Read the paragraph. Highlight the parts of the paragraph. The topic sentence is green. Supporting details and transition words are yellow. The elaborations are pink, and the conclusion is green. Circle the transition words, and label each part of the paragraph.

The Benefits of Exercise

Regular exercise benefits people's health in two important ways. One benefit is that exercise improves people's physical health. It makes the heart, lungs, bones, and muscles stronger and keeps people at a healthy weight. Exercise is also good for the mind. It makes people feel better about themselves and calms them down when they are angry or stressed. When people regularly do physical activities they enjoy, their bodies and minds stay fit, happy, and healthy.

Parts of a Paragraph (*cont.*)

Part B

Identify the elements within the paragraph. Highlight the topic sentence and concluding sentence green; the supporting details yellow; and the elaborations pink. Circle any transition words.

Kind, hard-working, and tough are three traits that describe Mrs. Luella Bates Washington Jones. Her kindness is revealed in surprising ways. In spite of Roger's actions, Mrs. Washington Jones sees a boy in need of guidance and care. She is determined to feed him and instill a basic level of respect for other people. She also works hard to support herself and take care of her apartment. The apartment is clean and tidy. Over dinner, she tells Roger about her job at the hotel beauty shop. Through her stories, she conveys a sense of history with her job. Another unexpected trait is her toughness. When Roger attempted to steal her purse, the last thing he expected was to be confronted by her. She was determined to make a lasting impression. Instead of being frightened, she knocked him down and then decided to teach him about the consequences of his actions. Mrs. Luella Bates Washington Jones unexpectedly embodies the traits of a hard worker along with kindness and toughness.

Elements of a Drama

Acts	An act is one of the main parts of a play.
Scenes	Acts are made up of scenes or episodes that occur in the same location. One act can have many scenes.
Flashback	A flashback is a literary device used when a scene changes the chronology of events to an event back in the past.
Characters	Characters in a play are called the cast members. In a play, characters' names are written in bold font or style to tell who performs the dialogue or actions.
Stage Directions	The information set in parentheses tells stage directions. Information in parentheses is not read aloud by the actors. The stage directions tell what happens before the actors speak, or tell about a change in the stage set. These references tell the actors what to do, how to do it, or how to say the words.
Symbols	In a play, the playwright doesn't have to describe a symbol because he or she can show it (such as the Star of David worn by the Jews). Characters often explain the significance of the symbols through their dialogue with other characters.

Read the text features of a novel. Write the corresponding element of a drama. The first one is done for you.

Novel: *The Outsiders*	Drama or play: *The Play of the Diary of Anne Frank*
author	playwright
chapters	
plot: telling thoughts through actions	
episodes	
characters	
dialogue is read	
quotation marks show who is talking	
symbol: description of greased hair	

Critical Understandings: Direction Words

Read the prompts and respond using complete sentences. Refer to the chart on page 66 to determine how to respond. Provide text evidence when requested.

1. Define the idiom "catches his eye."

   _____

   _____

2. Report how Mr. Frank is feeling.

   _____

   _____

3. Compare Miep Gies to Mrs. Jones from "Thank You, M'am."

   _____

   _____

4. Interpret the meaning of the phrase "all control is gone." Provide text evidence.

   _____

   _____

   Text Evidence: _____

   _____

An Author's Creative License

Read the excerpt taken from Anne Frank's diary. Determine the differences between the diary entry and the drama.

SATURDAY, 11 JULY, 1942

Dear Kitty,

. . . I expect you will be interested to hear what it feels like to "disappear"; well, all I can say is that I don't know myself yet. I don't think I shall ever feel really at home in this house, but that does not mean that I loathe it here, it is more like being on vacation in a very peculiar boarding-house. Rather a mad idea, perhaps, but that is how it strikes me. The "Secret Annex" is an ideal hiding place. Although it leans to one side and is damp, you'd never find such a comfortable hiding place anywhere in Amsterdam, no, perhaps not even in the whole of Holland. Our little room looked very bare at first with nothing on the walls; but thanks to Daddy who had brought my film-star collection and picture postcards on beforehand, and with the aid of paste pot and brush, I have transformed the walls into one gigantic picture. This makes it look much more cheerful, and, when the Van Daans come, we'll get some wood from the attic, and make a few little cupboards for the walls and other odds and ends to make it look more lively.

. . . The four of us went to the private office yesterday evening and turned on the radio. I was so terribly frightened that someone might hear it that I simply begged Daddy to come upstairs with me. Mummy understood how I felt and came too. We are very nervous in other ways, too, that the neighbors might hear us or see something going on. We made curtains straight away on the first day. Really one can hardly call them curtains, they are just light, loose strips of material, all different shapes, quality, and pattern, which Daddy and I sewed together in a most unprofessional way. These works of art are fixed in position with drawing pins, not to come down until we emerge from here . . .

Yours, Anne

Diary	Play

Passage Comprehension

Read the prompts and respond using complete sentences. Refer to the chart on page 66 to determine how to respond. Provide text evidence when requested.

1. Define *flashback*. Explain how this chronological text structure contributes to the development of the plot.

   _____

   _____

   _____

   _____

   _____

2. Report how the playwrights used stage directions to change point of view. Provide text evidence.

   _____

   _____

   _____

   Text Evidence: _____

   _____

3. Compare Otto Frank's relationship with the Van Daans to Darry's relationship with Ponyboy and Sodapop.

   _____

   _____

   _____

   _____

   _____

   _____

   _____

   _____

Passage Comprehension (*cont.*)

4. Interpret the change in Anne's tone when she realizes what it means to be in hiding. Provide text evidence.

_____

_____

Text Evidence: _____

_____

_____

_____

_____

5. List words and phrases that were used in another location or time period. Define them using a dictionary.

_____

_____

_____

_____

6. Examine Anne's quote "We all live with the objective of being happy; our lives are all different and yet the same." Describe how Anne Frank and Ponyboy are both outsiders.

_____

_____

_____

_____

_____

_____

_____

_____

_____

Close Reading

Read the text.

Excerpt from *The Play of the Diary of Anne Frank*

ACT ONE

Scene One

The top floors of a warehouse in Amsterdam, Holland. November 1945. Late afternoon.

MR FRANK enters. He is weak and ill and is making a supreme effort at self-control. His clothes are threadbare. He carries a small rucksack. A scarf catches his eye. He takes it down, puts it around his neck, then wanders towards the couch, but stops as he sees the glove. He picks it up. Suddenly all control is gone. He breaks down and weeps. MIEP GIES enters up the stairs. She is a Dutch girl of about twenty-two, pregnant now. She is compassionate and protective in her attitude towards MR FRANK. She has been a stenographer and secretary in his business. She has her coat and hat on, ready to go home. A small silver cross hangs at her throat.

MIEP   Are you all right, Mr. Frank?

MR FRANK   *(quickly controlling himself)* Yes, Miep, yes.

MIEP   Everyone in the office has gone home—it's after six. Don't stay up here, Mr. Frank. What's the use of torturing yourself like this?

MR FRANK   I've come to say good-bye—I'm leaving here, Miep.

MIEP   What do you mean? Where are you going? Where?

MR FRANK   I don't know yet. I haven't decided.

MIEP   Mr. Frank, you can't leave here. This is your home. Amsterdam is your home. Your business is here, waiting for you. You're needed here. Now that the war is over, there are things that . . .

MR FRANK   I can't stay in Amsterdam, Miep. It has too many memories for me. Everywhere there's something—the house we lived in—the school—the street organ playing out there. I'm not the person you used to know, Miep. I'm a bitter old man. Forgive me. I shouldn't speak to you like this—after all that you did for us—the suffering . . .

MIEP   No. No. It wasn't suffering. You can't say we suffered.

Close Reading (*cont.*)

	MR FRANK	I know what you went through, you and Mr. Kraler. I'll remember it as long as I live. Come, Miep. *(He remembers his rucksack, crosses below the table to the couch and picks up his rucksack.)*
30		

MIEP   Mr. Frank, did you see? There are some of your papers here. *(She takes a bundle of papers from the shelves, then crosses below the table to* MR FRANK.*)* We found them in a heap of rubbish on the floor after—after you left.

MR FRANK   Burn them. *(He opens his rucksack and puts the glove in it.)*

35   **MIEP**   But, Mr. Frank, there are letters, notes . . .

MR FRANK   Burn them. All of them.

MIEP   Burn this? *(She hands him a worn, velour-covered book.)*

MR FRANK   *(quietly)* Anne's diary. *(He opens the diary and reads.)* 'Monday, the sixth of July, nineteen hundred and forty-two.' *(To* MIEP.*)* Nineteen hundred and forty-two. Is it possible, Miep? Only three years ago. *(He reads.)* 'Dear Diary, since you and I are going to be great friends, I will start by telling you about myself. My name is Anne Frank. I am thirteen years old. I was born in Germany the twelfth of June, nineteen twenty-nine. As my family is Jewish, we emigrated to Holland when Hitler came to power.'

40

45   **MR FRANK**
ANNE'S VOICE } *(together)* 'My father started a business, importing spice and herbs. Things went well for us until nineteen forty. Then the War came and the Dutch—*(He turns the page.)* defeat, followed by the arrival of the Germans. Then things got very bad for the Jews.'

(MR FRANK'S voice dies out as ANNE'S VOICE *grows stronger.)*

50   **ANNE**   You could not do this and you could not do that. They forced father out of his business. We had to wear yellow stars. I had to turn in my bike. I couldn't go to a Dutch school any more. I couldn't go to the cinema, or ride in an automobile, or even on a streetcar, and a million other things. But somehow we children still managed to have fun. Yesterday, father told me we were going into hiding. Where, he wouldn't say. At five o'clock this morning mother woke me and told me to hurry and get dressed. I was to put on as many clothes as I could. It would look too suspicious if we walked along carrying suitcases. It wasn't until we were on our way that I learned where we were going. Our hiding place was to be upstairs in the building where father used to have his business. Three other people were coming in with us—the Van Daans and their son Peter. Father knew the Van Daans but we had never met them.

55

60

(The sound of distant ships' sirens is heard.)

Close Reading (*cont.*)

Scene Two
Early morning. July 1942.

65

The three members of the VAN DAAN *family are waiting for the* FRANKS *to arrive.* MR VAN DAAN *is smoking a cigarette and watching his wife with a nervous eye. His overcoat and suit are expensive and well-cut.* MRS VAN DAAN *is sitting on the couch. She is a pretty woman in her early forties and is clutching her possessions: a hat-box, a handbag and an attractive straw*

70

carry-all. PETER VAN DAAN *is standing at the window in the room. He is a shy,* **awkward** *boy of sixteen. He wears a cap, a short overcoat, and long Dutch trousers, like 'plus fours'. All the* VAN DAANS *have the* **conspicuous** *yellow Star of David on the left breast of their clothing.*

MRS V.DAAN   Something's happened to them. I know it.

75   **MR V.DAAN**   Now, Kerli!

MRS V.DAAN   Mr. Frank said they'd be here at seven o'clock. He said . . .

MR V.DAAN   They have two miles to walk. You can't expect . . .

MRS V.DAAN   They've been picked up.

(The door below opens.)

80

That's what happened. They've been taken.

*(*MR VAN DAAN *indicates that he hears someone coming.)*

MR V.DAAN   You see?

*(*MR FRANK *comes up the stairwell from below.)*

MR FRANK   Mrs. Van Daan, Mr. Van Daan. *(He shakes hands with them. He moves to* PETER *and shakes his hand.)* There were too many of the Green Police on the

85

streets—we had to take the long way round.

Close Reading (*cont.*)

90

*(MIEP, not pregnant now, MARGOT, MR KRALER, and MRS FRANK come up the stairs. MARGOT is eighteen, beautiful, quiet and shy. She carries a leatherette hold-all and a large brown paper bag, which she puts on the table. KRALER is a Dutchman, **dependable** and kindly. He wears a hearing aid in his ear and carries two brief-cases. MRS FRANK is a young mother, gently bred and reserved. She, like MR FRANK, has a slight German accent. She carries a leatherette shopping bag and her handbag. We see the Star of David conspicuous on the FRANKS' clothing. KRALER acknowledges the VAN DAANS, moves to the shelves and checks their contents. MIEP empties her straw bag of the clothes it contains and piles them on the table.)*

95

MRS FRANK   Anne?

(ANNE FRANK comes quickly up the stairs. She is thirteen, quick in her movements, interested in everything and mercurial in her emotions. She wears a cape, long wool socks and carries a school bag.)

100

MR FRANK   My wife, Edith. Mr. and Mrs. Van Daan.

(MRS FRANK shakes MR VAN DAAN'S hand, then hurries across to shake hands with MRS VAN DAAN. She then moves to the sink and inspects it.)

Their son, Peter—my daughters, Margot and Anne.

105

(ANNE gives a polite little curtsy as she shakes MR VAN DAAN'S hand. She puts her bag on the left end of the table then immediately starts off on a tour of investigation of her new home, going upstairs to the attic room.)

KRALER   I'm sorry there is still so much confusion.

MR FRANK   Please. Don't think of it. After all, we'll have plenty of **leisure** to arrange everything ourselves.

110

MIEP   *(indicating the sink cupboard)* We put the stores of food you sent in here. *(She crosses to the shelves.)* Your drugs are here—soap, linen, here.

MRS FRANK   Thank you, Miep.

MIEP   I made up the beds—the way Mr. Frank and Mr. Kraler said. Forgive me. I have to hurry. I've got to go to the other side of town to get some ration books for you.

115

Close Reading (*cont.*)

MRS V.DAAN	Ration books? If they see our names on ration books, they'll know we're here.
KRALER ⎫ MIEP ⎭ *(together)*	There isn't anything . . . Don't worry. Your names won't be on them. *(As she hurries out.)* I'll be up later.
MR FRANK	Thank you, Miep.
	(MIEP exits down the stairwell.)
MRS FRANK	It's illegal, then, the ration books? We've never done anything illegal.
MR FRANK	We won't be living exactly according to **regulations** here.
KRALER	This isn't the black market, Mrs. Frank. This is what we call the white market—helping all of the hundreds and hundreds who are hiding out in Amsterdam.
	(The carillon is heard playing the quarter hour before eight. KRALER looks at his watch. ANNE comes down from the attic, stops at the window and looks out through the curtains.)
ANNE	It's the Westertoren.
KRALER	I must go. I must be out of here and downstairs in the office before the workmen get here. Miep or I, or both of us, will be up each day to bring you food and news and find out what your needs are. Tomorrow I'll get you a better bolt for the door at the foot of the stairs. It needs a bolt that you can throw yourself and open only at our signal. *(To MR FRANK.)* Oh—you'll tell them about the noise?
MR FRANK	I'll tell them.
KRALER	Good-bye, then, for the moment. I'll come up again, after the workmen leave.
MR FRANK	*(shaking KRALER'S hand)* Good-bye, Mr. Kraler.
MRS FRANK	*(shaking KRALER'S hand)* How can we thank you?

Line numbers: 120, 125, 130, 135, 140

Close Reading (*cont.*)

KRALER   I never thought I'd live to see the day when a man like Mr. Frank would have to go into hiding. When you think . . .

145   (KRALER *breaks off and exits down the stairs.* MR FRANK *follows him down the stairs and bolts the door after him. In the* **interval** *before he returns,* PETER *goes to* MARGOT, *gives a stiff bow and shakes hands with her.* ANNE *watches, and as they complete their greeting, moves to* PETER *and holds out her hand.* PETER *does not see her and turns away.* MR FRANK *comes up the stairs.*)

MRS FRANK   What did he mean, about the noise?

150   **MR FRANK**   First, let's take off some of these clothes.

(ANNE *moves below the table, stands with her back to the audience, removes her cape and beret and puts them on the pile of clothes on the table. They all start to take off* **garment** *after garment. On each of their coats, sweaters, blouses, suits and dresses is another yellow Star of David.* MR *and* MRS FRANK
155   *are under-dressed quite simply. The others wear several things, sweaters, extra dresses, bathrobes, aprons, etc.* MRS FRANK *takes off her gloves, carefully folding them before putting them away.*)

MR V.DAAN   It's a wonder we weren't arrested, walking along the streets—Petronella with a fur coat in July—and that cat of Peter's crying all the way.

160   **ANNE**   (*removing a pair of panties*) A cat?

MRS FRANK   (*shocked*) Anne, please!

ANNE   It's all right. I've got on three more (*She removes two more pairs of panties. Finally, as they finish removing their surplus clothing, they settle down.*)

MR FRANK   Now. About the noise. While the men are in the building below, we must
165   have complete quiet. Every sound can be heard down there, not only in the workrooms, but in the offices, too. The men come about eight-thirty, and leave at about five-thirty. So, to be perfectly safe, from eight in the morning until six in the evening we must move only when it is necessary and then in stockinged feet. We must not speak above a whisper. We must not run any water. We
170   cannot use the sink, or even, forgive me, the WC. The pipes go down through the workrooms. It would be heard. No rubbish . . .

(*The sound of marching feet is heard.* MR FRANK, *followed by* ANNE, *peers out of the window. Satisfied that the marching feet are going away, he returns and continues.*)

175   No rubbish must ever be thrown out which might reveal that someone is living here—not even a potato paring. We must burn everything in the stove at night. This is the way we must live until it is over, if we are to survive.

Close Reading (*cont.*)

(There is a pause. MARGOT *accidentally drops the nightgown she is taking off.* PETER *jumps to pick it up for her.)*

180   **MRS FRANK**   Until it is over.

MR FRANK   After six we can move about—we can talk and laugh and have our supper and read and play games—just as we would at home. *(He looks at his watch.)* And now I think it would be wise if we all went to our rooms, and were settled before eight o'clock. Mrs. Van Daan, you and your husband will go

185   upstairs. I regret that there's no place up there for Peter. But he will be here, near us. This will be our common room, where we'll meet to talk and eat and read, like one family.

MRS V.DAAN   And where do you and Mrs. Frank sleep?

MR FRANK   This room is also our bedroom.

190   *(MRS VAN DAAN rises in protest.)*

MRS V.DAAN   **MR V.DAAN**   *(together)*   That isn't right. We'll sleep here and you take the room upstairs. It's your place.

MR FRANK   Please. I've thought this out for weeks. It's the best arrangement. The only arrangement.

195   *(MR VAN DAAN starts to load his arms with the clothes he and his wife have taken off and thrown across the couch.)*

MRS V.DAAN   *(shaking* MR FRANK'S *hand)* Never, never can we thank you. *(She moves to* MRS FRANK *and shakes her hand.)* I don't know what would have happened to us, if it hadn't been for Mr. Frank.

Close Reading (*cont.*)

| 200 | **MR FRANK** | You don't know how your husband helped me when I came to this country—knowing no-one—not able to speak the language. I can never repay him for that. May I help you with your things? |

MR V.DAAN No. No. *(He picks up the carton and moves towards the attic stairs. To* MRS VAN DAAN*)* Come along, liefje.

205 **MRS V.DAAN** You'll be all right, Peter? You're not afraid?

PETER *(embarrassed)* Please, Mother. *(He picks up his gear.* MRS FRANK *goes to the head of the stairwell and stares thoughtfully down.* MR *and* MRS VAN DAAN *go upstairs.)*

MR FRANK You, too, must have some rest, Edith. You didn't close your eyes last night.
210 Nor you, Margot.

ANNE I slept, Father. Wasn't that funny? I knew it was the last night in my own bed, and yet I slept soundly.

MR FRANK I'm glad, Anne. Now you'll be able to help me straighten things in here. *(To* MRS FRANK *and* MARGOT*.)* Come with me—you and Margot rest in this
215 room for the time being.

MRS FRANK You're sure? I could help, really. And Anne hasn't had her milk.

MR FRANK I'll give it to her. *(He crosses to the table and picks up the piles of clothes.)* Anne, Peter—it's best that you take off your shoes now, before you forget. *(He leads the way to the room, goes in and switches on the pendant light.* MARGOT
220 *goes into the room.* ANNE *and* PETER *remove their shoes.)*

MRS FRANK You're sure you're not tired, Anne?

ANNE I feel fine. I'm going to help father.

MRS FRANK Peter, I'm glad you are to be with us.

PETER Yes, Mrs. Frank.

Close Reading (*cont.*)

225   (MRS FRANK *goes into the room and closes the door. During the following scene* MR FRANK *helps* MARGOT *to hang up clothes.* PETER *takes his cat out of its case.*)

ANNE   What's your cat's name?

PETER   'Mouschi'.

230   ANNE   Mouschi! Mouschi! Mouschi! *(She picks up the cat.)* I love cats. I have one—a darling little cat. But they made me leave her behind. I left some food and a note for the neighbors to take care of her—I'm going to miss her terribly. What is yours? A him or a her?

PETER   He's a tom. He doesn't like strangers. *(He takes the cat from* ANNE, *and puts*
235   *it back in its carrier.)*

ANNE   Then I'll have to stop being a stranger, won't I? Is he fixed?

PETER   Huh?

ANNE   Did you have him altered?

PETER   No.

240   ANNE   Oh, you ought to—to keep him from fighting. Where did you go to school?

PETER   Jewish Secondary.

ANNE   But that's where Margot and I go. I never saw you around.

PETER   I used to see you—sometimes.

ANNE   You did?

245   PETER   In the school yard. You were always in the middle of a bunch of kids. *(He takes a penknife from his pocket.)*

ANNE   Why didn't you ever come over?

PETER   I'm sort of a lone wolf. *(He starts to rip off his Star of David.)*

Close Reading (*cont.*)

	ANNE	What are you doing?
250	PETER	Taking it off.
	ANNE	But you can't do that. *(She grabs his hands and stops him.)* They'll arrest you if you go out without your star.
	PETER	*(pulling away)* Who's going out? *(He crosses to the stove, lifts the lid and throws the star into the stove.)*
255	ANNE	Why, of course. You're right. Of course we don't need them any more. *(She takes* PETER'S *knife and removes her star.* PETER *waits for her star to throw it away.)*
		I wonder what our friends will think when we don't show up today?
	PETER	I didn't have any dates with anyone.
260	ANNE	*(**concentrating** on her star)* Oh, I did. I had a date with Jopie this afternoon to go and play ping-pong at her house. Do you know Jopie de Waal?
	PETER	No.
265	ANNE	Jopie's my best friend. I wonder what she'll think when she telephones and there's no answer? Probably she'll go over to the house—I wonder what she'll think—we left everything as if we'd suddenly been called away—breakfast dishes in the sink—beds not made . . . *(As she pulls off her star, the cloth underneath shows clearly the colour and form of the star.)* Look! It's still there. What're you going to do with yours?
270	PETER	Burn it. *(He moves to the stove and holds out his hand for* ANNE'S *star.* ANNE *starts to give the star to* PETER, *but cannot.)*
	ANNE	It's funny. I can't throw it away. I don't know why.
	PETER	You can't throw . . . ? Something they branded you with? That they made you wear so they could spit on you?
	ANNE	I know. I know. But after all, it is the Star of David, isn't it?

Close Reading (*cont.*)

275   *(The* VAN DAANS *have arranged their things, have put their clothes in the wardrobe and are sitting on the bed, fanning themselves.)*

PETER   Maybe it's different for a girl.

*(*ANNE *puts her star in her school bag.)*

MR FRANK   Forgive me, Peter. Now, let me see. We must find a bed for your cat. I'm glad
280   you brought your cat. Anne was feeling so badly about hers.

(He sees a small worn wash-tub and pulls it from the top shelf.)

Here we are. Will it be comfortable in that?

PETER   Thanks.

MR FRANK   And here is your room. But I warn you, Peter, you can't grow any more.
285   Not at inch, or you'll have to sleep with your feet out of the skylight. Are
you hungry?

PETER   No.

MR FRANK   We have some bread and butter.

PETER   No, thank you.

290   **MR FRANK**   *(with a friendly pat on* PETER'S *shoulder)* You can have it for luncheon, then.
And tonight we will have a real supper—our first supper together.

PETER   Thanks. Thanks. *(He goes into his room.* MR FRANK *closes the door after*
PETER, *then sits and removes his shoes.)*

MR FRANK   That's a nice boy, Peter.

295   **ANNE**   He's awfully shy, isn't he?

MR FRANK   You'll like him, I know.

ANNE   I certainly hope so, since he's the only boy I'm likely to see for months and
months.

Close Reading (*cont.*)

MR FRANK   Anne, there's a box there. Will you open it?

300   *(The sound of children playing is heard from the street below. MR FRANK goes to the sink and pours a glass of milk from the thermos bottle.)*

ANNE   You know the way I'm going to think of it here? I'm going to think of it as a boarding-house. A very **peculiar** Summer boarding-house, like the one that we . . . *(She breaks off as she looks in the box.)* Father! Father! My film stars. I 305   was wondering where they were—and Queen Wilhelmina. How wonderful!

MR FRANK   There's something more. Go on. Look further.

(ANNE digs deeper into the box and brings out a velour-covered book. She examines it in delighted silence for a moment, then opens the cover slowly, and looks up at MR FRANK with shining eyes.)

310   ANNE   A diary! *(She throws her arms around him.)* I've never had a diary. And I've always longed for one. *(She rushes to the table and looks for a pencil.)* Pencil, pencil, pencil, pencil. *(She darts across to the stair-well and starts down the stairs.)* I'm going down to the office to get a pencil.

MR FRANK   Anne! No! *(He strides to ANNE and catches her arm. MRS FRANK aware of the* 315   *sudden movement and sounds, sits up. After a moment she rises, goes to the window and looks out, then returns and sits on the bed.)*

ANNE   *(startled)* But there's no-one in the building now.

MR FRANK   It doesn't matter. I don't want you ever to go beyond that door.

ANNE   *(sobered)* Never? Not even at night time, when everyone is gone? Or on 320   Sundays? Can't I go down to listen to the radio?

MR FRANK   Never. I am sorry, Anneke. It isn't safe. No, you must never go beyond that door.

ANNE   I see. *(For the first time she realizes what 'going into hiding' means.)*

Close Reading (*cont.*)

MR FRANK 325	It'll be hard, I know. But always remember this, Anneke. There are no walls, there are no bolts, no locks that anyone can put on your mind. Miep will bring us books. We will read history, poetry, mythology. *(He gives* ANNE *the glass of milk.)* Here's your milk.	

(MR FRANK puts his arm about ANNE, *and crosses with her to the couch, where they sit side by side.)*

330

As a matter of fact, between us, Annie, being here has certain advantages for you. For instance you remember the battle you had with your mother the other day on the subject of goloshes? You said you'd rather die than wear goloshes. But in the end you had to wear them. Well now, you see for as long as we are here, you will never have to wear goloshes. Isn't that good? And the

335

coat that you inherited from Margot—

(ANNE makes a wry face.)

—you won't have to wear that. And the piano. You won't have to practice on the piano. I tell you, this is going to be a fine life for you.

(ANNE'S panic is gone. PETER *appears in the doorway of his room, with a*

340

saucer in one hand and the cat in the other.)

PETER   I—I—I thought I'd better get some water for Mouschi before . . .

MR FRANK   Of course.

Close Reading (*cont.*)

345

350

355

360

(The carillon begins its melody and strikes eight. As it does so, MR FRANK motions for PETER and ANNE to be quiet, tiptoes to the window in the rear wall and peers down. MR VAN DAAN rises and moves to the head of the attic stairs. MR FRANK puts his finger to his lips, indicating to ANNE and PETER that they must be silent, then steps down towards PETER indicating he can draw no water. PETER starts back to his room. ANNE rises and crosses below the table to PETER. MR FRANK crosses quietly towards the girls' room. As PETER reaches the door of his room a board creaks under his foot. The three are frozen for a minute in fear. ANNE then continues over to PETER on tiptoe and pours some milk in the saucer. PETER squats on the floor, putting the milk down before the cat and encouraging him to drink. MR FRANK crosses to them, gives ANNE his fountain pen, then crosses to the girls' room, goes inside, sits on the bed and puts a comforting arm around MRS FRANK. ANNE squats for a moment beside PETER, watching the cat, then opens her diary and writes. All are silent and motionless, except MR VAN DAAN who returns to MRS VAN DAAN and fans her with a newspaper. The Westertoren finishes tolling the hour. As ANNE begins to write, her voice is heard faintly at first, then with growing strength.)

ANNE   I expect I should be describing what it feels like to go into hiding. But I really don't know yet, myself. I only know it's funny never to be able to go outdoors—never to breathe fresh air—never to run and shout and jump. It's the silence in the night that frightens me most. Every time I hear a creak in the house, or a step on the street outside, I'm sure they're coming for us. The days aren't so bad. At least we know that Miep and Mr. Kraler are down there below us in the office. Our protectors, we call them. I asked father what would happen to them if the Nazis found out they were hiding us. Pim said that they would suffer the same fate that we would. Imagine! They know this and yet when they come up here, they're always cheerful and gay as if there were nothing in the world to bother them. Friday, the twenty-first of August, nineteen forty-two. Today I'm going to tell you our general news. Mother is unbearable. She insists on treating me like a baby, which I loathe. Otherwise things are going better. The weather is . . .

365

370

Prepare to Write: Explanatory Paragraph

Part A. Study the Prompt

Read the prompt. Identify the topic, directions, and purpose for writing.

The war is over, and Mr. Frank is no longer in hiding. Write a paragraph that explains why Mr. Frank seems to have lost his will to live. Choose several details from the text that reveal his state of mind.

Topic: _____

Directions: _____

_____

Purpose for writing: _____

_____

Part B. Introduce Position Topic Sentence

Starting Words or Phrases					
If	After	Since	Before	So that	Because
Whenever	As long as	In order that	Even though	Although	Wherever
Unless	While	When	Even	As if	As soon as
As	Where	Though	Even if	Until	

Part C. Write Position Topic Sentence

Use a word or phrase from the chart in Part B to develop a position topic sentence.

Occasion (event/circumstance): _____

_____

Position (prove/explain): _____

_____

Topic Sentence: _____

_____

_____

Prepare to Write: Explanatory Paragraph (*cont.*)

Part D. Prove the Position

Losses	Physical Appearance	Behaviors

Part E. Write Concluding Sentence

Develop a concluding sentence by restating the topic sentence. Restate the occasion and position by choosing another word or phrase from the box in Part B.

_____

_____

_____

_____

_____

_____

Position Topic Sentences

Use the words in the chart on page 140 to combine the following sentences to create topic sentences that express a position.

Example:

Occasion/Event: I have enjoyed all of our family vacations.

Position/Consequence: My favorite was our trip to the mountains.

Topic Sentence: While I have enjoyed all of our family vacations, my favorite was our trip to the mountains.

1. Occasion/Event: Windmills produce clean energy.

    Position/Consequence: Many people are opposed to them.

    Topic Sentence: _____

    _____

2. Occasion/Event: Martha is class president.

    Position/Consequence: We will have many class functions.

    Topic Sentence: _____

    _____

3. Occasion/Event: Cell phones are a convenient way to stay in touch.

    Position/Consequence: Many people stay glued to their phones.

    Topic Sentence: _____

    _____

4. Occasion/Event: Children jump on trampolines.

    Position/Consequence: Safety nets should be used.

    Topic Sentence: _____

    _____

5. Occasion/Event: She went to the library to study.

    Position/Consequence: Her grades improved.

    Topic Sentence: _____

    _____

The Writer's Checklist

Trait	Yes	No	Did the writer . . .?
Ideas and Content			focus all sentences on the topic
			provide supporting details for the topic sentence
Organization			write a topic sentence
			tell things in an order that makes sense
			write a concluding sentence
Voice and Audience Awareness			think about the audience and purpose for writing
Word Choice			try to find a unique way to say things
Sentence Fluency			write complete sentences
Conventions			capitalize words correctly:
			capitalize the first word of each sentence
			capitalize proper nouns, including people's names
			punctuate correctly:
			put a period or question mark at the end of each sentence
			use grammar correctly:
			use the correct verb tense
			make sure the verb agrees with the subject in number
			use correct spelling

Let's Focus: "The Circuit"

Content Focus
pursuit of happiness; the value of education

Type of Text
informational—autobiography; short story

Author's Name _____

Author's Purpose _____

Big Ideas
Consider the following Big Idea questions. Write your answer for each question.

Is the American Dream a possibility for everyone? Explain.

_____

_____

What are the negative effects of a transient lifestyle?

_____

_____

Autobiography Preview Checklist: "The Circuit" on pages 147–153.

☐ Title: What clue does it provide about the passage?

☐ Pictures: What additional information is added here?

☐ Margin Information: What vocabulary is important to understand this story?

Enduring Understandings
After reading the text . . .

_____

_____

_____

_____

_____

_____

Key Passage Vocabulary: "The Circuit"

Read each word. Write it in column 3. Then, circle a number to rate your knowledge of the word.

Vocabulary	Part of Speech	Write the Word	Rate the Word
exchange	(v)		0 1 2 3
populated	(adj)		0 1 2 3
motionless	(adj)		0 1 2 3
drone	(n)		0 1 2 3
design	(n)		0 1 2 3
instinctively	(adv)		0 1 2 3
murmur	(v)		0 1 2 3
savor	(v)		0 1 2 3
introduce	(v)		0 1 2 3
enthusiastically	(adv)		0 1 2 3

THE CIRCUIT
by Francisco Jiménez

A family of migrant farmworkers finished picking the last of the strawberry crop. Now they are seeking work from a vineyard owner whose grapes are ready to harvest.

exchange

to trade; to give one thing for another

populated

lived in; filled with

At sunset we drove into a labor camp near Fresno.
5 Since Papá did not speak English, Mamá asked the camp foreman if he needed any more workers. "We don't need no more," said the foreman, scratching his head. "Check with Sullivan down the road. Can't miss him. He lives in a big white house with a fence
10 around it."

When we got there, Mamá walked up to the house. She went through a white gate, past a row of rose bushes, up the stairs to the front door. She rang the doorbell. The porch light went on and a tall husky
15 man came out. They **exchanged** a few words. After the man went in, Mamá clasped hands and hurried back to the car. "We have work! Mr. Sullivan said we can stay there the whole season," she said, gasping and pointing to an old garage near the stables. ∎1

20 The garage was worn out by the years. It had no windows. The walls, eaten by termites, strained to support the roof full of holes. The dirt floor, **populated** by earthworms, looked like a gray road map.

25 That night, by the light of a kerosene lamp, we unpacked and cleaned our new home. Roberto swept away the loose dirt, leaving the hard ground. Papá plugged the holes in the walls with old newspapers and tin can tops. Mamá fed my little
30 brothers and sisters. Papá and Roberto then brought in the mattress and placed it on the far corner of the garage. "Mamá, you and the little ones sleep on the mattress. Roberto, Panchito, and I will sleep outside under the trees," Papá said. ∎2

35 Early next morning, Mr. Sullivan showed us where his crop was, and after breakfast, Papá, Roberto, and I headed for the vineyard to pick.

Around nine o'clock, the temperature had risen to almost one hundred degrees. I was completely
40 soaked in sweat, and my mouth felt as if I had been

1 Why is Mamá excited about an old garage?

2 What is the narrator's name?

chewing on a handkerchief. I walked over to the end of the row, picked up the jug of water we had brought, and began drinking. "Don't drink too much; you'll get sick," Roberto shouted. No sooner
45 had he said that than I felt sick to my stomach. I dropped to my knees and let the jug roll off my hands. I remained **motionless** with my eyes glued on the hot sandy ground. All I could hear was the **drone** of insects. Slowly I began to recover. I poured
50 water over my face and neck and watched the black mud run down my arms and hit the ground.

I still felt a little dizzy when we took a break to eat lunch. It was past two o'clock and we sat underneath a large walnut tree that was on the side of the road.
55 While we ate, Papá jotted down the number of boxes we had picked. Roberto drew **designs** on the ground with a stick. Suddenly I noticed Papá's face turn pale as he looked down the road. "Here comes the school bus," he whispered loudly in alarm.
60 **Instinctively**, Roberto and I ran and hid in the vineyards. We did not want to get in trouble for not going to school. The yellow bus stopped in front of Mr. Sullivan's house. Two neatly dressed boys about my age got off. They carried books under their arms.
65 After they crossed the street, the bus drove away. Roberto and I came out from hiding and joined Papá. "*Tienen que tener cuidado*," he warned us. **3**

After lunch, we went back to work. The sun kept beating down. The buzzing insects, the wet sweat,
70 and the hot dry dust made the afternoon seem to last forever. Finally the mountains around the valley reached out and swallowed the sun. Within an hour it was too dark to continue picking. The vines blanketed the grapes, making it difficult to
75 see the bunches. "*Vámonos,*" said Papá, signaling to us that it was time to quit work. Papá then took out a pencil and began to figure out how much we had earned our first day. He wrote down numbers, crossed some out, wrote down some more. "*Quince,*"
80 he **murmured**. **4**

motionless
still; not moving

drone
a low, humming noise

design
a pattern or drawing

instinctively
without thinking; in a natural or automatic way

murmur
to speak softly

3 Why didn't the boys go to school?

4 Why do they work from morning until it is too dark to see?

savor

to enjoy something deeply

---

5 Did they have a bathroom? How do you know?

When we arrived home, we took a cold shower underneath a waterhose. We then sat down to eat dinner around some wooden crates that served as a table. Mamá had cooked a special meal for us.

85 We had rice and tortillas with *"carne con chile,"* my favorite dish. **5**

The next morning I could hardly move. My body ached all over. I felt little control over my arms and legs. This feeling went on every morning for days,

90 until my muscles finally got used to the work.

It was Monday, the first week of November. The grape season was over and I could now go to school. I woke up early that morning and lay in bed, looking at the stars and **savoring** the thought of not going

95 to work and of starting sixth grade for the first time that year. Since I could not sleep, I decided to get up and join Papá and Roberto at breakfast. I sat at the table across from Roberto, but I kept my head down. I did not want to look up and face him. I knew he

100 was sad. He was not going to school today. He was not going tomorrow, or next week, or next month. He would not go until the cotton season was over, and that was sometime in February. I rubbed my hands together and watched the dry, acid-stained

105 skin fall to the floor in little rolls. **6**

6 Why do you think the narrator wasn't expected to pick cotton?

When Papá and Roberto left for work, I felt relief. I walked to the top of a small grade next to the shack and watched the *Carcachita* disappear in the distance in a cloud of dust.

110 Two hours later, around eight o'clock, I stood by the side of the road waiting for school bus number twenty. When it arrived I climbed in. No one noticed me. Everyone was busy either talking or yelling. I sat in an empty seat in the back.

115 When the bus stopped in front of the school, I felt very nervous. I looked out the bus window and saw boys and girls carrying books under their arms. I felt empty. I put my hands in my pants pockets and

walked to the principal's office. When I entered, I
120 heard a woman's voice say: "May I help you?" I was
startled. I had not heard English for months. For a
few seconds I remained speechless. I looked at the
lady who waited for an answer. My first instinct was
to answer her in Spanish, but I held back. Finally,
125 after struggling for English words, I managed to
tell her that I wanted to enroll in the sixth grade.
After answering many questions, I was led to the
classroom. **7**

Mr. Lema, the sixth grade teacher, greeted me and
130 assigned me to a desk. He then **introduced** me
to the class. I was so nervous and scared at that
moment when everyone's eyes were on me that
I wished I were with Papá and Roberto picking
cotton. After taking roll, Mr. Lema gave the class
135 the assignment for the first hour. "The first thing
we have to do this morning is finish reading the
story we began yesterday," he said **enthusiastically**.
He walked up to me, handed me an English book,
and asked me to read. "We are on page 125," he said
140 politely. When I heard this, I felt my blood rush to
my head; I felt dizzy. "Would you like to read?" he
asked hesitantly. I opened the book to page 125.
My mouth was dry. My eyes began to water. I could
not begin. "You can read later," Mr. Lema said
145 understandingly.

For the rest of the reading period, I kept getting
angrier and angrier with myself. I should have read,
I thought to myself. **8**

During recess, I went into the restroom and opened
150 my English book to page 125. I began to read in
a low voice, pretending I was in class. There were
many words I did not know. I closed the book and
headed back to the classroom.

introduce

to present one
person to another
person or to a
group

enthusiastically

with great energy
and excitement

7 Why was the
narrator
struggling with
his English?

8 Why was he
disappointed
with himself for
not reading?

Mr. Lema was sitting at his desk correcting papers.
155 When I entered he looked up at me and smiled. I
felt better. I walked up to him and asked if he could
help me with the new words. "Gladly," he said.

The rest of the month, I spent my lunch hours
working on English with Mr. Lema, my best friend
160 at school. **9**

9 What did the narrator value more than making friends?

One Friday during lunch hour, Mr. Lema asked me
to take a walk with him to the music room. "Do you
like music?" he asked me as we entered the building.

"Yes, I like Mexican *corridos*," I answered. He then
165 picked up a trumpet, blew on it, and handed it to
me. The sound gave me goose bumps. I knew that
sound. I had heard it in many Mexican *corridos*.
"How would you like to learn to play it?" he asked.

He must have read my face, because before I could
170 answer, he added: "I'll teach you how to play it
during our lunch hours."

That day I could hardly wait to get home to tell Papá
and Mamá the great news. As I got off the bus, my
little brothers and sisters ran up to meet me. They
175 were yelling and screaming. I thought they were
happy to see me, but when I opened the door to our
shack, I saw that everything we owned was neatly
packed in cardboard boxes. **10**

10 Predict what will happen next.

Francisco Jiménez

When Francisco Jiménez was 4 years old, his parents brought him and his brother to the United States illegally. They were fleeing the poverty of their small village in Mexico. But without the proper papers, the family had to earn a meager living picking crops. They did not have a permanent home for years. "I came to realize that learning and knowledge were the only stable things in my life," says Jiménez. "Whatever I learned in school, that knowledge would stay with me no matter how many times we moved." Jiménez became a U.S. citizen in 1965 and went on to become an award-winning author and well-respected college professor. He has taught at Harvard, Columbia, and Santa Clara universities. *The Circuit* has won many awards, including the American Library Association Best Book for Young Adults, and has been published in English, Spanish, Chinese, Japanese, Korean, and Italian.

Tense Timeline: Past and Present Tenses

Read the examples of different types of verbs. Write examples in the past progressive and the present progressive for each pronoun usage (as done with *helping*).

← Yesterday — Today — Tomorrow →

Past Tense	Present Tense	Future
I walked. She walked. We skipped. He skipped. They faded. It faded. We flossed. He flossed. I carried. He carried. I wrote. She wrote.	I walk. She walks. We skip. He skips. They fade. It fades. We floss. He flosses. I carry. He carries. I write. She writes.	
Past Progressive	**Present Progressive**	**Future**
I was helping. You were helping. He was helping. We were helping. They were helping. It was fading. I was skipping. We were carrying.	I am helping. You are helping. He is helping. We are helping. They are helping. It is fading. I am skipping. We are carrying.	

Verb Tense

Underline all of the past and present verbs/verb phrases in each sentence. Write the verbs in the correct column in the chart.

> **Examples:**
> He <u>was</u> not <u>going</u> to school today.
>
> That night by the light of the kerosene lamp, we <u>unpacked</u> and <u>cleaned</u> our new home.

1. Now they are seeking work from a vineyard owner.

2. At sunset we drove into a labor camp near Fresno.

3. Mamá asked the camp foreman if he needed any more workers.

4. "He lives in a big white house with a fence around it."

5. She went through a white gate, past a row of rose bushes, up the stairs, to the front door.

6. Mamá clasped her hands and hurried back to the car.

7. When we arrived home, we took a cold shower underneath a waterhose.

8. Mr. Lema was sitting at his desk.

9. "Yes, I like Mexican *corridos*," I answered.

10. They were yelling and screaming.

Past		Past Progressive	Present	Present Progressive
unpacked	cleaned	was going		

Linking Verb or Helping Verb

Underline the verb or verb phrase in each sentence. Write the verb or verb phrase in the proper column in the chart.

> **Examples:**
>
> Everyone <u>was</u> busy.
>
> We <u>were hiding</u> from the bus.

1. The grapes are ready for harvest.

2. I was planning to talk to my parents about my trumpet lessons.

3. It was after two o'clock.

4. I was reading to myself in the bathroom.

5. We are on page 125.

6. My mouth was dry.

7. I was so nervous and scared at that moment.

8. Boys and girls were carrying books under their arms.

9. Mr. Lema was sitting at his desk.

10. They were happy to see me.

Linking Verb	Helping Verb + Main Verb
was	were hiding

Masterpiece Sentences: Stage 5—Paint Your Words

Rewrite the following sentences by replacing the underlined words with more descriptive words or phrases.

1. After fixing the barn, the <u>tired man sat</u> in the chair on the porch.

New sentence: _____

_____

2. During lunch, the <u>nice</u> teacher <u>worked</u> with the new student.

New sentence: _____

_____

3. When we got there, Mamá <u>walked</u> up to the <u>house</u>.

New sentence: _____

_____

4. <u>At sunset</u>, we <u>drove</u> into a labor camp near Fresno.

New sentence: _____

_____

5. After <u>lunch</u>, we <u>went</u> back to <u>work</u>.

New sentence: _____

_____

6. <u>When we arrived home</u>, we took a <u>cold</u> shower underneath a waterhose.

New sentence: _____

_____

7. My mouth was <u>dry</u>.

New sentence: _____

8. I <u>walked up to</u> him and <u>asked if he could help me</u> with the new words.

New sentence: _____

_____

Masterpiece Sentences: Stages 1–5

Using one of the pictures, work through the five stages to write a masterpiece sentence.

Stage	Process	Questions to Answer	Answers
Stage 1: Prepare Your Canvas	Choose a noun for the subject. Choose a verb for the predicate.	Who did it? Did what? To what?	
Stage 2: Paint Your Predicate	Tell more about what happened.	When? Where? How?	
Stage 3: Move the Predicate Painters	Improve sentence structure by moving painters.		
Stage 4: Paint Your Subject	Tell more about the subject.	Which one? What kind? How many?	
Stage 5: Paint Your Words	Select words or phrases in the sentence and replace them with more descriptive words or phrases.		
New Sentence			

Passage Comprehension

Read the prompts and respond using complete sentences. Refer to the chart on page 66 to determine how to respond. Provide text evidence when requested.

1. Define *circuit* as it relates to migrant farmers. Provide evidence from the text to support your answer.

   _____

   _____

   _____

   Text Evidence: _____

   _____

   _____

2. Interpret the choices Panchito's parents made regarding the education of their children. Use text evidence from the story and background knowledge about the historical and cultural circumstances surrounding Mexican migrant farm workers at the time the story was written.

   _____

   _____

   _____

   _____

   _____

   _____

   _____

   _____

   _____

   _____

   _____

   _____

   _____

   _____

Passage Comprehension (*cont.*)

3. Report the obstacles that migrant children faced when trying to get a good education.

_____

_____

_____

_____

4. Compare Panchito's point of view on education with your point of view on education.

_____

_____

_____

_____

5. Interpret the meaning of the quote "the mountains reached out and swallowed the sun."

_____

_____

_____

_____

6. Compare Panchito's point of view when he saw the packed boxes with Anne Frank's point of view when she learned they would be moving into the annex.

_____

_____

_____

_____

Close Reading

Read the text.

"The Circuit"

A family of migrant farmworkers finished picking the last of the strawberry crop. Now they are seeking work from a vineyard owner whose grapes are ready to harvest.

At sunset we drove into a labor camp near Fresno. Since Papá did not
5 speak English, Mamá asked the camp foreman if he needed any more
workers. "We don't need no more," said the foreman, scratching his head.
"Check with Sullivan down the road. Can't miss him. He lives in a big
white house with a fence around it."

When we got there, Mamá walked up to the house. She went through a
10 white gate, past a row of rose bushes, up the stairs to the front door. She
rang the doorbell. The porch light went on and a tall husky man came
out. They **exchanged** a few words. After the man went in, Mamá
clasped hands and hurried back to the car. "We have work! Mr. Sullivan
said we can stay there the whole season," she said, gasping and pointing
15 to an old garage near the stables.

The garage was worn out by the years. It had no windows. The walls,
eaten by termites, strained to support the roof full of holes. The dirt floor,
populated by earthworms, looked like a gray road map.

That night, by the light of a kerosene lamp, we unpacked and cleaned our
20 new home. Roberto swept away the loose dirt, leaving the hard ground.
Papá plugged the holes in the walls with old newspapers and tin can tops.
Mamá fed my little brothers and sisters. Papá and Roberto then brought
in the mattress and placed it on the far corner of the garage. "Mamá, you
and the little ones sleep on the mattress. Roberto, Panchito, and I will
25 sleep outside under the trees," Papá said.

Early next morning, Mr. Sullivan showed us where his crop was, and after
breakfast, Papá, Roberto, and I headed for the vineyard to pick.

Close Reading (*cont.*)

Around nine o'clock, the temperature had risen to almost one hundred degrees. I was completely soaked in sweat, and my mouth felt as if I had
30 been chewing on a handkerchief. I walked over to the end of the row, picked up the jug of water we had brought, and began drinking. "Don't drink too much; you'll get sick," Roberto shouted. No sooner had he said that than I felt sick to my stomach. I dropped to my knees and let the jug roll off my hands. I remained **motionless** with my eyes glued on the hot
35 sandy ground. All I could hear was the **drone** of insects. Slowly I began to recover. I poured water over my face and neck and watched the black mud run down my arms and hit the ground.

I still felt a little dizzy when we took a break to eat lunch. It was past two o'clock and we sat underneath a large walnut tree that was on the side of
40 the road. While we ate, Papá jotted down the number of boxes we had picked. Roberto drew **designs** on the ground with a stick. Suddenly I noticed Papá's face turn pale as he looked down the road. "Here comes the school bus," he whispered loudly in alarm. **Instinctively**, Roberto and I ran and hid in the vineyards. We did not want to get in trouble for not
45 going to school. The yellow bus stopped in front of Mr. Sullivan's house. Two neatly dressed boys about my age got off. They carried books under their arms. After they crossed the street, the bus drove away. Roberto and I came out from hiding and joined Papá. "*Tienen que tener cuidado,*" he warned us.

50 After lunch, we went back to work. The sun kept beating down. The buzzing insects, the wet sweat, and the hot dry dust made the afternoon seem to last forever. Finally the mountains around the valley reached out and swallowed the sun. Within an hour it was too dark to continue picking. The vines blanketed the grapes, making it difficult to see the
55 bunches. "*Vámonos,*" said Papá, signaling to us that it was time to quit work. Papá then took out a pencil and began to figure out how much we had earned our first day. He wrote down numbers, crossed some out, wrote down some more. "*Quince,*" he **murmured**.

Close Reading (*cont.*)

60 When we arrived home, we took a cold shower underneath a waterhose. We then sat down to eat dinner around some wooden crates that served as a table. Mamá had cooked a special meal for us. We had rice and tortillas with "*carne con chile*," my favorite dish.

The next morning, I could hardly move. My body ached all over. I felt little control over my arms and legs. This feeling went on every morning 65 for days, until my muscles finally got used to the work.

It was Monday, the first week of November. The grape season was over and I could now go to school. I woke up early that morning and lay in bed, looking at the stars and **savoring** the thought of not going to work and of starting sixth grade for the first time that year. Since I could not 70 sleep, I decided to get up and join Papá and Roberto at breakfast. I sat at the table across from Roberto, but I kept my head down. I did not want to look up and face him. I knew he was sad. He was not going to school today. He was not going tomorrow, or next week, or next month. He would not go until the cotton season was over, and that was sometime in 75 February. I rubbed my hands together and watched the dry, acid-stained skin fall to the floor in little rolls.

When Papá and Roberto left for work, I felt relief. I walked to the top of a small grade next to the shack and watched the *Carcachita* disappear in the distance in a cloud of dust.

80 Two hours later, around eight o'clock, I stood by the side of the road waiting for school bus number twenty. When it arrived I climbed in. No one noticed me. Everyone was busy either talking or yelling. I sat in an empty seat in the back.

When the bus stopped in front of the school, I felt very nervous. I looked 85 out the bus window and saw boys and girls carrying books under their arms. I felt empty. I put my hands in my pants pockets and walked to the principal's office. When I entered, I heard a woman's voice say: "May I help you?" I was startled. I had not heard English for months. For a few seconds I remained speechless. I looked at the lady who waited for an 90 answer. My first instinct was to answer her in Spanish, but I held back. Finally, after struggling for English words, I managed to tell her that I wanted to enroll in the sixth grade. After answering many questions, I was led to the classroom.

Close Reading (*cont.*)

95 Mr. Lema, the sixth grade teacher, greeted me and assigned me to a desk. He then **introduced** me to the class. I was so nervous and scared at that moment when everyone's eyes were on me that I wished I were with Papa and Roberto picking cotton. After taking roll, Mr. Lema gave the class the assignment for the first hour. "The first thing we have to do this morning is finish reading the story we began yesterday," he said **enthusiastically**.

100 He walked up to me, handed me an English book, and asked me to read. "We are on page 125," he said politely. When I heard this, I felt my blood rush to my head; I felt dizzy. "Would you like to read?" he asked hesitantly. I opened the book to page 125. My mouth was dry. My eyes began to water. I could not begin. "You can read later," Mr. Lema said

105 understandingly.

For the rest of the reading period, I kept getting angrier and angrier with myself. I should have read, I thought to myself.

During recess, I went into the restroom and opened my English book to page 125. I began to read in a low voice, pretending I was in class. There

110 were many words I did not know. I closed the book and headed back to the classroom.

Mr. Lema was sitting at his desk correcting papers. When I entered he looked up at me and smiled. I felt better. I walked up to him and asked if he could help me with the new words. "Gladly," he said.

Close Reading (*cont.*)

115 The rest of the month, I spent my lunch hours working on English with Mr. Lema, my best friend at school.

One Friday during lunch hour, Mr. Lema asked me to take a walk with him to the music room. "Do you like music?" he asked me as we entered the building.

120 "Yes, I like Mexican *corridos*," I answered. He then picked up a trumpet, blew on it, and handed it to me. The sound gave me goose bumps. I knew that sound. I had heard it in many Mexican *corridos*. "How would you like to learn to play it?" he asked.

He must have read my face, because before I could answer, he added: "I'll
125 teach you how to play it during our lunch hours."

That day I could hardly wait to get home to tell Papá and Mamá the great news. As I got off the bus, my little brothers and sisters ran up to meet me. They were yelling and screaming. I thought they were happy to see me, but when I opened the door to our shack, I saw that everything we
130 owned was neatly packed in cardboard boxes.

Quick Write in Response to Reading

Imagine you are Panchito and you write in a journal every day. Tonight's journal entry is a paragraph about holding a trumpet in your hand for the first time and returning home in a fog of excitement to see packed boxes. Use evidence from the text in your journal entry.

_____

_____

_____

_____

_____

_____

_____

_____

_____

_____

_____

_____

_____

_____

_____

_____

_____

_____

_____

_____

_____

Let's Focus: Excerpt from *The Autobiography of Malcolm X*

Content Focus
enlightenment; the power of literacy

Type of Text
informational—autobiography

Authors' Names _____

Authors' Purposes _____

Big Ideas
Consider the following quote and Big Idea questions. Write your answer for each question.

"Education is the passport to the future, for tomorrow belongs to those who prepare for it today."—Malcolm X

Is education the passport to the future? Explain.

_____

_____

Is code-switching necessary? Explain.

_____

_____

Autobiography Preview Checklist: the excerpt from *The Autobiography of Malcolm X* on pages 169–173.

- ☐ Title: What clue does it provide?

- ☐ Pictures: What additional information is added here?

- ☐ Margin Information: What vocabulary is important to understand this story?

- ☐ Features: What other text features do you notice?

Enduring Understandings
After reading the text . . .

_____

_____

_____

_____

Key Passage Vocabulary: Excerpt from *The Autobiography of Malcolm X*

Read each word. Write it in column 3. Then, circle a number to rate your knowledge of the word.

Vocabulary	Part of Speech	Write the Word	Rate the Word
acquire	(v)		0 1 2 3
functional	(adj)		0 1 2 3
envy	(n)		0 1 2 3
eventually	(adv)		0 1 2 3
inevitable	(adj)		0 1 2 3
correspondence	(n)		0 1 2 3
debate	(n)		0 1 2 3
emphasis	(n)		0 1 2 3
isolation	(n)		0 1 2 3
adjust	(v)		0 1 2 3

from
The Autobiography of
Malcolm X

with Alex Haley

Malcolm X was a Black Muslim minister, a militant, a social and political activist, and a hero to many. His journey toward activism began in prison, where he first learned to read with understanding and
5 *write with precision.*

It was because of my letters that I happened to stumble upon starting to **acquire** some kind of a homemade education. I became increasingly frustrated at not being able to express what I wanted
10 to convey in letters that I wrote, especially those to Mr. Elijah Muhammad. In the street, I had been the most articulate hustler out there—I had commanded attention when I said something. But now, trying to write simple English, I not only wasn't articulate, I
15 wasn't even **functional**. How would I sound writing in slang, the way I would say it, something such as "Look, daddy, let me pull your coat about cat, Elijah Muhammad—" **1**

Many who today hear me somewhere in person
20 or on television, or those who read something I've said, will think I went to school far beyond the eighth grade. This impression is due entirely to my prison studies. **2**

It had really begun back in the Charlestown Prison,
25 when Bimbi first made me feel **envy** of his stock of knowledge. Bimbi had always taken charge of any conversations he was in, and I had tried to emulate him. But every book I picked up had few sentences which didn't contain anywhere from
30 one to nearly all of the words that might as well

acquire
to gain; to earn; to come by

functional
in working order; able to do a task or job

envy
the feeling of wanting what someone else has

1 Why didn't Malcolm X want to write the way he spoke?

2 Where did Malcolm X get a homemade education?

have been in Chinese. When I just skipped those words, of course, I really ended up with little idea of what the book said. So I had come to the Norfolk Prison Colony still going through only book-reading
35 motions. Pretty soon, I would have quit even these motions, unless I had received the motivation that I did. **3**

I saw that the best thing I could do was get hold of a dictionary—to study, to learn some words. I was
40 lucky enough to reason also that I should try to improve my penmanship. It was sad. I couldn't even write in a straight line. It was both ideas together that moved me to request a dictionary along with some tablets and pencils from the Norfolk Prison
45 Colony school.

I spent two days just riffling uncertainly through the dictionary's pages. I'd never realized so many words existed! I didn't know *which* words I needed to learn. Finally, just to start some kind of action,
50 I began copying.

In my slow, painstaking, ragged handwriting, I copied into my tablet everything printed on that first page, down to the punctuation marks.

I believe it took me a day. Then, aloud, I read back,
55 to myself, everything I'd written on the tablet. Over and over, aloud, to myself, I read my own handwriting. **4**

I woke up the next morning, thinking about those words—immensely proud to realize that not
60 only had I written so much at one time, but I'd written words that I never knew were in the world. Moreover, with a little effort, I also could remember what many of these words meant. I reviewed the words whose meanings I didn't remember.
65 Funny thing, from the dictionary's first page right now, that *aardvark* springs to my mind. The dictionary had a picture of it, a long-tailed, long-

3 Why didn't Malcolm X understand what he read?

4 Malcolm X hoped to accomplish two things with his dictionary efforts. What were they?

> " Education is the passport to the future, for tomorrow belongs to those who prepare for it today. "

70 eared, burrowing African mammal, which lives
off termites caught by sticking out its tongue as an
anteater does for ants.

I was so fascinated that I went on—I copied the
dictionary's next page. And the same experience
came when I studied that. With every succeeding
75 page, I also learned of people and places and events
from history. Actually the dictionary is like a
miniature encyclopedia. Finally the dictionary's
A section had filled a whole tablet—and I went on
into the B's. That was the way I started copying
what **eventually** became the entire dictionary.
80 It went a lot faster after so much practice helped
me to pick up handwriting speed. Between what I
wrote in my tablet, and writing letters, during the
rest of my time in prison I would guess I wrote a
million words. **5**

85 I suppose it was **inevitable** that as my word base
broadened, I could for the first time pick up a book
and read and now begin to understand what the
book was saying. Anyone who has read a great deal
can imagine the new world that opened. Let me tell
90 you something: From then until I left that prison,
in every free moment I had, if I was not reading in
the library, I was reading on my bunk. You couldn't
have gotten me out of books with a wedge. Between
Mr. Muhammad's teachings, my **correspondence**,
95 my visitors—usually Ella and Reginald—and my
reading of books, months passed without my even
thinking about being imprisoned. In fact, up to
then, I never had been so truly free in my life. **6**

The Norfolk Prison Colony's library was in the
100 school building. A variety of classes was taught
there by instructors who came from such places
as Harvard and Boston universities. The weekly
debates between inmate teams were also held
in the school building. You would be astonished

5 How would copying the dictionary help a person?

eventually
over time; in the end

inevitable
to be expected; hard to keep from happening

correspondence
written messages to and from other people

debate
a contest in which two sides argue the pros and cons of an issue

6 What newfound ability made Malcolm X feel truly free though he was in prison?

emphasis

the weight, value, or importance put on something

isolation

the state of being totally alone

7 How did inmates challenge the knowledge of one another?

8 What did the prison staff believe would happen to an inmate if he was interested in books?

> **My Alma mater was books, a good library . . . I could spend the rest of my life reading, just satisfying my curiosity.**

105 to know how worked up convict debaters and audiences would get over subjects like "Should Babies Be Fed Milk?" **7**

Available on the prison library's shelves were books on just about every general subject. Much of the big 110 private collection that Parkhurst had willed to the prison was still in crates and boxes in the back of the library—thousands of old books. Some of them looked ancient: covers faded, old-time parchment-looking binding. Parkhurst, I've mentioned, seemed 115 to have been principally interested in history and religion. He had the money and the special interest to have a lot of books that you wouldn't have in general circulation. Any college library would have been lucky to get that collection.

120 As you can imagine, especially in a prison where there was heavy **emphasis** on rehabilitation, an inmate was smiled upon if he demonstrated an unusually intense interest in books. There was a sizable number of well-read inmates, especially the 125 popular debaters. Some were said by many to be practically walking encyclopedias. They were almost celebrities. No university would ask any student to devour literature as I did when this new world opened to me, of being able to read and *understand*. **8**

130 I read more in my room than in the library itself. An inmate who was known to read a lot could check out more than the permitted maximum number of books. I preferred reading in the total **isolation** of my own room.

135 When I had progressed to really serious reading, every night at about 10:00 p.m. I would be outraged with the "lights out." It always seemed to catch me right in the middle of something engrossing.

adjust

to get used to something

140 Fortunately, right outside my door was a corridor light that cast a glow into my room. The glow was enough to read by, once my eyes **adjusted** to it. So when "lights out" came, I could sit on the floor where I could continue reading in that glow. **9**

> **9** What did Malcolm X choose to do instead of sleep?

145 At one-hour intervals the night guards paced past every room. Each time I heard the approaching footstep, I jumped into bed and feigned sleep. And as soon as the guard passed, I got back out of bed onto the floor area of that light-glow, where I would read for another fifty-eight minutes—until the

150 guard approached again. That went on until three or four every morning. Three or four hours of sleep a night was enough for me. Often in the years in the streets, I had slept less than that. **10**

> **10** Malcolm X was used to very little sleep. Tell the difference between his reasons for staying up while on the streets and while in prison. Which reason was more beneficial?

Malcolm X was born Malcolm Little in 1925. His father, Earl, was a Baptist minister who believed that black and white people should not integrate. The family was harassed by white supremacists, and Malcolm saw his house burned to the ground by the Ku Klux Klan. Soon after, Earl Little was brutally murdered.

Perhaps because of these tragedies, Malcolm hoped to become a lawyer. Though he was a good student, his English teacher told him that because of his race, he would never succeed. Shattered by this, Malcolm quit school. He turned to drugs and robbery. He gained a reputation as a smart, tough hustler. Three months before he turned 21 years old, he was sent to prison for burglary. There, he continued his drug use and reckless behavior until he met another inmate, Bimbi, who introduced him to the prison library. In prison, he learned about the work of Elijah Muhammad. Malcolm adopted the name Malcolm X, converted to the Black Muslim faith, and became an outspoken supporter of Elijah Muhammad's Nation of Islam. Elijah Muhammad taught that the only response to racism was for a black man to separate from white society. Malcolm X eventually came to disagree with Elijah Muhammad. He left the Nation of Islam and formed his own group.

Malcolm X was an electrifying speaker and had many followers. However, his popularity made others jealous. He received many death threats. Just before one of his speeches, in 1965, Malcolm X was shot to death. Three Black Muslims were convicted of his murder.

Central Idea

Identify the main idea of each section of the excerpt from *The Autobiography of Malcolm X*. Then, use the main ideas to determine the central idea of the text.

Introduction:

_____

_____

_____

Desire to Write Articulately:

_____

_____

_____

Dictionary Study:

_____

_____

_____

Love of Reading:

_____

_____

_____

Central Idea:

_____

_____

_____

Critical Understandings

Read the first three paragraphs of the excerpt from *The Autobiography of Malcolm X*. Read the prompts and respond using complete sentences. Refer to the chart on page 66 to determine how to respond. Provide text evidence when requested.

1. Identify three positions held by Malcolm X. Provide text evidence.

_____

_____

_____

Text Evidence: _____

_____

2. Infer the level of Malcolm X's formal education. Provide text evidence.

_____

_____

_____

Text Evidence: _____

_____

3. Summarize Malcolm's motivation to learn to read and write.

_____

_____

_____

4. Contrast the illiterate prisoner with the articulate street hustler.

_____

_____

_____

_____

_____

_____

_____

Using Transition Words

Examples of Transition Families			
One Another Finally	First Next At last	First of all The second A third	First Second Third
One Also Another Finally	Start by Next Then Finally	Initially Then After Later	In the spring In the summer In the fall In the winter
My first choice My second choice	First of all More importantly	A good An even better The best	One important Equally important
During the week On the weekend	With my friends With my family On my own	I first heard I also heard	One Another
One example Another example A third example	In the beginning As By the time Then	One good choice Another choice The best choice	Early each morning Throughout the day In the evening
To begin After that Then Next Finally	One example A better example The best example	One difference A second difference The most obvious difference	Before winter break During winter break After winter break

Read the following paragraph and circle all of the transition words and the commas.

Recycling is an important habit for several reasons. First, our landfills are overflowing with trash. Much of this trash is recyclable. Recycling paper and aluminum cans would significantly reduce the amount of trash sitting in landfills. Secondly, our earth's resources are not infinite. Recycling provides us with a way to maximize precious resources. Even though trees are a renewable resource, deforestation is negatively impacting our climate. In addition to positively impacting the environment, recycling can positively impact our pocketbooks. Consuming less costs less, and recycling centers actually pay for recycled paper and aluminum. For a variety of reasons, recycling is a habit worth forming.

Passage Comprehension

Read the prompts and respond using complete sentences. Refer to the chart on page 66 to determine how to respond. Provide text evidence when requested.

1. Identify the strategy that Malcolm X used to learn to read and write.

   _____

   _____

   _____

2. Infer why Malcolm X did not want to write the way he spoke. Provide text evidence.

   _____

   _____

   _____

   _____

   Text Evidence: _____

   _____

   _____

   _____

3. Use your knowledge of the historical and cultural setting in which Malcolm X was raised to infer why he did not value education.

   _____

   _____

   _____

   _____

   _____

   _____

   _____

   _____

   _____

Passage Comprehension (*cont.*)

4. Summarize the excerpt from *The Autobiography of Malcolm X* using an IVF topic sentence strategy.

_____

_____

_____

_____

_____

_____

_____

5. Contrast Malcolm as a hustler and Malcolm as a prisoner.

_____

_____

_____

_____

_____

_____

_____

_____

6. Consider Malcolm's quote "Education is the passport to the future, for tomorrow belongs to the those who prepare for it today." Contrast Malcolm's point of view regarding education with the pool players at the Golden Shovel in the poem "We Real Cool."

_____

_____

_____

_____

_____

_____

_____

Close Reading

Read the text.

---

from *The Autobiography of Malcolm X*

Malcolm X was a Black Muslim minister, a militant, a social and political activist, and a hero to many. His journey toward activism began in prison, where he first learned to read with understanding and write with precision.

5   It was because of my letters that I happened to stumble upon starting to **acquire** some kind of a homemade education. I became increasingly frustrated at not being able to express what I wanted to convey in letters that I wrote, especially those to Mr. Elijah Muhammad. In the street, I had been the most articulate hustler out there—I had commanded
10 attention when I said something. But now, trying to write simple English, I not only wasn't articulate, I wasn't even **functional**. How would I sound writing in slang, the way I would say it, something such as "Look, daddy, let me pull your coat about cat, Elijah Muhammad—"

  Many who today hear me somewhere in person or on television, or those
15 who read something I've said, will think I went to school far beyond the eighth grade. This impression is due entirely to my prison studies.

Close Reading (*cont.*)

It had really begun back in the Charlestown Prison, when Bimbi first made me feel **envy** of his stock of knowledge. Bimbi had always taken charge of any conversations he was in, and I had tried to emulate him.

20 But every book I picked up had few sentences which didn't contain anywhere from one to nearly all of the words that might as well have been in Chinese. When I just skipped those words, of course, I really ended up with little idea of what the book said. So I had come to the Norfolk Prison Colony still going through only book-reading motions. Pretty soon, I

25 would have quit even these motions, unless I had received the motivation that I did.

I saw that the best thing I could do was get hold of a dictionary—to study, to learn some words. I was lucky enough to reason also that I should try to improve my penmanship. It was sad. I couldn't even write in a straight

30 line. It was both ideas together that moved me to request a dictionary along with some tablets and pencils from the Norfolk Prison Colony school.

I spent two days just riffling uncertainly through the dictionary's pages. I'd never realized so many words existed! I didn't know *which* words

35 I needed to learn. Finally, just to start some kind of action, I began copying.

In my slow, painstaking, ragged handwriting, I copied into my tablet everything printed on that first page, down to the punctuation marks.

I believe it took me a day. Then, aloud, I read back, to myself, everything

40 I'd written on the tablet. Over and over, aloud, to myself, I read my own handwriting.

Close Reading (*cont.*)

I woke up the next morning, thinking about those words—immensely proud to realize that not only had I written so much at one time, but I'd written words that I never knew were in the world. Moreover, with
45 a little effort, I also could remember what many of these words meant. I reviewed the words whose meanings I didn't remember. Funny thing, from the dictionary's first page right now, that *aardvark* springs to my mind. The dictionary had a picture of it, a long-tailed, long-eared, burrowing African mammal, which lives off termites caught by sticking
50 out its tongue as an anteater does for ants.

I was so fascinated that I went on—I copied the dictionary's next page. And the same experience came when I studied that. With every succeeding page, I also learned of people and places and events from history. Actually the dictionary is like a miniature encyclopedia. Finally
55 the dictionary's A section had filled a whole tablet—and I went on into the B's. That was the way I started copying what **eventually** became the entire dictionary. It went a lot faster after so much practice helped me to pick up handwriting speed. Between what I wrote in my tablet, and writing letters, during the rest of my time in prison I would guess I wrote
60 a million words.

I suppose it was **inevitable** that as my word base broadened, I could for the first time pick up a book and read and now begin to understand what the book was saying. Anyone who has read a great deal can imagine the new world that opened. Let me tell you something: From then until I left
65 that prison, in every free moment I had, if I was not reading in the library, I was reading on my bunk. You couldn't have gotten me out of books with a wedge. Between Mr. Muhammad's teachings, my **correspondence**, my visitors—usually Ella and Reginald—and my reading of books, months passed without my even thinking about being imprisoned. In fact, up to
70 then, I never had been so truly free in my life.

Close Reading (*cont.*)

The Norfolk Prison Colony's library was in the school building. A variety of classes was taught there by instructors who came from such places as Harvard and Boston universities. The weekly **debates** between inmate teams were also held in the school building. You would be astonished
75 to know how worked up convict debaters and audiences would get over subjects like "Should Babies Be Fed Milk?"

Available on the prison library's shelves were books on just about every general subject. Much of the big private collection that Parkhurst had willed to the prison was still in crates and boxes in the back of the
80 library—thousands of old books. Some of them looked ancient: covers faded, old-time parchment-looking binding. Parkhurst, I've mentioned, seemed to have been principally interested in history and religion. He had the money and the special interest to have a lot of books that you wouldn't have in general circulation. Any college library would have been
85 lucky to get that collection.

As you can imagine, especially in a prison where there was heavy **emphasis** on rehabilitation, an inmate was smiled upon if he demonstrated an unusually intense interest in books. There was a sizable number of well-read inmates, especially the popular debaters. Some were said by many
90 to be practically walking encyclopedias. They were almost celebrities. No university would ask any student to devour literature as I did when this new world opened to me, of being able to read and *understand*.

I read more in my room than in the library itself. An inmate who was known to read a lot could check out more than the permitted maximum
95 number of books. I preferred reading in the total **isolation** of my own room.

Close Reading (*cont.*)

When I had progressed to really serious reading, every night at about 10:00 p.m. I would be outraged with the "lights out." It always seemed to catch me right in the middle of something engrossing.

100 Fortunately, right outside my door was a corridor light that cast a glow into my room. The glow was enough to read by, once my eyes **adjusted** to it. So when "lights out" came, I could sit on the floor where I could continue reading in that glow.

At one-hour intervals the night guards paced past every room. Each time
105 I heard the approaching footstep, I jumped into bed and feigned sleep. And as soon as the guard passed, I got back out of bed onto the floor area of that light-glow, where I would read for another fifty-eight minutes— until the guard approached again. That went on until three or four every morning. Three or four hours of sleep a night was enough for me. Often
110 in the years in the streets, I had slept less than that.

Prepare to Write: Time-Order Paragraph

Part A. Study the Prompt

Read the prompt and identify the topic, directions, and purpose for writing.

Write a paragraph that explains how Malcolm X used his time in prison as an opportunity for personal growth. Use transition words.

Topic: _____

_____

Directions: _____

Purpose for writing: _____

_____

Part B. Write a Topic Sentence (when or where + statement)

When?	Where?	Statement

Topic Sentence: _____

Prepare to Write: Time-Order Paragraph (*cont.*)

Part C. Sequence Events

Write the steps Malcolm X followed to improve himself and the specific purpose of each step.

2-Column Notes	
Step	**Purpose**

Prepare to Write: Time-Order Paragraph (*cont.*)

Part D. Write a Concluding Sentence

Develop a concluding sentence by restating the topic sentence. Choose a word from the chart below to start your sentence. Use a comma to separate the word or phrase from the rest of the sentence.

Concluding Words and Phrases				
As a result	Consequently	Finally	In closing	In conclusion
In summary	In the end	So	Therefore	Thus

_____

_____

_____

_____

_____

_____

_____

The Writer's Checklist

Trait	Yes	No	Did the writer . . .?
Ideas and Content			focus all sentences on the topic
			provide supporting details for the topic sentence
Organization			write a topic sentence
			tell things in an order that makes sense
			use transition words and/or phrases
			write a concluding sentence
Voice and Audience Awareness			think about the audience and purpose for writing
Word Choice			try to find a unique way to say things
			use words that are lively and specific to the content
Sentence Fluency			write complete sentences
			expand some sentences by painting the subject and/or predicate
Conventions			capitalize words correctly:
			capitalize the first word of each sentence
			capitalize proper nouns, including people's names
			punctuate correctly:
			put a period or question mark at the end of each sentence
			put an apostrophe before the s for a singular possessive noun
			use a comma after a long adverb phrase at the beginning of a sentence
			use grammar correctly:
			use the correct verb tense
			make sure the verb agrees with the subject in number
			use correct spelling

Let's Focus: Excerpt from *Breaking Night*

Content Focus
triumph

Type of Text
informational—memoir

Author's Name _____

Author's Purpose _____

Big Ideas

Consider the following Big Idea questions. Write your answer for each question.

Are suffering and normalcy relative? Explain.

_____

_____

Which plays a bigger part in who we are: things we are born with or things we are surrounded by? Explain.

_____

_____

Narrative Preview Checklist: Excerpt from *Breaking Night* on pages 191–196.

☐ Title: What clue does it provide about the passage?

☐ Pictures: What additional information is added here?

☐ Margin Information: What vocabulary is important to understand this story?

Enduring Understandings

After reading the text . . .

_____

_____

_____

_____

_____

_____

Key Passage Vocabulary: Excerpt from *Breaking Night*

Read each word. Write the word in column 3. Then, circle a number to rate your knowledge of the word.

Vocabulary	Part of Speech	Write the Word	Knowledge Rating
anticipation	(n)		0 1 2 3
consistency	(n)		0 1 2 3
qualify	(v)		0 1 2 3
invaluable	(adj)		0 1 2 3
ailment	(n)		0 1 2 3
portion	(n)		0 1 2 3
clamor	(v)		0 1 2 3
reassuring	(adj)		0 1 2 3
elaborate	(adj)		0 1 2 3
abundant	(adj)		0 1 2 3

from Breaking Night by Liz Murray

By the time I was almost five years old, we had become a functional, government-dependent family of four. The first of the month, the day Ma's stipend from welfare was due, held all the ritual and
5 celebration of Christmas morning. Our collective **anticipation** of the money filled the apartment with a kind of electricity, guaranteeing that Ma and Daddy would be agreeable and upbeat for at least twenty-four hours each month. It was my parents'
10 one **consistency**. **1**

The government gave the few hundred dollars monthly to those who, for one reason or another, were unable to work for a living—although I often saw our able-bodied neighbors crowded beside the
15 mailboxes, eagerly watching as they were stuffed with the thin, blue envelopes. Ma, who was legally blind due to a degenerative eye disease she'd had since birth, happened to be one of SSI's legitimate recipients. I know, because I went with her the day
20 she interviewed to **qualify**. **2**

The woman behind the desk told her that she was so blind that if she ever drove a car, she would "probably end the life of every living thing in her path."

25 Then she shook Ma's hand and congratulated her both for qualifying and for her ability to successfully cross the street.

"Sign right here. You can expect your checks on the first of every month."

30 And we did. In fact, there was nothing our family looked forward to more than Ma's check. The mailman's arrival had a domino effect, setting the whole day, and our treasured ritual, in motion. It was my job to lean my head out of my bedroom
35 window, which faced the front, and to call out any sighting of the mailman to Ma and Daddy.

anticipation
a feeling of excitement about something that is about to happen

consistency
something done in the same way, time after time

qualify
to show that you have the right to do or have something

1 Why was the first of the month like a holiday?

2 Why did they receive a check?

invaluable

extremely useful or precious and hard to replace

3 What is Ma like?

4 Who is the "planner" in the family?

"Lizzy, let me know when you see *any* sign of him. Remember, look *left*."

40 If Ma could know a few minutes earlier that he was coming, she could grab her welfare ID out of the junk drawer, snatch her check from the mailbox, and be the first in line at the check-cashing store. The role I played in those days became an **invaluable** part of the routine.

45 Elbows jutting behind me, I would clutch the rusted window guard and extend my neck as far as possible into the sun, over and over again throughout the morning. The task gave me a sense of importance. When I saw the blue uniform appear over the hill—

50 an urban Santa Claus pushing his matching cart—I could not wait to announce him. In the meantime, I'd listen to the sound of my parents waiting.

Ma in her oversize worry chair, picking out yellow stuffing. 3

55 "Damn. Damn. He's dragging his ass."

Daddy going over the details of their plans a hundred times, pacing, weaving circles in the air as though to somehow shorten the feel of his wait.

"Okay, Jeanie, we're going to stop off to buy coke,
60 then we take care of the electric bill with Con Edison. Then we can get a half pound of bologna for the kids. And I need money for tokens." 4

The moment I spotted the mailman, I could tell them the very second I knew, or I could wait just a
65 little longer. It was the difference between having their attention and giving it away—relinquishing the one moment when I was as significant as they were, as necessary as the mailman or even the money itself. But I could never hold back; the moment I saw
70 him round the corner I'd shout, "He's coming! I see him! He's coming!" Then we could all move on to the next stage of our day.

Behind the gaudy glass storefront of the check-cashing place, there was something for everyone.
75 Children gravitated to the twenty-five-cent machines, a row of clear boxes on metal poles with toys jumbled inside. They waited impatiently for quarters to free the plastic spider on a ring, the man who expanded to ten times his size in water,
80 or the wash-away tattoos of butterflies, comic book heroes, or pink and red hearts. Tacked up high near the register were lottery tickets for stray men with gambling **ailments** or hopeful women who allotted just a few of the family's dollars to the allure of
85 a lucky break. Often these ladies dramatically waved the sign of the cross over themselves before scratching away with a loose dime or penny. But for many, even the smallest item was completely unaffordable until their turn in line. **5**

90 Women made up that endless line; women clutching the monthly bills, women frowning, women with children. Their men (if present at all) stood off to the side, leaning coolly on the metal walls. Either they came in with the women but stood back,
95 waiting for the check to be cashed, or they arrived beforehand, anticipating the routine, sure to shake down their wives or girlfriends for a **portion**. The women would fend them off to the best of their ability, giving up what they had to and making the
100 most of what was left. Lisa and I became so used to the chaos that we hardly looked up at the adults **clamoring** with one another. **6**

Lisa lingered by the quarter machines, captivated by the glittery stickers. I stayed close to our parents,
105 who were different from the other adults in that they functioned as a team, having arrived in pursuit of a shared goal. I was a participant in their giddiness, eager to make their excitement my own.

ailment
a sickness or something that causes pain and discomfort

portion
one part of a greater whole

clamor
to demand something in a noisy or angry way

5 How would this life seem to a five-year-old child?

6 Why do you think it was mostly women in line?

reassuring

comforting; causing you to feel less worried

elaborate

very complex; having many parts

7 Why did Ma need Lizzy at home and at the check-cashing store?

8 Where are they now? Why are they not in line anymore?

If I could break the joy of check day down into small
110 segments, then nothing topped the time Ma and I
spent together in line. As she waited for her turn at
the counter, again I was her helper. In these urgent
moments, full of anticipation, Ma relied on me
most. It was my moment to shine, and I always rose
115 to the occasion. **7**

"Eight more ahead of us, Ma. Seven. Don't worry,
the cashier's moving fast."

Her smile as I delivered the progress report
belonged to me. Calling out the numbers in a
120 **reassuring** tone determined the amount of attention
she paid me. I would have traded the rest of check
day for ten more people in line ahead of us, because
for this guaranteed amount of time, she wasn't going
anywhere. I wouldn't have to worry about Ma's habit
125 of leaving us in the middle of things.

Once, the four of us walked over to Loews
Paradise Theater on the Grand Concourse to see a
discounted showing of *Alice in Wonderland*. Daddy
explained on the walk over that the Concourse
130 used to be an area of luxury, a strip of **elaborate**
architecture that attracted the wealthy. But all
I could see as we walked were vast, dirty brick
buildings with the occasional tarnished cherubs
or gargoyles over doorways, chipped and cracked
135 but still hanging on. We sat down in a nearly
empty theater. **8**

Ma didn't stay until the end. It's not that she
didn't try; she got up once, twice, three times for
a "smoke." Then she got up for a final time and
140 didn't come back. When we returned home that
evening, the record player was spinning a woman's
sad, throaty singing. Ma was taking a pull off her
cigarette and studying her own slender, naked body
in the full-length mirror.

145 "Where were you guys?" she asked naturally, and I
wondered if I might have imagined that she'd come
with us at all.

But in the check line, she wasn't going anywhere. As
much as she fidgeted, Ma wouldn't leave without the
150 money. So I took the opportunity to hold her hand
and to ask her questions about herself when she was
my age. **9**

"I don't know, Lizzy. I was bad when I was a kid. I
stole things and cut school. How many more people
155 in front of us, pumpkin?"

Each time I faced her, Ma motioned toward the
cashier, urging me to keep an eye out. Holding
her attention was tricky, a balancing act between
slipping in questions and showing that I was on top
160 of things. I always assured her that we were almost
there; privately, I wished she'd have to wait as long
as possible, longer than anyone else.

"I don't know, Lizzy. You're a nicer kid, you never
cried when you were a baby. You just made this
165 noise like *eh, eh*. It was the cutest thing, almost
polite. Lisa would scream her head off and smash
everything, rip up my magazines, but you never
cried. I worried you were retarded, but they said
you were all right. You were always a good kid. How
170 many more people, pumpkin?" **10**

Even if I was told and retold the same stories, I
never tired of asking.

"What was my first word?"

"'Mommy.' You handed me your bottle and said
175 'Mommy,' like you were telling me to fill 'er up. You
were a riot."

"How old was I?"

"Ten months."

> **9** Why did Lizzy enjoy the time with Ma in the check line more than at the theater?

> **10** What is Lizzy like?

abundant

available in large amounts; more than enough

11 Why didn't Ma answer Lizzy's last question?

"How long have we lived in our house?"

180 "Years."

"How many?"

"Lizzy, move over, my turn's coming." **11**

At home, we split off into two rooms: the living room for us kids, and next to it, the kitchen for Ma
185 and Daddy. Unlike most times, on that first day of the month, food was **abundant**. Lisa and I dined on Happy Meals in front of the black-and-white TV, to the sound of spoons clanking on the nearby table, chairs being pulled in—and those elongated
190 moments of silence when we knew what they were concentrating on. Daddy had to do it for Ma because with her bad eyesight she could never find a vein.

At last, the four of us enjoyed the second-best part
195 of the day. We sat together, all spread around the living room, facing the flickering TV. Outside, the ice cream truck rattled its loop of tinny music and children gathered, scrambled, gathered, and scrambled again in a game of tag.

12 How much of the check do you think is left after the first day?

200 The four of us together. French-fry grease on my fingertips. Lisa chewing on a cheeseburger. Ma and Daddy, twitching and shifting just behind us, euphoric. **12**

Nouns: Multiple Functions

Sort the underlined nouns in the following sentences according to their function. Write them in the proper column in the chart.

> **Examples:**
> A milling <u>crowd</u> of adults surrounded me.
> I raised my <u>head</u> to look down the street.
>
> The mailman had a flag on his <u>uniform</u>.
> In our neighborhood, he was a famous <u>man</u>.

1. The mailman was walking toward us, his boots noisy on the <u>street</u>.

2. He wore a <u>flag</u> on his arm.

3. There were many hungry <u>kids</u> in the streets outside our apartment.

4. <u>Dad</u> patiently waits for Ma to cash the check.

5. I looked out the window and saw the mailman walk around the <u>corner</u>.

6. The two <u>girls</u> watched TV and listened to their parents.

7. As Ma and I waited in line, I held tightly onto her <u>hand</u>.

8. The sight of the mailman started a chain <u>reaction</u>.

9. The check is a <u>blessing</u> to each one of us.

10. The first of the month was my favorite <u>day</u>.

Subject Noun	Direct Object	Predicate Noun	Object of the Preposition
crowd	head	man	uniform

Conjunctions

Complete the following sentences with the correct conjunction. Determine if the sentence has a compound subject, compound predicate, or compound object. Circle the correct answer.

Example: Lisa _____*and*_____ Liz ate Happy Meals in the living room.
(Compound Subject)   Compound Predicate   Compound Object

1. We cashed the check _____ bought Happy Meals.
   Compound Subject   Compound Predicate   Compound Object

2. Either Ma _____ Dad will pay the electric bill.
   Compound Subject   Compound Predicate   Compound Object

3. Ma could risk her life walking _____ stay home.
   Compound Subject   Compound Predicate   Compound Object

4. Liz could eat a bologna sandwich _____ a cheeseburger.
   Compound Subject   Compound Predicate   Compound Object

5. The parents _____ kids waited in line together.
   Compound Subject   Compound Predicate   Compound Object

Write a sentence containing the element listed.

1. (Compound Subject) _____

   _____

   _____

2. (Compound Predicate)_____

   _____

   _____

3. (Compound Object)_____

   _____

   _____

Masterpiece Sentences: Stages 1–6

Choose one of the Stage 1 sentences and complete the chart for the remaining stages to write a masterpiece sentence.

Stage 1 Sentences:

• Ma and Dad waited. • The girls ate burgers and fries. • The girl watched and waited.

Stage	Process	Questions to Answer	Sentence
Stage 1: Prepare Your Canvas	Choose a noun for the subject. Choose a verb for the predicate. Add a direct object if it is needed.	Who did it? Did what? To what?	
Stage 2: Paint Your Predicate	Tell more about what happened.	When? Where? How?	
Stage 3: Move Your Predicate Painters	Improve sentence structure by moving painters.		
Stage 4: Paint Your Subject	Tell more about the subject.	Which one? What kind? How many?	
Stage 5: Paint Your Words	Select words or phrases in the sentence and replace them with more descriptive words or phrases.		
Stage 6: Finishing Touches	Move sentence parts; check spelling and punctuation.		

Masterpiece Sentences With Compound Elements

Use the following painter questions and information about yourself or the people in the text to create sentences with a variety of structures and elements.

Who?	Did what?	How?	**AND**	Did what?	To what?	Where?

When?	Who?	**AND**	Who?	Did what?	Where?

What?	**OR**	What?	How?	Did what?	To what?

Who?	Will do what?	To what?	How?	**OR**	Will do what?	To what?	How?

Where?	What kind?	Who?	Did what?	To what?	**AND**	To what?	When?

Passage Comprehension

Reread the excerpt from *Breaking Night*. Respond to each prompt using complete sentences. Refer to the chart on page 66 to determine how to respond to each prompt. Provide text evidence when requested.

1. Infer Daddy's rationale for paying the electricity bill last.

   _____

   _____

2. Contrast Ma's mood before and after the check arrived each month.

   _____

   _____

   _____

   _____

   _____

   Text Evidence: _____

   _____

   _____

   _____

   _____

3. Identify the family ritual on check day.

   _____

   _____

   _____

   _____

   _____

   _____

   _____

   _____

   _____

Passage Comprehension (*cont.*)

4. Infer what Daddy did for Ma when they returned home on check day.

_____

_____

_____

Text Evidence: _____

_____

_____

_____

_____

5. Summarize the excerpt from *Breaking Night* as it relates to a monthly circuit.

_____

_____

_____

_____

_____

_____

_____

6. Compare and contrast Liz Murray's parents with Panchito's parents in "The Circuit."

_____

_____

_____

_____

_____

_____

_____

_____

Close Reading

Read the text.

from *Breaking Night*

By the time I was almost five years old, we had become a functional, government-dependent family of four. The first of the month, the day Ma's stipend from welfare was due, held all the ritual and celebration of Christmas morning. Our collective **anticipation** of the money filled the
5   apartment with a kind of electricity, guaranteeing that Ma and Daddy would be agreeable and upbeat for at least twenty-four hours each month. It was my parents' one **consistency**.

The government gave the few hundred dollars monthly to those who, for one reason or another, were unable to work for a living—although I often
10 saw our able-bodied neighbors crowded beside the mailboxes, eagerly watching as they were stuffed with the thin, blue envelopes. Ma, who was legally blind due to a degenerative eye disease she'd had since birth, happened to be one of SSI's legitimate recipients. I know, because I went with her the day she interviewed to **qualify**.

15 The woman behind the desk told her that she was so blind that if she ever drove a car, she would "probably end the life of every living thing in her path."

Then she shook Ma's hand and congratulated her both for qualifying and for her ability to successfully cross the street.

20 "Sign right here. You can expect your checks on the first of every month."

Close Reading (*cont.*)

And we did. In fact, there was nothing our family looked forward to more than Ma's check. The mailman's arrival had a domino effect, setting the whole day, and our treasured ritual, in motion. It was my job to lean my head out of my bedroom window, which faced the front, and to call out
25 any sighting of the mailman to Ma and Daddy.

"Lizzy, let me know when you see *any* sign of him. Remember, look *left.*"

If Ma could know a few minutes earlier that he was coming, she could grab her welfare ID out of the junk drawer, snatch her check from the mailbox, and be the first in line at the check-cashing store. The role I
30 played in those days became an **invaluable** part of the routine.

Elbows jutting behind me, I would clutch the rusted window guard and extend my neck as far as possible into the sun, over and over again throughout the morning. The task gave me a sense of importance. When I saw the blue uniform appear over the hill—an urban Santa Claus
35 pushing his matching cart—I could not wait to announce him. In the meantime, I'd listen to the sound of my parents waiting.

Ma in her oversize worry chair, picking out yellow stuffing.

"Damn. Damn. He's dragging his ass."

Daddy going over the details of their plans a hundred times, pacing,
40 weaving circles in the air as though to somehow shorten the feel of his wait.

"Okay, Jeanie, we're going to stop off to buy coke, then we take care of the electric bill with Con Edison. Then we can get a half pound of bologna for the kids. And I need money for tokens."

45 The moment I spotted the mailman, I could tell them the very second I knew, or I could wait just a little longer. It was the difference between having their attention and giving it away—relinquishing the one moment when I was as significant as they were, as necessary as the mailman or even the money itself. But I could never hold back; the moment I saw him
50 round the corner I'd shout, "He's coming! I see him! He's coming!" Then we could all move on to the next stage of our day.

Close Reading (*cont.*)

Behind the gaudy glass storefront of the check-cashing place, there was something for everyone. Children gravitated to the twenty-five-cent machines, a row of clear boxes on metal poles with toys jumbled inside.
55 They waited impatiently for quarters to free the plastic spider on a ring, the man who expanded to ten times his size in water, or the wash-away tattoos of butterflies, comic book heroes, or pink and red hearts. Tacked up high near the register were lottery tickets for stray men with gambling **ailments** or hopeful women who allotted just a few of the family's dollars
60 to the allure of a lucky break. Often these ladies dramatically waved the sign of the cross over themselves before scratching away with a loose dime or penny. But for many, even the smallest item was completely unaffordable until their turn in line.

Women made up that endless line; women clutching the monthly bills,
65 women frowning, women with children. Their men (if present at all) stood off to the side, leaning coolly on the metal walls. Either they came in with the women but stood back, waiting for the check to be cashed, or they arrived beforehand, anticipating the routine, sure to shake down their wives or girlfriends for a **portion**. The women would fend them off
70 to the best of their ability, giving up what they had to and making the most of what was left. Lisa and I became so used to the chaos that we hardly looked up at the adults **clamoring** with one another.

Lisa lingered by the quarter machines, captivated by the glittery stickers. I stayed close to our parents, who were different from the other adults
75 in that they functioned as a team, having arrived in pursuit of a shared goal. I was a participant in their giddiness, eager to make their excitement my own.

Close Reading (*cont.*)

If I could break the joy of check day down into small segments, then nothing topped the time Ma and I spent together in line. As she waited 80 for her turn at the counter, again I was her helper. In these urgent moments, full of anticipation, Ma relied on me most. It was my moment to shine, and I always rose to the occasion.

"Eight more ahead of us, Ma. Seven. Don't worry, the cashier's moving fast."

Her smile as I delivered the progress report belonged to me. Calling out 85 the numbers in a **reassuring** tone determined the amount of attention she paid me. I would have traded the rest of check day for ten more people in line ahead of us, because for this guaranteed amount of time, she wasn't going anywhere. I wouldn't have to worry about Ma's habit of leaving us in the middle of things.

90 Once, the four of us walked over to Loews Paradise Theater on the Grand Concourse to see a discounted showing of *Alice in Wonderland*. Daddy explained on the walk over that the Concourse used to be an area of luxury, a strip of **elaborate** architecture that attracted the wealthy. But all I could see as we walked were vast, dirty brick buildings with the 95 occasional tarnished cherubs or gargoyles over doorways, chipped and cracked but still hanging on. We sat down in a nearly empty theater.

Ma didn't stay until the end. It's not that she didn't try; she got up once, twice, three times for a "smoke." Then she got up for a final time and didn't come back. When we returned home that evening, the record player was 100 spinning a woman's sad, throaty singing. Ma was taking a pull off her cigarette and studying her own slender, naked body in the full-length mirror.

"Where were you guys?" she asked naturally, and I wondered if I might have imagined that she'd come with us at all.

Close Reading (*cont.*)

But in the check line, she wasn't going anywhere. As much as she
105 fidgeted, Ma wouldn't leave without the money. So I took the opportunity
to hold her hand and to ask her questions about herself when she was
my age.

"I don't know, Lizzy. I was bad when I was a kid. I stole things and cut
school. How many more people in front of us, pumpkin?"

110 Each time I faced her, Ma motioned toward the cashier, urging me
to keep an eye out. Holding her attention was tricky, a balancing act
between slipping in questions and showing that I was on top of things.
I always assured her that we were almost there; privately, I wished she'd
have to wait as long as possible, longer than anyone else.

115 "I don't know, Lizzy. You're a nicer kid, you never cried when you were a
baby. You just made this noise like *eh*, *eh*. It was the cutest thing, almost
polite. Lisa would scream her head off and smash everything, rip up my
magazines, but you never cried. I worried you were retarded, but they said
you were all right. You were always a good kid. How many more people,
120 pumpkin?"

Even if I was told and retold the same stories, I never tired of asking.

"What was my first word?"

"'Mommy.' You handed me your bottle and said 'Mommy,' like you were
telling me to fill 'er up. You were a riot."

125 "How old was I?"

"Ten months."

"How long have we lived in our house?"

"Years."

"How many?"

130 "Lizzy, move over, my turn's coming."

Close Reading (*cont.*)

At home, we split off into two rooms: the living room for us kids, and next to it, the kitchen for Ma and Daddy. Unlike most times, on that first day of the month, food was **abundant**. Lisa and I dined on Happy Meals in front of the black-and-white TV, to the sound of spoons clanking on
135 the nearby table, chairs being pulled in—and those elongated moments of silence when we knew what they were concentrating on. Daddy had to do it for Ma because with her bad eyesight she could never find a vein.

At last, the four of us enjoyed the second-best part of the day. We sat together, all spread around the living room, facing the flickering TV.
140 Outside, the ice cream truck rattled its loop of tinny music and children gathered, scrambled, gathered, and scrambled again in a game of tag.

The four of us together. French-fry grease on my fingertips. Lisa chewing on a cheeseburger. Ma and Daddy, twitching and shifting just behind us, euphoric.

Quick Write in Response to Reading

Write a paragraph describing Lizzy, the narrator of the excerpt from *Breaking Night*. Identify three character traits and include evidence from the text to support the selected traits. Begin the paragraph with a Number Topic Sentence.

_____

_____

_____

_____

_____

_____

_____

_____

_____

_____

_____

_____

_____

_____

_____

_____

_____

_____

_____

_____

_____

_____

_____

_____

_____

Let's Focus: "From Homeless to Harvard"

Content Focus
triumph; willpower

Type of Text
informational

Author's Name _____

Author's Purpose _____

Big Ideas
Consider the following Big Idea questions. Write your answer for each question.

At what age are our personality and belief system formed?

_____

_____

To what degree is our future shaped by the people whom we live with as children?

_____

_____

Informational Preview Checklist: "From Homeless to Harvard" on pages 212–215.

☐ Title: What clue does it provide?

☐ Pictures: What additional information is added here?

☐ Headings: What will you learn about in each section?

☐ Features: What other text features do you notice?

Enduring Understandings
After reading the text . . .

_____

_____

_____

_____

Key Passage Vocabulary: "From Homeless to Harvard"

Read each word. Write the word in column 3. Then, circle a number to rate your knowledge of the word.

Vocabulary	Part of Speech	Write the Word	Knowledge Rating
outcome	(n)		0 1 2 3
diagnose	(v)		0 1 2 3
conditions	(n)		0 1 2 3
alternative	(adj)		0 1 2 3
motivated	(adj)		0 1 2 3
apply	(v)		0 1 2 3
opportunity	(n)		0 1 2 3
strategy	(n)		0 1 2 3
lecture	(v)		0 1 2 3
inspiration	(n)		0 1 2 3

From Homeless to Harvard

outcome
a result or the way something ends

The winter evening is cold and windy with crisp-looking stars shining over Bronx, New York. Liz Murray, just 12 years
5 old, doesn't want to go home because her parents are doing drugs again. She is walking the streets, alone, headed for the home of a friend. She knocks
10 on an apartment door, hoping to spend the night on the sofa in her friend's apartment. Hopefully, her friend's parents won't mind. Maybe she'll go
15 home to check on her mother in the morning, or maybe she'll go to school. ■

What could the future hold for a child who lives like this?
20 Could a person whose life began in a background of parental drug addiction and poverty hope to be educated at a famous university and
25 become a public success? That **outcome** is unlikely, but Liz Murray made it possible.

1 Why doesn't Liz want to go home?

Liz Murray inspires the audience at a speaking engagement.

Born into Poverty

Liz Murray was born into a life of poverty and addiction in the Bronx in 1980. An eye disease soon left her mom legally blind. As a result of her disability, she received welfare from the government and relied on Liz to take care of her and "be her eyes." Liz was forced to do things such as watch for the mailman on the first of every month and stand in line at the check-cashing store with the other welfare recipients—while other kids her age were playing innocent games of tag and hide and seek. Once the check was cashed, her drug-addicted parents used the money for drugs and began the cycle of neglect and mistreatment of their children.

Liz remembers eating well on the first of each month. However, during the rest of the month, her parents used their support to feed their drug addictions instead of their children. Some months, after spending their welfare check on drugs, her parents only had $30 left to feed Liz and her sister. **2**

When Liz was growing up, she lived in filthy conditions. Because of this, Liz was unbathed, wore unclean clothing, and often had lice. Liz was aware of the smell she gave off and the unwelcome stares from kids at school. The shame of this caused Liz to hate school and plead to stay home. Often, her mother agreed. She loved her parents and felt fortunate that they loved her back. **3**

Death Brings Realization

Eventually, her parents separated. Liz's older sister, Lisa, went to live with their mom and her new boyfriend. Liz stayed with her father because she didn't want him to be alone. When Liz was 11, her mother was **diagnosed** with HIV and died five years later.

While her mother grew more sick, Liz's father moved to a shelter for the homeless. Liz was sent to a group home, but **conditions** at the home were so bad that she didn't stay long. Living on

diagnose
to find out and name what is wrong with someone or something

conditions
all the things in the surroundings that affect how a person acts or feels

2 Liz's parents sacrificed the well-being of their children for what?

3 Why did Liz miss school?

Liz's mother (top) and Liz with her dad (bottom)

alternative

different from other things of its kind

motivated

focused on reaching one or more goals

apply

to ask for something in writing or by filling out a form

4 How did Liz's life dramatically change at age 16?

5 How did Liz determine to improve her life?

6 What kind of high school did Liz attend? How long did it take her to graduate?

7 How was Liz able to go to an expensive school like Harvard?

95 the streets of New York, she found food in garbage bins and shelter in friends' homes or on subway trains. **4**

After her mother's death, Liz suddenly realized that 100 she was truly on her own. Her mother had said many times, "Someday life will get better." But Liz realized her mother died before she 105 could fix anything, so Liz resolved to change her life for the better before it was too late. She began to think seriously about her own life. 110 She wondered if she could rise out of her background of poverty and improve her life with education. This idea pushed her forward. **5**

Getting an Education

115 At 17, Liz heard about **alternative** high schools. She researched different schools and finally found one that would accept her. 120 Because she was intelligent and **motivated** and had taught herself to read, Liz did well in school despite her lack of previous schooling. 125 She determined to graduate in two years instead of the usual four. Because of her willingness to study often, anywhere she could—school 130 hallways, libraries, stairwells in apartment buildings—she did it.

During this time, she was still homeless, sleeping out 135 on the streets sometimes and working at odd jobs to earn money. At school, her teachers encouraged her. She began to believe in 140 herself, but she never let anyone know how she was living. Then, something happened that set the course of her life. **6**

145 A teacher chose her and a few other students to visit Boston, Massachusetts. While there, she visited Harvard University, a respected Ivy 150 League university known for academic excellence. As she stood gazing at the campus, her teacher told her that it was possible for her to go 155 to school at Harvard, and she believed him. Liz would later write in her memoir, *Breaking Night*, that it was a good thing he didn't tell 160 her how hard it was to get accepted to this university. Then, she heard about a *New York Times* scholarship for needy students and **applied** 165 for it. Applicants had to write an essay describing any hardships they had overcome to achieve academic success. Liz was one of six students 170 who received the scholarship. She applied and was accepted to Harvard. **7**

Liz enrolled at Harvard in the fall of 2000 and completed several semesters of academic study. Then, in 2003, her father became sick with AIDS, and she returned to New York to take care of him. **8**

A New Direction

Despite what appeared to be a setback in New York, Liz continued her education at Columbia University. The unexpected changes in her life also brought many exciting **opportunities**. The *New York Times* published a story about her scholarship, then the television show "20/20" told her story, and Oprah Winfrey interviewed her. Also in 2003, a television movie was made about her life. **9**

Liz's father died in 2006, having finally overcome his drug addiction. Liz returned to Harvard in May 2008 to complete her degree. She realized that her story might have the power to help others. But, even better, her experiences and her knowledge might allow her to create **strategies** to help people cope with hardships. People might use these ways to move beyond their hardships to a meaningful life. **10**

Today, Liz has a company. Through workshops, she **lectures** to groups throughout the country, encouraging others to rise to their own dreams. Her sister also graduated from college and is a teacher. Whatever their dreams are, whatever background they come from, however hard they need to work, Liz Murray gives people **inspiration** to change their lives. **11**

NEW YORK TIMES BESTSELLER

"A white-knuckle account of survival... full of heart and deeply moving" — THE NEW YORK TIMES BOOK REVIEW (EDITORS' CHOICE)

Breaking Night

A Memoir of Forgiveness, Survival, and My Journey from Homeless to Harvard

LIZ MURRAY

Murray's memoir was published in 2010.

opportunity
a chance to do something you want to do

strategy
a plan for doing something over time

lecture
to give an organized talk in public

inspiration
energy to do something new or creative

8 Why did Liz have to leave Harvard?

9 Why did Liz become a subject of the media?

10 What did Liz's father do before he died that would have made Liz proud?

11 Why do you think Liz is interested in helping others?

Critical Understandings

Respond to each prompt using complete sentences. Refer to the chart on page 66 to determine how to respond to each prompt.

1. Paraphrase the introduction.

   _____

   _____

   _____

   _____

   _____

2. Determine the main idea of the section Death Brings Realization.

   _____

   _____

   _____

   _____

   _____

3. Create a timeline of Liz's life from 1980 to 2000.

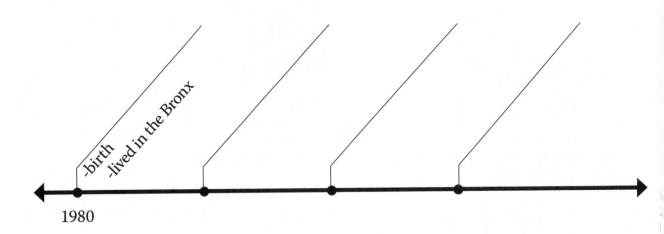

1980

Critical Understandings (*cont.*)

4. Delineate evidence of obstacles in Liz's life through high school.

Obstacle	Text Evidence

Passage Comprehension

Reread "From Homeless to Harvard." Respond to each prompt using complete sentences. Refer to the chart on page 66 to determine how to respond to each prompt.

1. Delineate the evidence that supports the claim that a child without parental supervision can become a successful adult.

   _____

   _____

   _____

   _____

   _____

   _____

   _____

2. Determine Liz's strengths that allowed her to break the cycle of poverty and addiction.

   _____

   _____

   _____

3. Paraphrase the last sentence in "From Homeless to Harvard" to explain Liz Murray's hopes for her company.

   _____

   _____

   _____

4. Create a timeline of Liz's life from 2003 to today.

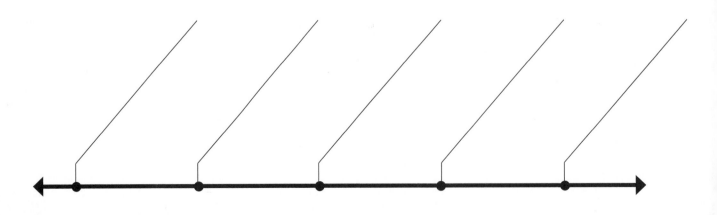

Passage Comprehension (*cont.*)

5. Delineate Liz's path to a college degree.

Step	Text Evidence

Passage Comprehension (*cont.*)

6. Create an invitation to a speaking engagement featuring Liz Murray. Include information about the speaker as well as topics that will be covered.

Close Reading

Read the text.

> ### "From Homeless to Harvard"
>
> The winter evening is cold and windy with crisp-looking stars shining over Bronx, New York. Liz Murray, just 12 years old, doesn't want to go home because her parents are doing drugs again. She is walking the streets, alone, headed for the home of a friend. She knocks on an apartment door, hoping
> 5 to spend the night on the sofa in her friend's apartment. Hopefully, her friend's parents won't mind. Maybe she'll go home to check on her mother in the morning, or maybe she'll go to school.
>
> What could the future hold for a child who lives like this? Could a person whose life began in a background of parental drug addiction and poverty
> 10 hope to be educated at a famous university and become a public success? That **outcome** is unlikely, but Liz Murray made it possible.

> ### Born into Poverty
>
> Liz Murray was born into a life of poverty and addiction in the Bronx in 1980. An eye disease soon left her mom legally blind. As a result of her disability, she received welfare from the government and relied on Liz
> 15 to take care of her and "be her eyes." Liz was forced to do things such as watch for the mailman on the first of every month and stand in line at the check-cashing store with the other welfare recipients—while other kids her age were playing innocent games of tag and hide and seek. Once the check was cashed, her drug-addicted parents used the money for drugs
> 20 and began the cycle of neglect and mistreatment of their children.
>
> Liz remembers eating well on the first of each month. However, during the rest of the month, her parents used their support to feed their drug addictions instead of their children. Some months, after spending their welfare check on drugs, her parents only had $30 left to feed Liz and
> 25 her sister.
>
> When Liz was growing up, she lived in filthy conditions. Because of this, Liz was unbathed, wore unclean clothing, and often had lice. Liz was aware of the smell she gave off and the unwelcome stares from kids at school. The shame of this caused Liz to hate school and plead to stay
> 30 home. Often, her mother agreed. She loved her parents and felt fortunate that they loved her back.

Close Reading (*cont.*)

Death Brings Realization

Eventually, her parents separated. Liz's older sister, Lisa, went to live with their mom and her new boyfriend. Liz stayed with her father because she didn't want him to be alone. When Liz was 11, her mother was
35 **diagnosed** with HIV and died five years later. While her mother grew more sick, Liz's father moved to a shelter for the homeless. Liz was sent to a group home, but **conditions** at the home were so bad that she didn't stay long. Living on the streets of New York, she found food in garbage bins and shelter in friends' homes or on subway trains.

40 After her mother's death, Liz suddenly realized that she was truly on her own. Her mother had said many times, "Someday life will get better." But Liz realized her mother died before she could fix anything, so Liz resolved to change her life for the better before it was too late. She began to think seriously about her own life. She wondered if she could rise out
45 of her background of poverty and improve her life with education. This idea pushed her forward.

Close Reading (*cont.*)

Getting an Education

At 17, Liz heard about **alternative** high schools. She researched different schools and finally found one that would accept her. Because she was intelligent and **motivated** and had taught herself to read, Liz did well in
50 school despite her lack of previous schooling. She determined to graduate in two years instead of the usual four. Because of her willingness to study often, anywhere she could—school hallways, libraries, stairwells in apartment buildings—she did it.

During this time, she was still homeless, sleeping out on the streets
55 sometimes and working at odd jobs to earn money. At school, her teachers encouraged her. She began to believe in herself, but she never let anyone know how she was living. Then, something happened that set the course of her life.

A teacher chose her and a few other students to visit Boston, Massachusetts.
60 While there, she visited Harvard University, a respected Ivy League university known for academic excellence. As she stood gazing at the campus, her teacher told her that it was possible for her to go to school at Harvard, and she believed him. Liz would later write in her memoir, *Breaking Night*, that it was a good thing he didn't tell her how hard it was
65 to get accepted to this university. Then, she heard about a *New York Times* scholarship for needy students and **applied** for it. Applicants had to write an essay describing any hardships they had overcome to achieve academic success. Liz was one of six students who received the scholarship. She applied and was accepted to Harvard.

70 Liz enrolled at Harvard in the fall of 2000 and completed several semesters of academic study. Then, in 2003, her father became sick with AIDS, and she returned to New York to take care of him.

Close Reading (*cont.*)

A New Direction

Despite what appeared to be a setback in New York, Liz continued her education at Columbia University. The unexpected changes in her
75 life also brought many exciting **opportunities**. The *New York Times* published a story about her scholarship, then the television show "20/20" told her story, and Oprah Winfrey interviewed her. Also in 2003, a television movie was made about her life.

Liz's father died in 2006, having finally overcome his drug addiction. Liz
80 returned to Harvard in May 2008 to complete her degree. She realized that her story might have the power to help others. But, even better, her experiences and her knowledge might allow her to create **strategies** to help people cope with hardships. People might use these ways to move beyond their hardships to a meaningful life.

85 Today, Liz has a company. Through workshops, she **lectures** to groups throughout the country, encouraging others to rise to their own dreams. Her sister also graduated from college and is a teacher. Whatever their dreams are, whatever background they come from, however hard they need to work, Liz Murray gives people **inspiration** to change
90 their lives.

Prepare to Write: Compare and Contrast Paragraph

Part A. Study the Prompt

Read the prompt and identify the topic, directions, and purpose for writing.

Often, writers present factual information in a different way. In this unit, we read Liz Murray's account of her own life as well as an informational text written by someone else.

How is Liz's life portrayed in each text? Consider the way Liz perceives what is normal and the way Liz was treated by her parents. Write a paragraph that compares the portrayal of both topics in the excerpt from *Breaking Night* and the passage "From Homeless to Harvard." Consider how the information provided differs from one text to the other. Include examples from the texts in your comparison. Use transition words as you move from one point to another.

Topic: _____

Directions: _____

_____

Purpose for writing: _____

_____

Part B. Write a Topic Sentence—Compare/Contrast Statement

Compare/Contrast Words		
different	the same	unlike
in common	better	alike
differences	similar	worse

_____

_____

_____

_____

_____

_____

_____

Prepare to Write: Compare and Contrast Paragraph (*cont.*)

Part C. Organize Information

Compare and contrast the information in both texts.

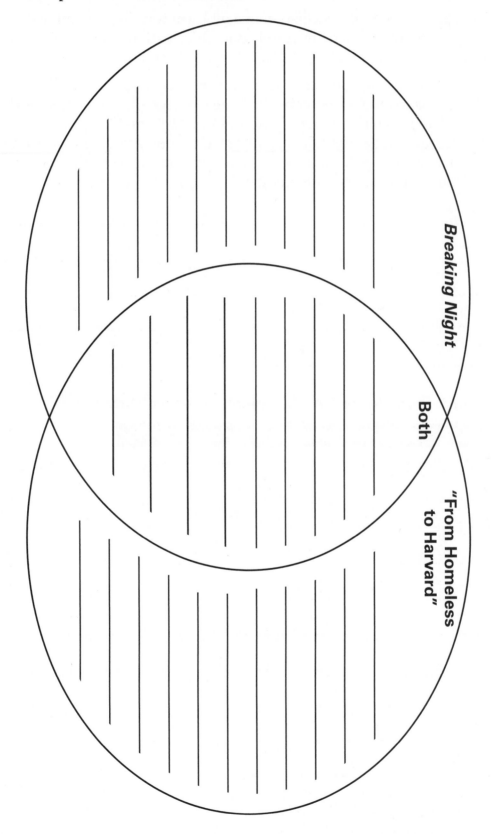

Prepare to Write: Compare and Contrast Paragraph (*cont.*)

Part D. Write a Concluding Sentence

Develop a concluding sentence by restating the topic sentence. Choose a word from the chart below to start your sentence. Use a comma to separate the word or phrase from the rest of the sentence.

Concluding Words and Phrases				
as a result	consequently	finally	in closing	in conclusion
in summary	in the end	so	therefore	thus

_____

_____

_____

_____

_____

_____

Part E. Use Transition Words to Illustrate and Compare

Use transition words in writing to help you move from one idea to the next.

Illustrate				
for example	for instance	as an illustration	in particular	as an example
Compare/Change Direction				
in contrast	although	instead	however	on the contrary

The Writer's Checklist

Trait	Yes	No	Did the writer . . .?
Ideas and Content			focus all sentences on the topic
			provide supporting details for the topic sentence
			include examples, evidence, and/or explanations to develop the supporting detail sentences
Organization			write a topic sentence
			tell things in an order that makes sense
			use transition words and/or phrases
			write a concluding sentence
Voice and Audience Awareness			think about the audience and purpose for writing
			write in a clear and engaging way that makes the audience want to read the work; write so the reader can "hear" the writer speaking
Word Choice			try to find a unique way to say things
			use words that are lively and specific to the content
Sentence Fluency			write complete sentences
			expand some sentences by painting the subject and/or predicate
Conventions			capitalize words correctly:
			capitalize the first word of each sentence
			capitalize proper nouns, including people's names
			punctuate correctly:
			put a period or question mark at the end of each sentence
			put an apostrophe before the s for a singular possessive noun
			use a comma after a long adverb phrase at the beginning of a sentence
			use grammar correctly:
			use the correct verb tense
			make sure the verb agrees with the subject in number
			use correct spelling

Let's Focus: "The Symbol of Freedom"

Content Focus
Nelson Mandela's struggle for justice in South Africa

Type of Text
informational

Author's Name _____

Author's Purpose _____

Big Ideas
Consider the following Big Idea questions. Write your answer for each question.

What causes stereotypes and prejudices?

_____

_____

What inspires people to take action?

_____

_____

Informational Preview Checklist: "The Symbol of Freedom" on pages 231–234.

☐ Title: What clue does it provide about the passage?

☐ Pictures: What additional information is added here?

☐ Headings: What will you learn about in each section?

☐ Features: What other text features do you notice?

Enduring Understandings
After reading the text . . .

_____

_____

_____

_____

_____

Key Passage Vocabulary: "The Symbol of Freedom"

Read each word. Write the word in column 3. Then, circle a number to rate your knowledge of the word.

Vocabulary	Part of Speech	Write the Word	Knowledge Rating
discrimination	(n)		0 1 2 3
resources	(n)		0 1 2 3
invent	(v)		0 1 2 3
access	(v)		0 1 2 3
impose	(v)		0 1 2 3
govern	(v)		0 1 2 3
impact	(v)		0 1 2 3
passive	(adj)		0 1 2 3
harmony	(n)		0 1 2 3
transform	(v)		0 1 2 3

The Symbol of Freedom

Nelson Mandela's lifelong fight for the cause of
freedom in South Africa is a tale of inspiration and
determination; it is a tale of struggle. During his
27 years in prison, he became a powerful symbol
5 of resistance to the racial **discrimination** that has
plagued South Africa, and he emerged as the first
black president of South Africa in 1994. **1**

South Africa's landscape and environment have been
described as the most enticing in the world. South
10 Africa has a mild climate, similar to that of the
San Francisco Bay. The land is fertile with plentiful
mineral **resources**. In fact, South African mines are
world leaders in the production of diamonds, gold,
and platinum. These qualities combined to make
15 South Africa attractive to European powers in the
17th, 18th, and 19th centuries.

South Africa had much to offer European powers
looking for natural resources and economic gain.
The land was colonized by the Dutch in the 1600s.
20 During the following century, England became
interested in the land and eventually defeated the
Dutch. South Africa remained a colony of England
until 1961. **2**

discrimination

the act of treating
some people worse
than others for
unfair reasons

resources

things that can
be sold to create
wealth

1 Nelson Mandela
was South
Africa's first
what?

2 Who ruled
South Africa
until 1961?

invent

to make up or think of

access

to find a way into; to gain entry to

impose

to force upon; to burden with

3 What were apartheid laws designed to do?

4 What happened to people who protested against apartheid laws?

Apartheid

25 The political parties in control of the country consisted primarily of white men of European ancestry. These groups **invented** apartheid as a means to control the 30 economy and the people. *Apartheid* is a Dutch word that means "separateness." Apartheid laws were aimed to keep the white, European 35 minority in power. The laws discriminated against the black people of African ancestry, who made up more than 70 percent of the nation's 40 population, as well as people of mixed race and Asian descent. **3**

These laws touched every aspect of social life. 45 Nonwhites could not go to white schools or hospitals or visit white beaches. They could not vote and were segregated from many jobs. 50 To **access** designated white areas, all black Africans were required to carry "pass books" containing fingerprints, a photo, and 55 personal information. Black Africans were forced to live in specific areas on the outskirts of South Africa and needed passports to enter the 60 rest of the country. They were treated as visiting foreigners in their own country.

The penalties **imposed** on those who protested 65 against the discrimination were severe. Thousands of individuals were tortured and killed. Those who were tried in court were typically 70 sentenced to death, exile, or life in prison—like Nelson Mandela. **4**

Apartheid and the People of South Africa		
	Blacks	**Whites**
Population	19 million	4.5 million
Land allocation	13%	87%
Annual expenditures on education per pupil	$45	$696
Teacher/pupil ratio	1/60	1/22

Disproportionate Treatment circa 1978. Source: Moraine Park Technical College

Mandela burning his pass book

Apartheid sign in English and Afrikaans; South African pass book

A Means to an End

When Mandela was 12 years old, his father died of lung disease, causing his life to abruptly change. He was adopted by a tribal chief. He lived in a palace and learned African history from elder chiefs who visited. He learned how the African people had lived in relative peace until the coming of the Europeans. According to the elders, the people of South Africa had lived as brothers, but the white man shattered this fellowship. While the black man shared his land, air, and water with the white man, the white man took all of these things for himself.

At age 16, Mandela heard a tribal leader speak with great sadness about the future of young men in South Africa. The tribal leader explained that because the land was controlled by white men, the young black men would struggle to earn a living and never have the power to **govern** themselves. This speech profoundly **impacted** Mandela and set the course for his life of activism.

After years of performing well at various schools, Mandela enrolled in law school, where he met people of all races and backgrounds. He was exposed to liberal and Africanist thought in addition to racism and discrimination. This experience served to further fuel his passion for politics. In 1944, he joined the African National Congress to become a voice for those who didn't have one. **5**

Mandela Challenges the Apartheid Government

As more and more laws were passed to limit the progress of black South Africans, the ANC staged a campaign against apartheid laws that was structured around the theory of **passive** resistance. Mandela opened a law practice and campaigned against apartheid. Soon after, Mandela was charged with high treason, but the charges were eventually dropped. Mandela continued his important mission. The resistance to apartheid grew stronger, as did the commitment by the government to maintain white rule.

Tension with the government continued to grow. It peaked in 1960 when 69 black people were shot dead by police. The government declared a state of emergency and banned the ANC. In response, the ANC abandoned its policy of non-violence, and Mandela helped lead the armed struggle for freedom. **6**

govern
to rule; to direct

impact
to have an effect on

passive
not taking action; letting something happen to you

5 What organization did Mandela join? What kind of organization was this?

Top: *Entrance to the high-security prison at Robben Island, South Africa, now a national and World Heritage Site*

Bottom: *The inside of Mandela's prison cell as it was when he was imprisoned in 1964*

6 What policy did the ANC abandon in 1960? Why?

harmony

friendly agreement;
the working
together of all parts

transform

to change into
something new

7 For what ideal
was Mandela
prepared to die?
What was his
actual sentence?

8 What landmark
event took place
in South Africa
in 1994?

9 Mandela was
the symbol of
what?

Imprisonment

After playing a minor role in
a workers' strike and illegally
155 leaving the country in 1961,
Mandela began a five-year
prison sentence. During
that time, Mandela and
other members of the ANC
160 were tried for plotting to
overthrow the government by
violence. Mandela defended
himself during his trial with
words about democracy,
165 freedom, and equality. "I
have cherished the ideal of a
democratic and free society
in which all persons live
together in **harmony** and
170 with equal opportunities,"
he said. "It is an ideal for
which I hope to live and to
see realized. But if needs be,
it is an ideal for which I am
175 prepared to die." The verdict
was life in prison. **7**

Apartheid Ends

Mandela's fight did not end.
During his years in prison,
he became an international
180 symbol of resistance to
apartheid. In 1990, the
South African government
responded to international
pressure and released
185 Mandela. Talks of
transforming the old-style
government of South Africa to
a new multiracial democracy
began. In 1994, for the first
190 time in South Africa's history,
all races voted in democratic
elections, and Mandela was
elected president. **8**

Nelson Mandela struggled
195 to end apartheid in South
Africa. He led the charge,
became the face of resistance,
and shared the hopes and
dreams of many; he was the
200 symbol of freedom. Jailed
for 27 years, he emerged to
become the country's first
black president and play a
leading role in the drive for
205 human rights across the
world. **9**

Action, Linking, or Helping Verbs

Read each sentence and underline the verb or verb phrase. Write the verbs in the proper column in the chart below.

1. He was the symbol of freedom.

2. All black Africans were required to carry "pass books."

3. He learned how the African people had lived in relative peace until the coming of the Europeans.

4. He was adopted by a tribal chief.

5. South Africa remained a colony of England until 1961.

6. This group invented apartheid as a means to control the economy and the people.

7. The verdict was life in prison.

8. Thousands of individuals were tortured and killed.

9. Mandela opened a law practice and campaigned against apartheid.

10. Nelson Mandela's lifelong fight for the cause of freedom in South Africa is a tale of inspiration and determination.

Action Verb		Linking Verb	Helping Verb + Main Verb

Tense Timeline: Future and Future Progressive Tenses

Complete the sentences for the future and future progressive tense with the verb *speak*.

Yesterday	Today	Tomorrow

Past	Present	Future
		will + verb
I spoke.	I speak.	I will speak.
You spoke.	You speak.	You
She spoke.	She speaks.	She
We spoke.	We speak.	We
They spoke.	They speak.	They
Past Progressive	**Present Progressive**	**Future Progressive**
		will + be + -ing
I was speaking.	I am speaking.	I will be speaking.
You were speaking.	You are speaking.	You
She was speaking.	She is speaking.	She
We were speaking.	We are speaking.	We
They were speaking.	They are speaking.	They

Verb Tenses

Underline the verb in each sentence. Rewrite the sentence, changing the tense as indicated in the parentheses. Underline the verb in the new sentence.

> **Examples:**
> The government <u>declared</u> a state of emergency. (future)
> The government <u>will declare</u> a state of emergency.
>
> Mandela <u>served</u> a five-year prison sentence. (future progressive)
> Mandela <u>will be serving</u> a five-year prison sentence.

1. These laws touched every aspect of social life. (future progressive)

   _____

   _____

2. Mandela enrolled in law school. (future)

   _____

   _____

3. The resistance to apartheid grew stronger. (future)

   _____

   _____

4. Mandela continued his important mission. (future progressive)

   _____

   _____

5. The South African government responded to international pressure and released Mandela. (future)

   _____

   _____

Conjunctions

Conjunctions join words, phrases, or clauses in a sentence. They also join sentences.

Coordinating Conjunctions

Coordinating conjunctions are the most common type of conjunction. They connect words that have the same function. Common coordinating conjunctions are **and**, **but**, and **or**.

- The conjunction **and** relates two similar ideas.

> Nelson closed his eyes to rest. His friends left.
>
> Nelson closed his eyes to rest, **and** his friends left.

- The conjunction **but** signals contrasting ideas.

> Nelson was arrested. His family was safe.
>
> Nelson was arrested, **but** his family was safe.

- The conjunction **or** signals an alternative choice.

> Mandela will give up the fight for equality.
> The government will punish him for treason.
>
> Mandela will give up the fight for equality, **or** the government will punish him for treason.

Coordinating Conjunctions

Circle the conjunction(s) in each sentence. Determine the meaning of the conjunction and place a check mark in the corresponding column.

	Similar Ideas	Contrasting Ideas	Alternative Choices
Ex: Nelson Mandela was sentenced to life in prison, (and) the fight for freedom was in danger.	✓		
1. Mandela could allow the government to end his campaign, or he could continue the fight, risking imprisonment.			
2. The government hoped to end the fight against apartheid, but the people continued the struggle against injustice.			
3. Nonwhites could not go to white schools or hospitals or visit white beaches.			
4. The ANC abandoned its policy of non-violence, and Mandela helped lead the armed struggle for freedom.			
5. The people of South Africa had lived as brothers, but the white man shattered this fellowship.			
6. The white people controlled the wealth, and the black Africans lived in poverty.			
7. Mandela was charged with high treason, but the charges were dropped.			

Spotlight on Punctuation: Commas with Conjunctions

Circle the conjunction in each sentence. Add a comma where needed.

1. South Africa's landscape and environment have been described as the most enticing in the world.

2. Mandela opened a law practice and the people came to him for help.

3. Nonwhites could not go to white schools or visit white beaches.

4. Black Africans were allowed to visit other areas of South Africa but needed a passport.

5. The government imprisoned Mandela to end his campaigns but Mandela emerged more powerful than ever.

6. All races voted in democratic elections and Mandela was elected president.

7. Black Africans wanted equal rights but they were continually denied.

8. It is an ideal that I hope to live for and to see realized.

9. Black Africans were treated as foreigners and the government felt justified.

10. Black Africans could not vote and were segregated from many jobs.

Masterpiece Sentences Using Conjunctions

Use the following painter questions and information about Nelson Mandela to create sentences with a variety of structures and elements.

Who?	Did what?	How?	**AND**	Who?	Did what?	How?

Who?	Did what?	To what?	**BUT**	Who?	Did what?	To what?

Who?	Did what?	To what?	**AND**	Who?	Did what?	To what?

What?	Did what?	Where?	**BUT**	Who?	Did what?	To what?	How?

When?	Who?	Will do what?	To what?	**OR**	Who?	Will do what?	To what?

Comma or Semicolon

Read the compound sentences and decide if the sentence needs a comma or a semicolon. Fill in the blank with the proper punctuation mark.

> **Example:**
> The whites were treated as native South Africans __;__ the nonwhites were treated as foreigners.

1. The government punished protestors ____ the people protested anyway.

2. Whites were allowed to live anywhere ____ but nonwhites were forced to live on the outskirts of South Africa.

3. Mandela was charged with high treason ____ the charges were dropped.

4. Mandela was sentenced to life in prison ____ so his fight against apartheid came to an end.

5. The struggle continued in Mandela's absence ____ and eventually the laws were changed.

6. New laws were passed that dictated where black Africans could live and work ____ so the resistance to apartheid grew stronger.

7. The government sought to limit Mandela's popularity ____ the people's love of him grew.

8. Mandela could see the injustice ____ but the government remained ignorant.

9. Mandela was jailed for 27 years ____ but the international fight against apartheid continued.

10. The government wished to keep the people apart ____ the people wished to unite.

Passage Comprehension

Reread "The Symbol of Freedom." Respond to each prompt using complete sentences. Refer to the chart on page 66 to determine how to respond to each prompt. Provide text evidence when requested.

1. Paraphrase the first paragraph.

    _____

    _____

    _____

    _____

    _____

    _____

2. Delineate the events that led to apartheid in South Africa.

    _____

    _____

    _____

    _____

    _____

    _____

3. Delineate the events in Mandela's youth that led him to join the African National Congress (ANC). Write the events in the boxes.

	→	→

    Joined the ANC

Passage Comprehension (*cont.*)

4. Create a poster persuading people to join the African National Congress (ANC).

Passage Comprehension (*cont.*)

5. Determine the meaning of the following sentence from the text:
    According to the elders, the people of South Africa had lived as brothers, but the white man shattered this fellowship.

    _____

    _____

    _____

    _____

    _____

    _____

    _____

    _____

6. Determine whether Mandela's activism was successful and the reason for this success or failure. Provide text evidence to support your answer.

    _____

    _____

    _____

    _____

    _____

    _____

    Text Evidence: _____

    _____

    _____

    _____

    _____

    _____

    _____

Close Reading

Read the text.

The Symbol of Freedom

Nelson Mandela's lifelong fight for the cause of freedom in South Africa
is a tale of inspiration and determination; it is a tale of struggle. During
his 27 years in prison, he became a powerful symbol of resistance to the
racial **discrimination** that has plagued South Africa, and he emerged as
5 the first black president of South Africa in 1994.

South Africa's landscape and environment have been described as the most
enticing in the world. South Africa has a mild climate, similar to that of the
San Francisco Bay. The land is fertile with plentiful mineral **resources**. In
fact, South African mines are world leaders in the production of diamonds,
10 gold, and platinum. These qualities combined to make South Africa
attractive to European powers in the 17th, 18th, and 19th centuries.

South Africa had much to offer European powers looking for natural
resources and economic gain. The land was colonized by the Dutch in the
1600s. During the following century, England became interested in the
15 land and eventually defeated the Dutch. South Africa remained a colony
of England until 1961.

Close Reading (*cont.*)

Apartheid

The political parties in control of the country consisted primarily of white men of European ancestry. These groups **invented** apartheid as a means to control the economy and the people. *Apartheid* is a Dutch word that
20 means "separateness." Apartheid laws were aimed to keep the white, European minority in power. The laws discriminated against the black people of African ancestry, who made up more than 70 percent of the nation's population, as well as people of mixed race and Asian descent.

These laws touched every aspect of social life. Nonwhites could not
25 go to white schools or hospitals or visit white beaches. They could not vote and were segregated from many jobs. To **access** designated white areas, all black Africans were required to carry "pass books" containing fingerprints, a photo, and personal information. Black Africans were forced to live in specific areas on the outskirts of South Africa and
30 needed passports to enter the rest of the country. They were treated as visiting foreigners in their own country.

The penalties **imposed** on those who protested against the discrimination were severe. Thousands of individuals were tortured and killed. Those who were tried in court were typically sentenced to death, exile, or life in
35 prison—like Nelson Mandela.

Close Reading (*cont.*)

A Means to an End

When Mandela was 12 years old, his father died of lung disease, causing his life to abruptly change. He was adopted by a tribal chief. He lived in a palace and learned African history from elder chiefs who visited. He learned how the African people had lived in relative peace until the coming
40 of the Europeans. According to the elders, the people of South Africa had lived as brothers, but the white man shattered this fellowship. While the black man shared his land, air, and water with the white man, the white man took all of these things for himself.

At age 16, Mandela heard a tribal leader speak with great sadness about
45 the future of young men in South Africa. The tribal leader explained that because the land was controlled by white men, the young black men would struggle to earn a living and never have the power to **govern** themselves. This speech profoundly **impacted** Mandela and set the course for his life of activism.

50 After years of performing well at various schools, Mandela enrolled in law school, where he met people of all races and backgrounds. He was exposed to liberal and Africanist thought in addition to racism and discrimination. This experience served to further fuel his passion for politics. In 1944, he joined the African National Congress to become a
55 voice for those who didn't have one.

Close Reading (*cont.*)

Mandela Challenges the Apartheid Government

As more and more laws were passed to limit the progress of black South Africans, the ANC staged a campaign against apartheid laws that was structured around the theory of **passive** resistance. Mandela opened a law practice and campaigned against apartheid. Soon after, Mandela was
60 charged with high treason, but the charges were eventually dropped. Mandela continued his important mission. The resistance to apartheid grew stronger, as did the commitment by the government to maintain white rule.

Tension with the government continued to grow. It peaked in 1960 when
65 69 black people were shot dead by police. The government declared a state of emergency and banned the ANC. In response, the ANC abandoned its policy of non-violence, and Mandela helped lead the armed struggle for freedom.

Close Reading (*cont.*)

Imprisonment

After playing a minor role in a workers' strike and illegally leaving the
70 country in 1961, Mandela began a five-year prison sentence. During that
time, Mandela and other members of the ANC were tried for plotting to
overthrow the government by violence. Mandela defended himself during
his trial with words about democracy, freedom, and equality. "I have
cherished the ideal of a democratic and free society in which all persons
75 live together in **harmony** and with equal opportunities," he said. "It is an
ideal for which I hope to live and to see realized. But if needs be, it is an
ideal for which I am prepared to die." The verdict was life in prison.

Apartheid Ends

Mandela's fight did not end. During his years in prison, he became an
international symbol of resistance to apartheid. In 1990, the South African
80 government responded to international pressure and released Mandela.
Talks of **transforming** the old-style government of South Africa to a new
multiracial democracy began. In 1994, for the first time in South Africa's
history, all races voted in democratic elections, and Mandela was elected
president.

85 Nelson Mandela struggled to end apartheid in South Africa. He led the
charge, became the face of resistance, and shared the hopes and dreams
of many; he was the symbol of freedom. Jailed for 27 years, he emerged to
become the country's first black president and play a leading role in the
drive for human rights across the world.

Quick Write in Response to Reading

Nelson Mandela helped end apartheid in South Africa. Write a paragraph summarizing what apartheid was and how Mandela's activism led to its demise. Include major turning points and events in Mandela's life.

_____

_____

_____

_____

_____

_____

_____

_____

_____

_____

_____

_____

_____

_____

_____

_____

_____

_____

_____

_____

_____

_____

Let's Focus: "I Am Prepared to Die"

Content Focus
Nelson Mandela's trial statement

Type of Text
informational—speech

Author's Name _____

Author's Purpose _____

Big Ideas
Consider the following Big Idea questions. Write your answer for each question.

What is worth dying for? Do you think you could ever let it happen?

_____

_____

When, and for what reasons, is violence justified?

_____

_____

Speech Preview: "I Am Prepared to Die" on pages 255–266.

☐ Title: What clue does it provide about the passage?

☐ Pictures: What additional information is added here?

☐ Epigraph: What do you know from reading this?

Predict what tone of voice Mandela will use in his speech.

_____

_____

Enduring Understandings
After reading the text . . .

_____

_____

_____

_____

Public Speaking

When speakers are trying to persuade an audience to take action or agree with certain ideas, they use strategies. One of the strategies is fallacy, which has many different varieties.

Strategies	Explanation
Change in tone	variance in speaking voice for effect (from forceful to soft; from compassionate to irate)
Declaration of purpose	statement of the central idea (can be directly stated or led to indirectly)
Proof	evidence, facts, and figures
Connections	stories and examples that the audience will connect with
Counterclaims	evidence, stories, or proof to debunk the opposing side
Word craft	figurative language; repeated words or phrases to make an impression or a point; aphorisms (memorable phrases)
Fallacy	errors in logic

Fallacy	Explanation
Exaggeration	overstating; making an action or idea of the opponent's seem bigger than it really is
Stereotype	treating a whole group or category of people as if they all act, think, or look the same
Overgeneralization	claims about all the members of a group or category; claims that use *all*, *none*, or *never*
Irrelevant facts	distracting facts that are "beside the point" but may sway audience's thinking
Loaded terms	words that bring up strong feelings, memories, or associations
Caricature	oversimplifying the opponent or their ideas
Leading questions	questions that force an audience to think a certain way or imply that they already think that way
False assumptions	taking something for granted that isn't true; acting as if the audience believes something they might not
Incorrect premises	beginning from a starting point that isn't true or correct
Ad hominem	an attack on the arguer, not the argument

Key Passage Vocabulary: "I Am Prepared to Die"

Read each word. Write the word in column 3. Then, circle a number to rate your knowledge of the word.

Vocabulary	Part of Speech	Write the Word	Knowledge Rating
contribution	(n)		0 1 2 3
exploitation	(n)		0 1 2 3
defy	(v)		0 1 2 3
suspend	(v)		0 1 2 3
policy	(n)		0 1 2 3
massive	(adj)		0 1 2 3
prospect	(n)		0 1 2 3
legacy	(n)		0 1 2 3
hamper	(v)		0 1 2 3
irrelevant	(adj)		0 1 2 3

Mandela supporters await the verdict at the Rivonia Trial.

I Am Prepared to Die

An abridged version of Nelson Mandela's speech "I Am Prepared to Die," April 20, 1964, from the opening of the Rivonia Trial

I am the first accused. I am a convicted prisoner
5 serving five years for leaving the country without a
permit and for inciting people to go on strike at the
end of May 1961.

At the outset, I want to say that the suggestion that
the struggle in South Africa is under the influence
10 of foreigners or communists is wholly incorrect. I
have done whatever I did because of my experience
in South Africa and my own proudly felt African
background.

contribution

something given in support of an effort or cause

exploitation

the act of using someone for your own selfish gain

defy

to boldly resist; to challenge

In my youth, I listened to the elders of my tribe
15 telling stories of wars fought by our ancestors in
defense of the fatherland. I hoped then that life
might offer me the opportunity to serve my people
and make my own humble **contribution** to their
freedom struggle.

20 Some of the things so far told to the court are true
and some are untrue. I do not, however, deny that
I planned sabotage. I did not plan it in a spirit of
recklessness, nor because I love violence. I planned
it as a result of a calm assessment of the political
25 situation that had arisen after many years of
tyranny, **exploitation**, and oppression of my people
by the whites.

I admit that I was one of the persons who helped to
form Umkhonto we Sizwe. I deny that Umkhonto
30 was responsible for a number of acts which have
been charged in the indictment against us. We felt
that without sabotage there would be no way open
to the African people to succeed in their struggle
against white supremacy. All lawful modes of
35 expressing opposition had been closed by legislation,
and we were placed in a position in which we had
either to accept permanent inferiority or to **defy** the
government. We chose to defy the government. **1**

1 What does
Mandela admit
he helped to
plan? What
reasons does he
give for this?

We first broke the law in a way which avoided
40 violence; when this form was legislated against,
and the government resorted to a show of force to
crush opposition, only then did we decide to answer
violence with violence. But the violence we chose
was not terrorism. We who formed Umkhonto were
45 all members of the African National Congress and
had behind us the ANC tradition of non-violence.

The African National Congress was formed in 1912
to defend the rights of the African people, which
had been seriously curtailed. For 37 years—that is,
50 until 1949—it adhered strictly to a constitutional
struggle. It put forward demands and resolutions;

it sent delegations to the government in the belief
that African grievances could be settled through
peaceful discussion. But white governments
55 remained unmoved, and the rights of Africans
became less instead of becoming greater.

suspend
to put off or do
away with

policy
a rule; a way of
doing things

*The founding members of
the ANC, originally known
as the South African Native
National Congress (SANNC)*

Even after 1949, the ANC remained determined to
avoid violence. At this time, however, a decision was
taken to protest against apartheid by peaceful, but
60 unlawful, demonstrations. More than 8,500 people
went to jail. Yet there was not a single instance of
violence. I and nineteen colleagues were convicted,
but our sentences were **suspended** mainly because
the judge found that discipline and non-violence
65 had been stressed throughout. **2**

2 The ANC was
determined not
to use what?

During the defiance campaign, the Public Safety
Act and the Criminal Law Amendment Act were
passed. These provided harsher penalties for
offenses against the laws. Despite this, the protests
70 continued and the ANC adhered to its **policy** of
non-violence.

In 1956, 156 leading members of the Congress
Alliance, including myself, were arrested. When the
court gave judgment some five years later, it found
75 that the ANC did not have a policy of violence. We
were acquitted.

> **massive**
> huge; on a very large scale

In 1960, there was the shooting at Sharpeville, which resulted in the declaration of the ANC as unlawful.* My colleagues and I, after careful
80 consideration, decided that we would not obey this decree. The African people were not part of the government and did not make the laws by which they were governed. We believed the words of the Universal Declaration of Human Rights, that "the
85 will of the people shall be the basis of authority of the government." The ANC refused to dissolve but instead went underground. **3**

> **3** What did the government declare the ANC to be? How did the ANC respond?

The government held a referendum which led to the establishment of the republic. Africans, who
90 constituted approximately 70% of the population, were not entitled to vote. I undertook to be responsible for organizing the national stay-at-home called to coincide with the declaration of the republic. The stay-at-home was to be a peaceful
95 demonstration. Careful instructions were given to avoid any recourse to violence.

The government's answer was to introduce new and harsher laws, to mobilize its armed forces, and to send armed vehicles into the townships in a
100 **massive** show of force. The government had decided to rule by force alone, and this decision was a milestone on the road to Umkhonto. **4**

> **4** What was the government's answer to the stay-at-home strike organized by Mandela?

What were we, the leaders of our people, to do? We had to continue the fight. Anything else would have
105 been surrender. Our problem was not whether to fight, but was how to continue the fight.

By this time, violence had become a feature of the South African political scene. There had been violence in 1957 when the women of Zeerust
110 were ordered to carry passes; there was violence in 1958 with the enforcement of cattle culling in Sekhukhuneland; there was violence in 1959 when the people of Cato Manor protested against pass raids; there was violence in 1960 when the
115 government attempted to impose Bantu authorities in Pondoland. Each disturbance pointed to the growth among Africans of the belief that violence

*Between 5,000 and 7,000 protestors went to the police station in Sharpeville to peacefully demonstrate against the Pass laws. The police opened fire on the protestors, killing 69 people.

Protesters run for safety after police open fire in the Sharpeville Massacre.

was the only way out. A government which uses
force to maintain its rule teaches the oppressed to
120 use force to oppose it.

I came to the conclusion that as violence was
inevitable, it would be unrealistic to continue
preaching peace and non-violence. This conclusion
was not easily arrived at. It was only when all
125 channels of peaceful protest had been barred that
the decision was made to embark on violent forms
of struggle. I can only say that I felt morally obliged
to do what I did. **5**

Four forms of violence are possible. There is
130 sabotage, there is guerrilla warfare, there is
terrorism, and there is open revolution. We chose to
adopt the first. Sabotage did not involve loss of life,
and it offered the best hope for future race relations.

5 Why did
Mandela stop
preaching peace
and non-
violence?

prospect

a possibility that something will happen soon

The initial plan was based on a careful analysis of
135 the political and economic situation of our country.
We believed that South Africa depended to a large
extent on foreign capital. We felt that planned
destruction of power plants, and interference with
rail and telephone communications, would scare
140 away capital from the country, thus compelling the
voters of the country to reconsider their position.
The selection of targets is proof of this policy. Had
we intended to attack life, we would have selected
targets where people congregated and not empty
145 buildings and power stations. **6**

6 Why did the ANC decide that sabotage was the form of violence they should use?

The whites failed to respond by suggesting change;
they responded to our call by suggesting the laager.
In contrast, the response of the Africans was one
of encouragement. Suddenly, there was hope again.
150 People began to speculate on how soon freedom
would be obtained.

But we in Umkhonto weighed the white response
with anxiety. The lines were being drawn. The
whites and blacks were moving into separate camps,
155 and the **prospect**s of avoiding a civil war were made
less. The white newspapers carried reports that
sabotage would be punished by death.

We felt it our duty to make preparations to use
force in order to defend ourselves against force.
160 We decided, therefore, to make provision for the
possibility of guerrilla warfare. All whites undergo
compulsory military training, but no such training
was given to Africans. It was in our view essential
to build up a nucleus of trained men who would be
165 able to provide the leadership if guerrilla warfare
started. **7**

7 What seemed inevitable, or likely to happen? How did Mandela's group prepare for this?

At this stage, the ANC decided that I should
attend the Conference of the Pan-African Freedom
Movement, which was to be held 1962. After the
170 conference, I would take a tour of the African states
with a view to whether facilities were available for
the training of soldiers. My tour was successful.

Wherever I went, I met sympathy for our cause and promises of help. All Africa was united against the
175 stand of white South Africa.

I started to make a study of the art of war and revolution and, while abroad, underwent a course in military training. If there was to be guerrilla warfare, I wanted to be able to fight with my people. On my
180 return, I found that there had been little alteration in the political scene save that the threat of a death penalty for sabotage had now become a fact. [8]

Another of the allegations made by the state is that the aims and objects of the ANC and the
185 Communist Party are the same. The allegation is false. The creed of the ANC is, and always has been, the creed of freedom and fulfillment for the African people in their own land. The most important document ever adopted by the ANC is
190 the Freedom Charter. It is by no means a blueprint for a socialist state. It calls for redistribution, but not nationalization, of land; it provides for nationalization of mines, banks, and monopoly industry because big monopolies are owned by
195 one race only, and without such nationalization, racial domination would be perpetuated. Under the Freedom Charter, nationalization would take place in an economy based on private enterprise. The realization of the Freedom Charter would open up
200 fresh fields for a prosperous African population.

As far as the Communist Party is concerned, and if I understand its policy correctly, it stands for the establishment of a state based on the principles of Marxism. The Communist Party's main aim was to
205 remove the capitalists and to replace them with a working-class government. The Communist Party sought to emphasize class distinctions, while the ANC seeks to harmonize them. This is a vital distinction. [9]

8 What did Mandela learn during his tour of the African states? What did he learn on his return home?

9 How is the ANC different from the Communist Party? (Remember, *harmony* means "all parts working together".)

The ANC Freedom Charter of 1955 laid the groundwork for change.

legacy

something passed down from earlier people or times

During my lifetime this struggle of the African against White domination. Black domination. I have democratic and free society together in harmony and is an ideal which I hope But if needs be, it is pared to die.

210 It is true that there has often been close cooperation between the ANC and the Communist Party. But cooperation is merely proof of a common goal—in this case, the removal of white supremacy—and is not proof of a complete community of interests.
215 The history of the world is full of similar examples. Perhaps the most striking is the cooperation between Great Britain, the United States, and the Soviet Union in the fight against Hitler. Nobody but Hitler would have dared to suggest that such cooperation
220 turned Churchill or Roosevelt into communists.

What is more, for many decades communists were the only political group in South Africa prepared to treat Africans as human beings and their equals; who were prepared to eat with us, talk with us, and
225 work with us. They were the only group prepared to work with the Africans for the attainment of political rights. **10**

10 Why did the ANC choose to work with the Communist Party? Give two reasons.

Because of this, many Africans today tend to equate freedom with communism. They are supported
230 in this belief by a legislature which brands all exponents of democratic government and African freedom as communists and banned many of them under the Suppression of Communism Act. Although I have never been a member of the
235 Communist Party, I myself have been convicted under that act.

I have always regarded myself, in the first place, as an African patriot. Today, I am attracted by the idea of a classless society, an attraction which springs
240 in part from my admiration of the structure of early African societies. The land belonged to the tribe. There were no rich or poor, and there was no exploitation.

11 Why do Mandela and his colleagues think some form of socialism— redistribution of wealth—is needed?

I and many leaders of the new independent states
245 accept the need for some form of socialism to enable our people to catch up with the advanced countries of this world and to overcome their **legacy** of extreme poverty. But this does not mean we are Marxists. **11**

250 Our fight is against real and not imaginary
hardships or, to use the language of the state
prosecutor, "so-called hardships." Basically, we fight
against two features of African life in South Africa:
poverty and lack of human dignity. We do not need
255 communists to teach us about these things.

South Africa is the richest country in Africa. But it
is a land of remarkable contrasts. The whites enjoy
the highest standard of living, while Africans live
in poverty and misery. The complaint of Africans,
260 however, is not only that they are poor and the
whites are rich, but that the laws are designed to
preserve this situation. **12**

There are two ways to break out of poverty. The
first is by formal education, and the second is by the
265 worker acquiring a greater skill at his work and thus
higher wages. As far as Africans are concerned,
both these avenues of advancement are deliberately
curtailed by legislation.

The government has always sought to **hamper**
270 Africans in their search for education. There is
compulsory education for all white children at
virtually no cost to their parents. But approximately
40% of African children between seven and fourteen
do not attend school. For those who do, the
275 standards are vastly different from those afforded
to white children.

The other main obstacle to the advancement of the
African is the industrial color bar under which all
the better jobs of industry are reserved for whites.
280 Moreover, Africans in the unskilled and semi-
skilled occupations are not allowed to form trade
unions. This means that they are denied the right of
collective bargaining permitted to white workers. **13**

---

hamper
to make it hard
for someone to do
something

12 What is the
main complaint
of black
Africans?

"There are two
ways to break
out of poverty.
The first is
by formal
education, and
the second is
by the worker
acquiring a
greater skill at
his work and
thus higher
wages."

13 How does the
African
government
hamper blacks'
opportunities
for
advancement?

– 60 –

irrelevant

unrelated; beside the point

During my lifetime
this struggle of the African
against White domination,
Black domination.   I have
democratic and free societ
together in harmony and w
is an ideal which I hope t
But if needs be, it is an
pared to die.

The government answers its critics by saying
285 that Africans in South Africa are better off than
inhabitants of other countries in Africa. Even if this
statement is true, it is **irrelevant**. Our complaint is
not that we are poor by comparison with people in
other countries, but that we are poor by comparison
290 with the white people in our own country, and that
we are prevented by legislation from altering this
imbalance.

The lack of human dignity experienced by Africans
is the direct result of the policy of white supremacy.
295 White supremacy implies black inferiority.
Legislation designed to preserve white supremacy
entrenches this notion. Menial tasks in South
Africa are invariably performed by Africans. When
anything has to be carried or cleaned, the white
300 man will look around for an African to do it for him.
Because of this sort of attitude, whites tend to regard
Africans as a separate breed. They do not look upon
them as people with families of their own; they do
not realize that we fall in love, that we want to be
305 with our wives and children, that we want to earn
enough money to support our families properly. **14**

14 How do whites view black Africans? Why?

Poverty and the breakdown of family have
secondary effects. Children wander the streets
because they have no schools to go to, or no
310 parents at home to see that they go, because both
parents, if there be two, have to work to keep the
family alive. This leads to a breakdown in moral
standards, to an alarming rise in illegitimacy, and
to violence. Not a day goes by without somebody
315 being stabbed or assaulted. And violence is carried
out of the townships into the white living areas.
People are afraid to walk the streets after dark.
Housebreakings and robberies are increasing,
despite the fact that the death sentence can now be
320 imposed for such offences. Death sentences cannot
cure the festering sore. **15**

15 What are some secondary effects of poverty?

The only cure is to alter the conditions under which
Africans are forced to live. Africans want to be paid
a living wage. Africans want to perform work which
325 they are capable of doing. We want to be allowed

to own land. We want to be part of the general population and not confined to ghettoes. We want to be allowed out after eleven o'clock at night and not to be confined to our rooms like children. We

330 want to be allowed to travel in our own country. We want security and a stake in society.

Above all, we want equal political rights because without them, our disabilities will be permanent. I know this sounds revolutionary to the whites in

335 this country because the majority of voters will be Africans. This makes the white man fear democracy.

Nelson Mandela addresses the All in Africa Conference in Pietermaritzburg, 1961.

But this fear cannot be allowed to stand in the way of the only solution which will guarantee racial harmony and freedom for all. It is not true

340 that the enfranchisement of all will result in racial domination. Political division, based on color, is entirely artificial. When it disappears, so will the domination of one color group by another. The ANC has spent half a century fighting against racialism.

345 When it triumphs, it will not change that policy. **16**

16 What do black South Africans want, above all? Why do white South Africans fear this?

Our struggle is a national one. It is a struggle of the African people, inspired by our own suffering and our own experience. It is a struggle for the right to live. During my lifetime, I have dedicated 350 myself to this struggle. I have fought against white domination, and I have fought against black domination. I have cherished the ideal of a democratic and free society in which all persons live together in harmony and with equal opportunities. 355 It is an ideal for which I hope to live and to see realized. But if needs be, it is an ideal for which I am prepared to die. **17**

> **17** For what is Nelson Mandela prepared to die?

> "Your long walk to freedom has ended in a physical sense. Our own journey continues. We have to continue working to build the kind of society you worked tirelessly to construct."
>
> **Jacob Zuma, South African President at Mandela's funeral**

Madiba (Nelson Mandela's clan name) died at his home in Johannesburg on December 5, 2013. Representatives from all over the world gathered to celebrate his life and legacy.

Critical Understandings

Reread lines 183–236 of "I Am Prepared to Die." Refer to the chart on page 66 to determine how to respond to each prompt. Respond using complete sentences.

1. Mandela argues that the ANC is not a communist group. His first piece of evidence is a document called the Freedom Charter. Evaluate the strength of this document as evidence.

_____

_____

_____

_____

_____

_____

_____

2. Distinguish between the goals of the Communist Party and the goals of the African National Congress.

_____

_____

_____

_____

_____

_____

_____

_____

_____

Critical Understandings (*cont.*)

3. Analyze the attraction of many black South Africans to communism.

_____

_____

_____

_____

_____

_____

_____

_____

_____

_____

_____

4. Assess the law that branded all supporters of democracy communists.

_____

_____

_____

_____

_____

_____

_____

_____

_____

_____

_____

_____

Passage Comprehension

Reread "I Am Prepared to Die." Respond to each prompt using complete sentences. Refer to the chart on page 66 to determine how to respond to each prompt.

1. Assess Mandela's reference to his youth as a way to begin the speech.

_____

_____

_____

_____

_____

_____

_____

_____

_____

2. Evaluate the ANC's policy of non-violence.

_____

_____

_____

_____

_____

_____

_____

_____

_____

_____

_____

_____

Passage Comprehension (*cont.*)

3. The ANC ultimately decided to use violence. Evaluate the reasons and evidence Mandela gives for this decision. Does he support them with evidence—facts and details from real life? Are his reasons and evidence sound?

Reason for decision	Evidence to support claims	Sound?

4. Distinguish between sabotage and the other three types of violence Mandela names.

_____

_____

_____

_____

_____

Passage Comprehension (*cont.*)

5. Evaluate whether Mandela's travels around the African continent were useful.

_____

_____

_____

_____

_____

_____

_____

_____

_____

_____

6. Distinguish between the lives and opportunities of white South Africans and black South Africans.

_____

_____

_____

_____

_____

_____

_____

_____

_____

_____

Passage Comprehension (*cont.*)

7. Analyze the secondary effects of poverty.

_____

_____

_____

_____

_____

_____

_____

_____

_____

_____

_____

8. Assess Mandela's willingness to die for the ideal of a free and democratic South Africa.

_____

_____

_____

_____

_____

_____

_____

_____

_____

_____

_____

_____

Close Reading

Read the text.

> ### I Am Prepared to Die
>
> *An abridged version of Nelson Mandela's speech "I Am Prepared to Die,"*
> *April 20, 1964, from the opening of the Rivonia Trial*
>
> I am the first accused. I am a convicted prisoner serving five years for
> leaving the country without a permit and for inciting people to go on strike
> 5 at the end of May 1961.
>
> At the outset, I want to say that the suggestion that the struggle in South
> Africa is under the influence of foreigners or communists is wholly
> incorrect. I have done whatever I did because of my experience in South
> Africa and my own proudly felt African background.
>
> 10 In my youth, I listened to the elders of my tribe telling stories of wars
> fought by our ancestors in defense of the fatherland. I hoped then that
> life might offer me the opportunity to serve my people and make my own
> humble **contribution** to their freedom struggle.
>
> Some of the things so far told to the court are true and some are untrue. I
> 15 do not, however, deny that I planned sabotage. I did not plan it in a spirit of
> recklessness, nor because I love violence. I planned it as a result of a calm
> assessment of the political situation that had arisen after many years of
> tyranny, **exploitation**, and oppression of my people by the whites.
>
> I admit that I was one of the persons who helped to form Umkhonto we
> 20 Sizwe. I deny that Umkhonto was responsible for a number of acts which
> have been charged in the indictment against us. We felt that without
> sabotage there would be no way open to the African people to succeed in
> their struggle against white supremacy. All lawful modes of expressing
> opposition had been closed by legislation, and we were placed in a position
> 25 in which we had either to accept permanent inferiority or to **defy** the
> government. We chose to defy the government.
>
> We first broke the law in a way which avoided violence; when this form was
> legislated against, and the government resorted to a show of force to crush
> opposition, only then did we decide to answer violence with violence. But the
> 30 violence we chose was not terrorism. We who formed Umkhonto were all
> members of the African National Congress and had behind us the ANC
> tradition of non-violence.

Close Reading (*cont.*)

35 The African National Congress was formed in 1912 to defend the rights of the African people, which had been seriously curtailed. For 37 years—that is, until 1949—it adhered strictly to a constitutional struggle. It put forward demands and resolutions; it sent delegations to the government in the belief that African grievances could be settled through peaceful discussion. But white governments remained unmoved, and the rights of Africans became less instead of becoming greater.

40 Even after 1949, the ANC remained determined to avoid violence. At this time, however, a decision was taken to protest against apartheid by peaceful, but unlawful, demonstrations. More than 8,500 people went to jail. Yet there was not a single instance of violence. I and nineteen colleagues were convicted, but our sentences were **suspended** mainly because the judge 45 found that discipline and non-violence had been stressed throughout.

During the defiance campaign, the Public Safety Act and the Criminal Law Amendment Act were passed. These provided harsher penalties for offenses against the laws. Despite this, the protests continued and the ANC adhered to its **policy** of non-violence.

50 In 1956, 156 leading members of the Congress Alliance, including myself, were arrested. When the court gave judgment some five years later, it found that the ANC did not have a policy of violence. We were acquitted.

In 1960, there was the shooting at Sharpeville, which resulted in the declaration of the ANC as unlawful.* My colleagues and I, after careful 55 consideration, decided that we would not obey this decree. The African people were not part of the government and did not make the laws by which they were governed. We believed the words of the Universal Declaration of Human Rights, that "the will of the people shall be the basis of authority of the government." The ANC refused to dissolve but instead 60 went underground.

The government held a referendum which led to the establishment of the republic. Africans, who constituted approximately 70% of the population, were not entitled to vote. I undertook to be responsible for organizing the national stay-at-home called to coincide with the declaration of the 65 republic. The stay-at-home was to be a peaceful demonstration. Careful instructions were given to avoid any recourse to violence.

The government's answer was to introduce new and harsher laws, to mobilize its armed forces, and to send armed vehicles into the townships in a **massive** show of force. The government had decided to rule by force 70 alone, and this decision was a milestone on the road to Umkhonto.

*Between 5,000 and 7,000 protestors went to the police station in Sharpeville to peacefully demonstrate against the Pass laws. The police opened fire on the protestors, killing 69 people.

Close Reading (*cont.*)

What were we, the leaders of our people, to do? We had to continue the fight. Anything else would have been surrender. Our problem was not
75 whether to fight, but was how to continue the fight.

By this time, violence had become a feature of the South African political scene. There had been violence in 1957 when the women of Zeerust were ordered to carry passes; there was violence in 1958 with the enforcement of cattle culling in Sekhukhuneland; there was violence in 1959 when the
80 people of Cato Manor protested against pass raids; there was violence in 1960 when the government attempted to impose Bantu authorities in Pondoland. Each disturbance pointed to the growth among Africans of the belief that violence was the only way out. A government which uses force to maintain its rule teaches the oppressed to use force to oppose it.

85 I came to the conclusion that as violence was inevitable, it would be unrealistic to continue preaching peace and non-violence. This conclusion was not easily arrived at. It was only when all channels of peaceful protest had been barred that the decision was made to embark on violent forms of struggle. I can only say that I felt morally obliged to do what I did.

90 Four forms of violence are possible. There is sabotage, there is guerrilla warfare, there is terrorism, and there is open revolution. We chose to adopt the first. Sabotage did not involve loss of life, and it offered the best hope for future race relations.

The initial plan was based on a careful analysis of the political and
95 economic situation of our country. We believed that South Africa depended to a large extent on foreign capital. We felt that planned destruction of power plants, and interference with rail and telephone communications, would scare away capital from the country, thus compelling the voters of the country to reconsider their position. The selection of targets is proof of
100 this policy. Had we intended to attack life, we would have selected targets where people congregated and not empty buildings and power stations.

Close Reading (*cont.*)

The whites failed to respond by suggesting change; they responded to our call by suggesting the laager. In contrast, the response of the Africans was one of encouragement. Suddenly, there was hope again. People began to
105 speculate on how soon freedom would be obtained.

But we in Umkhonto weighed the white response with anxiety. The lines were being drawn. The whites and blacks were moving into separate camps, and the **prospects** of avoiding a civil war were made less. The white newspapers carried reports that sabotage would be punished by death.

110 We felt it our duty to make preparations to use force in order to defend ourselves against force. We decided, therefore, to make provision for the possibility of guerrilla warfare. All whites undergo compulsory military training, but no such training was given to Africans. It was in our view essential to build up a nucleus of trained men who would be able to provide
115 the leadership if guerrilla warfare started.

At this stage, the ANC decided that I should attend the Conference of the Pan-African Freedom Movement, which was to be held 1962. After the conference, I would take a tour of the African states with a view to whether facilities were available for the training of soldiers. My tour was successful.
120 Wherever I went, I met sympathy for our cause and promises of help. All Africa was united against the stand of white South Africa.

I started to make a study of the art of war and revolution and, while abroad, underwent a course in military training. If there was to be guerrilla warfare, I wanted to be able to fight with my people. On my return, I found
125 that there had been little alteration in the political scene save that the threat of a death penalty for sabotage had now become a fact.

Another of the allegations made by the state is that the aims and objects of the ANC and the Communist Party are the same. The allegation is false. The creed of the ANC is, and always has been, the creed of freedom and
130 fulfillment for the African people in their own land. The most important document ever adopted by the ANC is the Freedom Charter. It is by no means a blueprint for a socialist state. It calls for redistribution, but not nationalization, of land; it provides for nationalization of mines, banks, and monopoly industry because big monopolies are owned by one race
135 only, and without such nationalization racial domination would be perpetuated. Under the Freedom Charter, nationalization would take place in an economy based on private enterprise. The realization of the Freedom Charter would open up fresh fields for a prosperous African population.

Close Reading (*cont.*)

As far as the Communist Party is concerned, and if I understand its
140 policy correctly, it stands for the establishment of a state based on the
principles of Marxism. The Communist Party's main aim was to remove
the capitalists and to replace them with a working-class government. The
Communist Party sought to emphasize class distinctions, while the ANC
seeks to harmonize them. This is a vital distinction.

145 It is true that there has often been close cooperation between the ANC
and the Communist Party. But cooperation is merely proof of a common
goal—in this case, the removal of white supremacy—and is not proof of a
complete community of interests. The history of the world is full of similar
examples. Perhaps the most striking is the cooperation between Great
150 Britain, the United States, and the Soviet Union in the fight against Hitler.
Nobody but Hitler would have dared to suggest that such cooperation
turned Churchill or Roosevelt into communists.

What is more, for many decades communists were the only political group
in South Africa prepared to treat Africans as human beings and their
155 equals; who were prepared to eat with us, talk with us, and work with
us. They were the only group prepared to work with the Africans for the
attainment of political rights.

Because of this, many Africans today tend to equate freedom with
communism. They are supported in this belief by a legislature which
160 brands all exponents of democratic government and African freedom
as communists and banned many of them under the Suppression
of Communism Act. Although I have never been a member of the
Communist Party, I myself have been convicted under that act.

I have always regarded myself, in the first place, as an African patriot.
165 Today, I am attracted by the idea of a classless society, an attraction which
springs in part from my admiration of the structure of early African
societies. The land belonged to the tribe. There were no rich or poor and
there was no exploitation.

I and many leaders of the new independent states accept the need for some
170 form of socialism to enable our people to catch up with the advanced
countries of this world and to overcome their **legacy** of extreme poverty.
But this does not mean we are Marxists.

Close Reading (*cont.*)

175 Our fight is against real and not imaginary hardships or, to use the language of the state prosecutor, "so-called hardships." Basically, we fight against two features of African life in South Africa: poverty and lack of human dignity. We do not need communists to teach us about these things.

South Africa is the richest country in Africa. But it is a land of remarkable contrasts. The whites enjoy the highest standard of living, while Africans live in poverty and misery. The complaint of Africans, however, is not only 180 that they are poor and the whites are rich, but that the laws are designed to preserve this situation.

There are two ways to break out of poverty. The first is by formal education, and the second is by the worker acquiring a greater skill at his work and thus higher wages. As far as Africans are concerned, both these avenues of 185 advancement are deliberately curtailed by legislation.

The government has always sought to **hamper** Africans in their search for education. There is compulsory education for all white children at virtually no cost to their parents. But approximately 40% of African children between seven and fourteen do not attend school. For those who do, the 190 standards are vastly different from those afforded to white children.

The other main obstacle to the advancement of the African is the industrial color bar under which all the better jobs of industry are reserved for whites. Moreover, Africans in the unskilled and semi-skilled occupations are not allowed to form trade unions. This means that they are denied the right of 195 collective bargaining permitted to white workers.

The government answers its critics by saying that Africans in South Africa are better off than inhabitants of other countries in Africa. Even if this statement is true, it is **irrelevant**. Our complaint is not that we are poor by comparison with people in other countries, but that we are poor by 200 comparison with the white people in our own country, and that we are prevented by legislation from altering this imbalance.

The lack of human dignity experienced by Africans is the direct result of the policy of white supremacy. White supremacy implies black inferiority. Legislation designed to preserve white supremacy entrenches this notion. 205 Menial tasks in South Africa are invariably performed by Africans. When anything has to be carried or cleaned the white man will look around for an African to do it for him. Because of this sort of attitude, whites tend to regard Africans as a separate breed. They do not look upon them as people with families of their own; they do not realize that we fall in love, that 210 we want to be with our wives and children, that we want to earn enough money to support our families properly.

Close Reading (*cont.*)

Poverty and the breakdown of family have secondary effects. Children wander the streets because they have no schools to go to, or no parents at home to see that they go, because both parents, if there be two, have
215 to work to keep the family alive. This leads to a breakdown in moral standards, to an alarming rise in illegitimacy, and to violence. Not a day goes by without somebody being stabbed or assaulted. And violence is carried out of the townships into the white living areas. People are afraid to walk the streets after dark. Housebreakings and robberies are increasing,
220 despite the fact that the death sentence can now be imposed for such offences. Death sentences cannot cure the festering sore.

The only cure is to alter the conditions under which Africans are forced to live. Africans want to be paid a living wage. Africans want to perform work which they are capable of doing. We want to be allowed to own land. We
225 want to be part of the general population and not confined to ghettoes. We want to be allowed out after eleven o'clock at night and not to be confined to our rooms like children. We want to be allowed to travel in our own country. We want security and a stake in society.

Above all, we want equal political rights because without them, our
230 disabilities will be permanent. I know this sounds revolutionary to the whites in this country because the majority of voters will be Africans. This makes the white man fear democracy.

But this fear cannot be allowed to stand in the way of the only solution which will guarantee racial harmony and freedom for all. It is not true
235 that the enfranchisement of all will result in racial domination. Political division, based on color, is entirely artificial. When it disappears, so will the domination of one color group by another. The ANC has spent half a century fighting against racialism. When it triumphs, it will not change that policy.

240 Our struggle is a national one. It is a struggle of the African people, inspired by our own suffering and our own experience. It is a struggle for the right to live. During my lifetime, I have dedicated myself to this struggle. I have fought against white domination, and I have fought against black domination. I have cherished the ideal of a democratic and
245 free society in which all persons live together in harmony and with equal opportunities. It is an ideal for which I hope to live and to see realized. But if needs be, it is an ideal for which I am prepared to die.

Prepare to Write: Multiparagraph Essay

Part A. Study the Prompt

Read the prompt and identify the topic, directions, and purpose for writing.

You have read the text version of Nelson Mandela's speech "I Am Prepared to Die." You have also viewed a multimedia version of excerpts from the speech. Write an essay that compares and contrasts the text and the video. In your essay, do the following:

- Analyze the impact of Mandela's words in each version.
- Evaluate the pros and cons of using each format to communicate Mandela's message.

Topic: _____

Directions: _____

_____

_____

Purpose for writing: _____

_____

_____

Part B. Write a Thesis Statement

Write at least two sentences that introduce the subject and identify the big ideas.

_____

_____

_____

_____

_____

_____

_____

_____

_____

_____

_____

Prepare to Write: Multiparagraph Essay (*cont.*)

Part C. Take Notes

Evaluate how well each version presents Mandela's argument, creates a mood, helps you understand apartheid, and persuades you to agree with Mandela.

How well did this version . . .	Text of Speech	Multimedia Version of Speech
present Mandela's claims and arguments?		
create a certain tone, mood, or feeling?		

Prepare to Write: Multiparagraph Essay (*cont.*)

How well did this version . . .	Text of Speech	Multimedia Version of Speech
persuade the reader or viewer to believe Mandela's message?		

Overall, I found the _____ more powerful because it

_____

_____ .

Part D. Write a Conclusion

Write at least two sentences that restate the thesis and summarize the key ideas.

_____

_____

_____

_____

_____

_____

_____

_____

Prepare to Write: Multiparagraph Essay (*cont.*)

Part E. Write Topic Sentences

Use your notes to write the topic sentences for each point of comparison between the two versions of the speech.

Paragraph #1

_____

_____

_____

Paragraph #2

_____

_____

_____

Paragraph #3

_____

_____

_____

The Expository Writer's Checklist

Trait	Yes	No	Did the writer . . .?
Ideas and Content			clearly state the topic of the composition
			focus each paragraph on the topic
			include examples, evidence, and/or explanations to develop each paragraph
Organization			Paragraph Level:
			tell things in an order that makes sense
			Report Level:
			write an introductory paragraph that states the topic and the plan
			use transition topic sentences to connect paragraphs
			write a concluding paragraph that restates the introductory paragraph
Voice and Audience Awareness			think about the audience and purpose for writing
			write in a clear and engaging way that makes the audience want to read the work
Word Choice			find a unique way to say things
			use words that are lively and specific to the content
Sentence Fluency			write complete sentences
			expand some sentences using the steps of Masterpiece Sentences
			use compound sentence elements and compound sentences
Conventions			capitalize words correctly:
			capitalize the first word of each sentence
			capitalize proper nouns, including people's names
			punctuate correctly:
			end sentences with a period, question mark, or exclamation mark
			use an apostrophe for possessive nouns and contractions
			use commas and/or semicolons correctly
			use grammar correctly:
			use the correct verb tense
			make sure the verb agrees with the subject in number
			use correct spelling

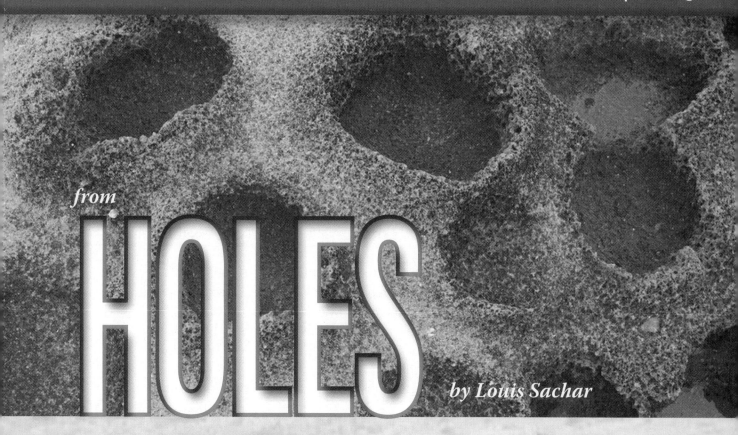

from

HOLES

by Louis Sachar

Stanley Yelnats is an overweight kid from a poor family. And he's being punished for a crime he didn't **commit**. The judge gave him an option: Either go to jail or go to Camp Green Lake. So Stanley chose Camp
5 Green Lake. After a long, lonely ride on a bus with no air-conditioning, Stanley has arrived at camp. What he finds is nothing like what he expected.

Stanley felt somewhat **dazed** as the guard unlocked his handcuffs and led him off the bus. He'd been on the
10 bus for over eight hours.

"Be careful," the bus driver said as Stanley walked down the steps.

Stanley wasn't sure if the bus driver meant for him to be careful going down the steps, or if he was telling
15 him to be careful at Camp Green Lake. "Thanks for the ride," he said. His mouth was dry and his throat hurt. He stepped onto the hard, dry dirt. There was a band of sweat around his wrist where the handcuff had been.

The land was **barren** and desolate. He could see a
20 few run-down buildings and some tents. Farther away there was a cabin beneath two tall trees. Those two trees were the only plant life he could see. There weren't even weeds. **1**

commit
to do something that is against the law or harmful

dazed
very confused and unable to think clearly

barren
without plant or animal life

1 What did Camp Green Lake look like?

juvenile

related to a person under 18 years of age

declare

to state something in a firm or official way

premises

the land and buildings owned by a person or company

aware

knowing something exists or is happening

2 Why is Stanley happy to enter the building?

3 Who do you think the new character is?

4 Why did the guard laugh?

5 Why does Stanley feel sorry for the guard and bus driver?

25 The guard led Stanley to a small building. A sign in front said, YOU ARE ENTERING CAMP GREEN LAKE **JUVENILE** CORRECTIONAL FACILITY. Next to it was another sign which **declared** that it was a violation of the Texas Penal Code to bring guns, explosives, weapons, drugs, or alcohol onto the **premises**.

30 As Stanley read the sign he couldn't help but think, *Well, duh!*

The guard led Stanley into the building, where he felt the welcome relief of air-conditioning. **2**

A man was sitting with his feet up on a desk. He
35 turned his head when Stanley and the guard entered, but otherwise didn't move. Even though he was inside, he wore sunglasses and a cowboy hat. He also held a can of soda, and the sight of it made Stanley even more **aware** of his own thirst.

40 He waited while the bus guard gave the man some papers to sign. **3**

"That's a lot of sunflower seeds," the bus guard said.

Stanley noticed a burlap sack filled with sunflower seeds on the floor next to the desk.

45 "I quit smoking last month," said the man in the cowboy hat. He had a tattoo of a rattlesnake on his arm, and as he signed his name, the snake's rattle seemed to wiggle. "I used to smoke a pack a day. Now I eat a sack of these every week."

50 The guard laughed. **4**

There must have been a small refrigerator behind his desk, because the man in the cowboy hat produced two more cans of soda. For a second Stanley hoped that one might be for him, but the man gave one to the guard and
55 said the other was for the driver.

"Nine hours here, and now nine hours back," the guard grumbled. "What a day."

Stanley thought about the long, miserable bus ride and felt a little sorry for the guard and the bus driver. **5**

60 The man in the cowboy hat spit sunflower seed shells into a wastepaper basket. Then he walked around the desk to Stanley. "My name is Mr. Sir," he said. "Whenever you speak to me you must call me by my name, is that clear?"

65 Stanley hesitated. "Uh, yes, Mr. Sir," he said, though he couldn't imagine that was really the man's name.

"You're not in the Girl Scouts anymore," Mr. Sir said. **6**

❖

70 Stanley had to remove his clothes in front of Mr. Sir, who made sure he wasn't hiding anything. He was then given two sets of clothes and a towel. Each set **consisted** of a long-sleeve orange jumpsuit, an orange T-shirt, and yellow socks. Stanley wasn't sure if the socks had been yellow originally.

75 He was also given white sneakers, an orange cap, and a canteen made of heavy plastic, which unfortunately was empty. The cap had a piece of cloth sewn on the back of it, for neck protection.

Stanley got dressed. The clothes smelled like soap.

Mr. Sir told him he should wear one set to work in 80 and one set for relaxation. Laundry was done every three days. On that day his work clothes would be washed. Then the other set would become his work clothes, and he would get clean clothes to wear while resting.

"You are to dig one hole each day, including Saturdays 85 and Sundays. Each hole must be five feet deep and five feet across in every direction. Your shovel is your measuring stick. Breakfast is served at 4:30." **7**

Stanley must have looked surprised, because Mr. Sir went on to explain that they started early to **avoid** the 90 hottest part of the day. "No one is going to baby-sit you," he added. "The longer it takes you to dig, the longer you will be out in the sun. If you dig up anything interesting, you are to report it to me or any other counselor. When you finish, the rest of the day is yours."

95 Stanley nodded to show he understood.

"This isn't a Girl Scout camp," said Mr. Sir.

He checked Stanley's backpack and allowed him to keep it. Then he led Stanley outside into the blazing heat.

"Take a good look around you," Mr. Sir said. "What 100 do you see?"

Stanley looked out across the **vast** wasteland. The air seemed thick with heat and dirt. "Not much," he said, then hastily added, "Mr. Sir."

Mr. Sir laughed. "You see any guard towers?"

105 "No."

consist
to be made up of

avoid
to stay away from something or someone

vast
extremely large

6 What kind of comment is this?

7 Predict the purpose of digging the holes.

"How about an electric fence?"

"No, Mr. Sir."

"There's no fence at all, is there?"

"No, Mr. Sir."

8 Why does Mr. Sir ask these questions?

110 "You want to run away?" Mr. Sir asked him. **8**

Stanley looked back at him, unsure what he meant.

"If you want to run away, go ahead, start running. I'm not going to stop you."

Stanley didn't know what kind of game Mr. Sir was 115 playing.

"I see you're looking at my gun. Don't worry. I'm not going to shoot you." He tapped his holster. "This is for yellow-spotted lizards. I wouldn't waste a bullet on you." **9**

9 How is Mr. Sir making Stanley feel?

120 "I'm not going to run away," Stanley said.

"Good thinking," said Mr. Sir. "Nobody runs away from here. We don't need a fence. Know why? Because we've got the only water for a hundred miles. You want to run away? You'll be buzzard food in three days."

125 Stanley could see some kids dressed in orange and carrying shovels dragging themselves toward the tents.

"You thirsty?" asked Mr. Sir.

"Yes, Mr. Sir," Stanley said gratefully.

"Well, you better get used to it. You're going 130 to be thirsty for the next eighteen months."

The Science
of Catching Criminals

In courts of law, the tiniest piece of **evidence** can bring a criminal to justice. Something as small as a **fiber** can connect a thief to a burglary. The science used to show a person's guilt or **innocence** is called forensics.

5 A forensic team is made up of different people. Some work at the crime scene itself. Others work in labs to study the evidence. All of them have the same goal: to use evidence to catch and **convict** a criminal.

At the Crime Scene

Anyone who commits a crime leaves evidence behind.

10 He or she may try to clean up, but usually some **trace** remains. It could be a fingerprint or a shoe print. It might be a bit of blood or skin. It may be a hair or thread. **1**

For this reason, a forensic investigation starts at the crime scene. First, police investigators **preserve** the scene.

15 They seal it off to make sure nobody changes it. Then, they gather evidence. Because evidence can be very small, the investigators must be very careful. They use special tools to scan every inch. They place tiny samples in clean containers. Even dust, pollen, or seeds can help break a

20 case. The examiners try not to overlook anything.

evidence
something that shows another thing happened or is true

fiber
a thin thread

innocence
the state of not being guilty

convict
to find someone guilty in a court of law

trace
a small sign that someone or something was present

preserve
to keep something the way it is

1 How can trace evidence lead to conviction of a criminal?

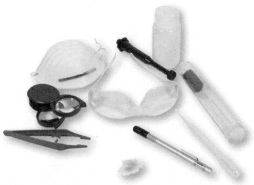

identify

to recognize; to match with a person or name

unique

one of a kind; different from all others

suspect

a person who police think may be guilty of a crime

witness

a person who saw something happen

2 Where can DNA be found?

3 What trace evidence was used to convict Buell?

4 The Ford Heights Four spent many years in prison and thought they were going to be killed. How would you feel if you were wrongly convicted of a terrible crime?

Back at the Lab

Once collected, the evidence is sent to a special lab. There, forensic scientists study it closely. They put it under microscopes. They run tests on it. They learn what it is made of and where it came from. If a piece
25 of evidence is from a human body, the scientists can **identify** its DNA.

All living things have DNA. It is in every cell of a person's body. It tells the cells how to grow. When blood, skin, or hair is left at a crime scene, the person's DNA is
30 left there too. Each person's DNA is **unique**, just like a fingerprint. If the DNA in a piece of evidence matches the DNA in a blood sample from a **suspect**, it can be evidence of guilt. If it doesn't, it can be evidence of innocence. **2**

The Power of Forensic Science

35 Whether it's a speck of fuzz or human blood, forensic evidence can make or break a case. Here are a couple of examples.

In 1982, orange fibers were found on the body of a murder victim in Ohio. Forensic scientists concluded that
40 they were carpet fibers from a van. Later, a woman was kidnapped by a man named Robert Anthony Buell, but she escaped and reported him to the police. Investigators learned that Buell had a van with orange carpeting. They took samples of the fibers for analysis. The fibers from
45 the van carpet matched the fibers on the victim. Buell was proven guilty. **3**

In another famous case, four men were convicted of a murder in Illinois. This crime happened before DNA testing could be done. The ruling was based on the
50 report of a **witness** who said she had seen the crime. The men were sentenced to a very long time in prison. Two were put on Death Row. Later, the witness confessed that her report had been a lie. By this time, DNA testing had been developed. It was used to show that the Ford
55 Heights Four were innocent and that another man was guilty.

Thanks to forensic science, justice was served. **4**

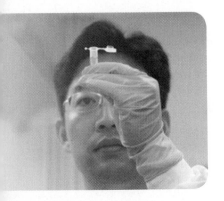

Thank You, M'am

by Langston Hughes

She was a large woman with a large purse that had everything in it but a hammer and nails. It had a long strap, and she carried it slung across her shoulder. It was about eleven o'clock at night, dark, and she was walking
5 alone, when a boy ran up behind her and tried to snatch her purse. The strap broke with the single tug the boy gave it from behind. But the boy's weight and the weight of the purse combined caused him to lose his **balance**. Instead of taking off full blast as he had hoped, the boy
10 fell on his back on the sidewalk, and his legs flew up. The large woman simply turned around and kicked him right square in his blue-jeaned sitter. Then she reached down, picked the boy up by his shirtfront, and shook him until his teeth rattled. **1**

15 After that the woman said, "Pick up my pocketbook, boy, and give it here."

She still held him tightly. But she bent down enough to **permit** him to stoop and pick up her purse. Then she said, "Now ain't you ashamed of yourself?"

20 Firmly gripped by his shirtfront, the boy said, "Yes'm."

The woman said, "What did you want to do it for?"

The boy said, "I didn't aim to."

She said, "You a lie!"

balance
the ability to stay steady and not fall

permit
to allow

1 What do you think the lady will do next?

release
to let go of; to set free

frail
weak and easily broken

furnished
having furniture, appliances, or basic supplies

2 Where is the lady taking the boy?

3 Why does Mrs. Jones want the boy to remember her?

25 By that time two or three people passed, stopped, turned to look, and some stood watching.

"If I turn you loose, will you run?" asked the woman.

"Yes'm," said the boy.

"Then I won't turn you loose," said the woman. She
30 did not **release** him.

"Lady, I'm sorry," whispered the boy.

"Um-hum! Your face is dirty. I got a great mind to wash your face for you. Ain't you got nobody home to tell you to wash your face?"

35 "No'm," said the boy.

"Then it will get washed this evening," said the large woman, starting up the street, dragging the frightened boy behind her. **2**

He looked as if he were fourteen or fifteen, **frail** and
40 willow-wild, in tennis shoes and blue jeans.

The woman said, "You ought to be my son. I would teach you right from wrong. Least I can do right now is to wash your face. Are you hungry?"

"No'm," said the being-dragged boy. "I just want you
45 to turn me loose."

"Was I bothering *you* when I turned that corner?" asked the woman.

"No'm."

"But you put yourself in contact with *me*," said the
50 woman. "If you think that that contact is not going to last awhile, you got another thought coming. When I get through with you, sir, you are going to remember Mrs. Luella Bates Washington Jones." **3**

Sweat popped out on the boy's face and he began to
55 struggle. Mrs. Jones stopped, jerked him around in front of her, put a half-nelson about his neck, and continued to drag him up the street. When she got to her door, she dragged the boy inside, down a hall, and into a large kitchenette-**furnished** room at the rear of the house. She
60 switched on the light and left the door open. The boy could hear other roomers laughing and talking in the large house. Some of their doors were open, too, so he knew he and the woman were not alone. The woman still had him by the neck in the middle of her room.

65 She said, "What is your name?"

"Roger," answered the boy.

"Then, Roger, you go to that sink and wash your face," said the woman, whereupon she turned him loose—at last. Roger looked at the door—looked at the woman—
70 looked at the door—*and went to the sink.* **4**

"Let the water run until it gets warm," she said. "Here's a clean towel."

"You gonna take me to jail?" asked the boy, bending over the sink.

75 "Not with that face, I would not take you nowhere," said the woman. "Here I am trying to get home to cook me a bite to eat, and you snatch my pocketbook! Maybe you ain't been to your supper either, late as it be. Have you?"

80 "There's nobody home at my house," said the boy.

"Then we'll eat," said the woman, "I believe you're hungry—or been hungry—to try to snatch my pocketbook!"

"I wanted a pair of blue **suede** shoes," said the boy. **5**

85 "Well, you didn't have to snatch *my* pocketbook to get some suede shoes," said Mrs. Luella Bates Washington Jones. "You could of asked me."

"M'am?"

The water dripping from his face, the boy looked at
90 her. There was a long pause. A very long pause. After he had dried his face and not knowing what else to do dried it again, the boy turned around, wondering what next. The door was open. He could make a dash for it down the hall. He could run, run, run, run, *run!*

95 The woman was sitting on the daybed. After a while she said, "I were young once and I wanted things I could not get." **6**

There was another long pause. The boy's mouth opened. Then he frowned, not knowing he frowned.

100 The woman said, "Um-hum! You thought I was going to say *but*, didn't you? You thought I was going to say, *but I didn't snatch people's pocketbooks.* Well, I wasn't going to say that." Pause. Silence. "I have done things, too, which I would not tell you, son—neither tell God,
105 if He didn't already know. Everybody's got something in common. So you set down while I fix us something to eat. You might run that comb through your hair so you will look **presentable**."

suede
soft, velvety leather

presentable
fit to appear in public

4 Why didn't Roger run?

5 Was Roger stealing to get something he wants or something he needs?

6 What is Mrs. Jones trying to do?

embarrass

to make someone uncomfortable or ashamed

latch

to grip; to fasten onto

stoop

a small porch

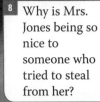 **7** Reread the last two sentences. What does this mean?

In another corner of the room behind a screen was
110 a gas plate and an icebox. Mrs. Jones got up and went
behind the screen. The woman did not watch the boy
to see if he was going to run now, nor did she watch her
purse, which she left behind her on the daybed. But the
boy took care to sit on the far side of the room, away
115 from the purse, where he thought she could easily see
him out of the corner of her eye if she wanted to. He did
not trust the woman *not* to trust him. And he did not
want to be mistrusted now. **7**

"Do you need somebody to go to the store," asked the
120 boy, "maybe to get some milk or something?"

"Don't believe I do," said the woman, "unless you just
want sweet milk yourself. I was going to make cocoa out
of this canned milk I got here."

"That will be fine," said the boy.

125 She heated some lima beans and ham she had in the
icebox, made the cocoa, and set the table. The woman
did not ask the boy anything about where he lived, or
his folks, or anything else that would **embarrass** him.
Instead, as they ate, she told him about her job in a
130 hotel beauty shop that stayed open late, what the work
was like, and how all kinds of women came in and out,
blondes, red-heads, and Spanish. Then she cut him a half
of her ten-cent cake.

"Eat some more, son," she said. **8**

135 When they were finished eating, she got up and
said, "Now, here, take this ten dollars and buy yourself
some blue suede shoes. And next time, do not make the
mistake of **latching** onto *my* pocketbook *nor nobody
else's*—because shoes come by devilish like that will burn
140 your feet. I got to get my rest now. But from here on in,
son, I hope you will behave yourself."

She led him down the hall to the front door and
opened it. "Goodnight! Behave yourself, boy!" she said,
looking out into the street as he went down the steps.

145 The boy wanted to say something else other than
"Thank you, m'am" to Mrs. Luella Bates Washington
Jones, but although his lips moved, he couldn't even say
that as he turned at the foot of the barren **stoop** and
looked up at the large woman in the door. Then she shut
150 the door. **9**

 **8** Why is Mrs. Jones being so nice to someone who tried to steal from her?

9 Is this how the story should have ended?

If I Were
In Charge of
the World

by Judith Viorst

If I were in **charge** of the world
I'd **cancel** oatmeal,
Monday mornings,
Allergy shots, and also
5 Sara Steinberg.

If I were in charge of the world
There'd be brighter night lights,
Healthier hamsters, and
Basketball baskets forty-eight inches lower.

10 If I were in charge of the world
You wouldn't have **lonely**.
You wouldn't have clean.
You wouldn't have bedtimes.
Or "Don't **punch** your sister."
15 You wouldn't even have sisters.

If I were in charge of the world
A chocolate sundae with whipped cream and nuts
    would be a vegetable.
All 007 movies would be G.
20 And a person who sometimes forgot to brush,
And sometimes forgot to flush,
Would still be **allowed** to be
In charge of the world.

charge
the responsibility of managing or controlling something

cancel
to stop something from happening or existing

allergy
an illness from eating, breathing, or touching something

healthy
in a good state or condition

lonely
sad from being without the company of others

punch
to hit hard with a fist

allow
to let something happen

We Real Cool

by Gwendolyn Brooks

THE POOL PLAYERS. SEVEN AT THE GOLDEN SHOVEL.

lurk
to wait in secret;
to hang out where
you shouldn't be

straight
in a firm and direct
way

sin
an offense against
religious or moral
law

We real cool. We
Left school. We

Lurk late. We
5 Strike straight. We

Sing sin. We
Thin gin. We

Jazz June. We
Die soon.

from

THE OUTSIDERS

by S. E. Hinton

Clockwise, starting at top left: Dallas, Two-Bit, Darry, Sodapop, Steve, Ponyboy, and Johnny

No one ever said life was easy. But Ponyboy is pretty sure that he's got things figured out. He knows that he can count on his brothers, Darry and Sodapop. And he knows that he can count on his friends—true friends
5 who would do anything for him, like Johnny and Two-Bit. And when it comes to the Socs—a vicious gang of rich kids who enjoy beating up on the "greasers" like him and his friends—he knows that he can count on them for trouble. But one night someone takes things too far, and
10 Ponyboy's world is turned upside down . . . **1**

1 What do you think will happen to Ponyboy?

The nurses wouldn't let us see Johnny. He was in critical condition. No visitors. But Two-Bit wouldn't take no for an answer. That was his buddy in there and he aimed to see him. We both begged and pleaded, but we
15 were getting nowhere until the doctor found out what was going on.

"Let them go in," he said to the nurse. "He's been asking for them. It can't hurt now."

Two-Bit didn't notice the expression in his voice.
20 It's true, I thought numbly, he is dying. We went in, practically on tiptoe, because the quietness of the hospital scared us. Johnny was lying still, with his eyes

closed, but when Two-Bit said, "Hey, Johnnykid," he opened them and looked at us, trying to grin. "Hey, y'all."

25 The nurse, who was pulling the shades open, smiled and said, "So he can talk after all."

Two-Bit looked around. "They treatin' you okay, kid?"

"Don't . . ."—Johnny gasped—"don't let me put enough grease on my hair."

30 "Don't talk," Two-Bit said, pulling up a chair, "just listen. We'll bring you some hair grease next time. We're havin' the big rumble tonight."

Johnny's huge black eyes widened a little, but he didn't say anything.

35 "It's too bad you and Dally can't be in it. It's the first big rumble we've had—not countin' the time we whipped Shepard's outfit." **2**

"He came by," Johnny said.

"Tim Shepard?"

40 Johnny nodded. "Came to see Dally."

Tim and Dallas had always been buddies.

"Did you know you got your name in the paper for being a hero?"

Johnny almost grinned as he nodded. "Tuff
45 enough," he managed, and by the way his eyes were glowing, I figured Southern gentlemen had nothing on Johnny Cade.

I could see that even a few words were tiring him out; he was as pale as the pillow and looked awful. Two-Bit
50 pretended not to notice.

"You want anything besides hair grease, kid?"

Johnny barely nodded. "The book"—he looked at me—"can you get another one?"

Two-Bit looked at me too. I hadn't told him about
55 *Gone with the Wind.*

"He wants a copy of *Gone with the Wind* so I can read it to him," I explained. "You want to run down to the drugstore and get one?" **3**

"Okay," Two-Bit said cheerfully. "Don't y'all run off."

60 I sat down in Two-Bit's chair and tried to think of something to say. "Dally's gonna be okay," I said finally. "And Darry and me, we're okay now."

I knew Johnny understood what I meant. We had always been close buddies, and those lonely days in the

2 Why can't Johnny and Dally be in the rumble?

3 Why does Johnny want Ponyboy to read to him?

falter

to fade off or stumble; to lose confidence

65 church strengthened our friendship. He tried to smile again, and then suddenly went white and closed his eyes tight.

"Johnny!" I said, alarmed. "Are you okay?"

He nodded, keeping his eyes closed. "Yeah, it just 70 hurts sometimes. It usually don't... I can't feel anything below the middle of my back . . ."

He lay breathing heavily for a moment. "I'm pretty bad off, ain't I, Pony?"

"You'll be okay," I said with fake cheerfulness. "You 75 gotta be. We couldn't get along without you."

The truth of that last statement hit me. We couldn't get along without him. We needed Johnny as much as he needed the gang. And for the same reason.

"I won't be able to walk again," Johnny started, then 80 **faltered**. "Not even on crutches. Busted my back."

"You'll be okay," I repeated firmly. Don't start crying, I commanded myself, don't start crying, you'll scare Johnny.

"You want to know something, Ponyboy? I'm scared 85 stiff. I used to talk about killing myself . . ." He drew a quivering breath. "I don't want to die now. It ain't long enough. Sixteen years ain't long enough. I wouldn't mind it so much if there wasn't so much stuff I ain't done yet and so many things I ain't seen. It's not fair. You know 90 what? That time we were in Windrixville was the only time I've been away from our neighborhood." **4**

4 Why does Johnny want to live?

"You ain't gonna die," I said, trying to hold my voice down. "And don't get juiced up, because the doc won't let us see you no more if you do."

95 Sixteen years on the streets and you can learn a lot. But all the wrong things, not the things you want to learn. Sixteen years on the streets and you see a lot. But all the wrong sights, not the sights you want to see.

Johnny closed his eyes and rested quietly for a 100 minute. Years of living on the East Side teaches you how to shut off your emotions. If you didn't, you would explode. You learn to cool it. **5**

5 What likely happens on the East Side that makes them have to shut off their emotions?

A nurse appeared in the doorway. "Johnny," she said quietly, "your mother's here to see you."

105   Johnny opened his eyes. At first they were wide with surprise, then they darkened. "I don't want to see her," he said firmly. **6**

"She's your mother."

"I said I don't want to see her." His voice was rising.
110 "She's probably come to tell me about all the trouble I'm causing her and about how glad her and the old man'll be when I'm dead. Well, tell her to leave me alone. For once"—his voice broke—"for once just to leave me alone." He was struggling to sit up, but he suddenly gasped, went
115 whiter than the pillowcase, and passed out cold.

The nurse hurried me out the door. "I was afraid of something like this if he saw anyone."

I ran into Two-Bit, who was coming in.

"You can't see him now," the nurse said, so Two-Bit
120 handed her the book. "Make sure he can see it when he comes around." She took it and closed the door behind her. Two-Bit stood and looked at the door a long time. "I wish it was any one of us except Johnny," he said, and his voice was serious for once. "We could get along without
125 anyone but Johnny."

Turning **abruptly**, he said, "Let's go see Dallas."

As we walked out into the hall, we saw Johnny's mother. I knew her. She was a little woman, with straight black hair and big black eyes like Johnny's. But that was
130 as far as the **resemblance** went. Johnnycake's eyes were fearful and sensitive; hers were cheap and hard. As we passed her she was saying, "But I have a right to see him. He's my son. After all the trouble his father and I've gone to raise him, this is our reward! He'd rather see
135 those no-count hoodlums than his own folks . . ." She saw us and gave us such a look of hatred that I almost backed up. "It was your fault. Always running around in the middle of the night getting jailed and heaven knows what else . . ." I thought she was going to cuss us out. I
140 really did. **7**

abruptly
in a sudden or unexpected way

resemblance
a similarity, or likeness, between two things

6 What kind of relationship does Johnny have with his mother?

7 Who does Johnny's mom blame for his condition?

deserve

to earn something by your words or actions

ornery

grouchy and bad-tempered

8 What can you speculate about Ponyboy's mother?

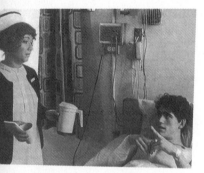

S. E. Hinton appeared as the nurse in the 1983 film version.

9 What happened at the church?

Two-Bit's eyes got narrow and I was afraid he was going to start something. I don't like to hear women get sworn at, even if they **deserve** it. "No wonder he hates your guts," Two-Bit snapped. He was going to tell her off
145 real good, but I shoved him along. I felt sick. No wonder Johnny didn't want to see her. No wonder he stayed overnight at Two-Bit's or at our house, and slept in the vacant lot in good weather. I remembered my mother . . . beautiful and golden, like Soda, and wise and firm,
150 like Darry. **8**

"Oh, lordy!" There was a catch in Two-Bit's voice and he was closer to tears than I'd ever seen him. "He has to live with that."

We hurried to the elevator to get to the next floor.
155 I hoped the nurse would have enough sense not to let Johnny's mother see him. It would kill him.

Dally was arguing with one of the nurses when we came in. He grinned at us. "Man, am I glad to see you! These —— hospital people won't let me smoke, and I
160 want out!"

We sat down, grinning at each other. Dally was his usual mean, **ornery** self. He was okay.

"Shepard came by to see me a while ago."

"That's what Johnny said. What'd he want?"
165 "Said he saw my picture in the paper and couldn't believe it didn't have 'Wanted Dead or Alive' under it. He mostly came to rub it in about the rumble. Man, I hate not bein' in that."

Only last week Tim Shepard had cracked three of
170 Dally's ribs. But Dally and Tim Shepard had always been buddies; no matter how they fought, they were two of a kind, and they knew it.

Dally was grinning at me. "Kid, you scared the devil outa me the other day. I thought I'd killed you."
175 "Me?" I said, puzzled. "Why?"

"When you jumped out of the church. I meant to hit you just hard enough to knock you down and put out the fire, but when you dropped like a ton of lead I thought I'd aimed too high and broke your neck." He thought for a
180 minute. "I'm glad I didn't, though." **9**

"I'll bet," I said with a grin. I'd never liked Dally—but
then, for the first time, I felt like he was my buddy. And
all because he was glad he hadn't killed me.

Dally looked out the window. "Uh . . ."—he sounded
185 very **casual**—"how's the kid?"

"We just left him," Two-Bit said, and I could tell that
he was debating whether to tell Dally the truth or not.
"I don't know about stuff like this . . . but . . . well, he
seemed pretty bad to me. He passed out cold before we
190 left him."

Dally's jaw line went white as he swore between
clenched teeth. **10**

"Two-Bit, you still got that fancy black-handled
switch?"

195 "Yeah."

"Give it here."

Two-Bit reached into his back pocket for his prize
possession. It was a jet-handled switchblade, ten inches
long, that would flash open at a mere breath. It was
200 the reward of two hours of walking aimlessly around a
hardware store to divert suspicion. He kept it razor sharp.
As far as I knew, he had never pulled it on anyone; he
used his plain pocketknife when he needed a blade. But
it was his showpiece, his pride and joy—every time he
205 ran into a new hood he pulled it out and showed off with
it. Dally knew how much that knife meant to Two-Bit,
and if he needed a blade bad enough to ask for it, well,
he needed a blade. That was all there was to it. Two-Bit
handed it over to Dally without a moment's **hesitation**. **11**

210 "We gotta win that fight tonight," Dally said. His
voice was hard. "We gotta get even with the Socs.
For Johnny."

He put the switch under his pillow and lay back,
staring at the ceiling. We left. We knew better than to
215 talk to Dally when his eyes were blazing and he was in a
mood like that.

We decided to catch a bus home. I just didn't feel
much like walking or trying to hitch a ride. Two-Bit left
me sitting on the bench at the bus stop while he went to
220 a gas station to buy some cigarettes. I was kind of sick to
my stomach and sort of groggy. I was nearly asleep

casual
relaxed; laid back

possession
something owned

hestitation
a delay or a pause

10 How does Dally feel about Johnny's condition?

11 Speculate why Dally wanted the knife.

strict

firm; having many rules and expecting to be obeyed

deny

to say something isn't true

12 Who does Ponyboy live with?

13 What does Ponyboy think about the rumble?

when I felt someone's hand on my forehead. I almost jumped out of my skin. Two-Bit was looking down at me worriedly. "You feel okay? You're awful hot."

225 "I'm all right," I said, and when he looked at me as if he didn't believe me, I got a little panicky. "Don't tell Darry, okay? Come on, Two-Bit, be a buddy. I'll be well by tonight. I'll take a bunch of aspirins."

"All right," Two-Bit said reluctantly. "But Darry'll kill 230 me if you're really sick and go ahead and fight anyway."

"I'm okay," I said, getting a little angry. "And if you keep your mouth shut, Darry won't know a thing."

"You know somethin'?" Two-Bit said as we were riding home on the bus. "You'd think you could get away 235 with murder, living with your big brother and all, but Darry's **stricter** with you than your folks were, ain't he?" **12**

"Yeah," I said, "but they'd raised two boys before me. Darry hasn't."

"You know, the only thing that keeps Darry from 240 bein' a Soc is us."

"I know," I said. I had known it for a long time. In spite of not having much money, the only reason Darry couldn't be a Soc was us. The gang. Me and Soda. Darry was too smart to be a greaser. I don't know how I knew, I 245 just did. And I was kind of sorry.

I was silent most of the way home. I was thinking about the rumble. I had a sick feeling in my stomach and it wasn't from being ill. It was the same kind of helplessness I'd felt that night Darry yelled at me for 250 going to sleep in the lot. I had the same deathly fear that something was going to happen that none of us could stop. As we got off the bus I finally said it. "Tonight— I don't like it one bit." **13**

Two-Bit pretended not to understand. "I never knew 255 you to play chicken in a rumble before. Not even when you was a little kid."

I knew he was trying to make me mad, but I took the bait anyway. "I ain't chicken, Two-Bit Mathews, and you know it," I said angrily. "Ain't I a Curtis, same as Soda 260 and Darry?"

Two-Bit couldn't **deny** this, so I went on: "I mean, I got an awful feeling something's gonna happen."

"Somethin' is gonna happen. We're gonna stomp the Socs' guts, that's what."

265   Two-Bit knew what I meant, but doggedly pretended not to. He seemed to feel that if you said something was all right, it immediately was, no matter what. He's been that way all his life, and I don't expect he'll change. Sodapop would have understood, and we would have
270 tried to figure it out together, but Two-Bit just ain't Soda. Not by a long shot.

from The Play of
THE DIARY OF
Anne Frank

by Frances Goodrich and Albert Hackett

List of Characters
(*in the order of their appearance*)

MR. FRANK	*Pronunciation:*	Frahnk
MIEP GIES	*Pronunciation:*	Meep
MRS. VAN DAAN	*Pronunciation:*	*Petronella,* Pet-row-nell'-ah
MR. VAN DAAN	*Pronunciation:*	Fahn Dahn
PETER VAN DAAN	*Pronunciation:*	Pay'-ter
MRS. FRANK	*Pronunciation:*	*Edith,* Ae'-dith
MARGOT FRANK	*Pronunciation:*	Mar'-gott
ANNE FRANK	*Pronunciation:*	Ah'-nah
MR. KRALER	*Pronunciation:*	Krah'-ler

ACT ONE

Scene One
The top floors of a warehouse in Amsterdam, Holland. November 1945. Late afternoon.

5

10

15

MR FRANK enters. He is weak and ill and is making a supreme effort at self-control. His clothes are threadbare. He carries a small rucksack. A scarf catches his eye. He takes it down, puts it around his neck, then wanders towards the couch, but stops as he sees the glove. He picks it up. Suddenly all control is gone. He breaks down and weeps. MIEP GIES *enters up the stairs. She is a Dutch girl of about twenty-two, pregnant now. She is compassionate and protective in her attitude towards* MR FRANK. *She has been a stenographer and secretary in his business. She has her coat and hat on, ready to go home. A small silver cross hangs at her throat.* **1**

1 What does the cross tell you about Miep?

MIEP Are you all right, Mr. Frank?

MR FRANK (*quickly controlling himself*) Yes, Miep, yes.

20	**MIEP**	Everyone in the office has gone home—it's after six. Don't stay up here, Mr. Frank. What's the use of torturing yourself like this?
	MR FRANK	I've come to say good-bye—I'm leaving here, Miep.
	MIEP	What do you mean? Where are you going? Where?
	MR FRANK	I don't know yet. I haven't decided.
25	**MIEP**	Mr. Frank, you can't leave here. This is your home. Amsterdam is your home. Your business is here, waiting for you. You're needed here. Now that the war is over, there are things that . . .
30	**MR FRANK**	I can't stay in Amsterdam, Miep. It has too many memories for me. Everywhere there's something— the house we lived in—the school—the street organ playing out there. I'm not the person you used to know, Miep. I'm a bitter old man. Forgive me. I shouldn't speak to you like this—after all that you did for us—the suffering . . .
35	**MIEP**	No. No. It wasn't suffering. You can't say we suffered.
40	**MR FRANK**	I know what you went through, you and Mr. Kraler. I'll remember it as long as I live. Come, Miep. *(He remembers his rucksack, crosses below the table to the couch and picks up his rucksack.)*
45	**MIEP**	Mr. Frank, did you see? There are some of your papers here. *(She takes a bundle of papers from the shelves, then crosses below the table to* MR FRANK.*)* We found them in a heap of rubbish on the floor after—after you left.
	MR FRANK	Burn them. *(He opens his rucksack and puts the glove in it.)*
	MIEP	But, Mr. Frank, there are letters, notes . . .
	MR FRANK	Burn them. All of them.
50	**MIEP**	Burn this? *(She hands him a worn, velour-covered book.)* **2**

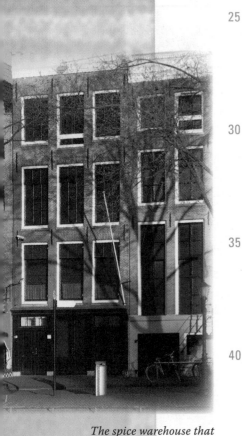

The spice warehouse that enclosed the secret annex

2 What does Miep know that Mr. Frank does not?

MR FRANK   (quietly) Anne's diary. (He opens the diary and
            reads.) 'Monday, the sixth of July, nineteen
            hundred and forty-two.' (To MIEP.) Nineteen
55   hundred and forty-two. Is it possible, Miep? Only
            three years ago. (He reads.) 'Dear Diary, since you
            and I are going to be great friends, I will start by
            telling you about myself. My name is Anne Frank.
            I am thirteen years old. I was born in Germany the
60   twelfth of June, nineteen twenty-nine. As my
            family is Jewish, we emigrated to Holland when
            Hitler came to power.' **3**

MR FRANK ⎫
ANNE'S VOICE ⎬ (together) 'My father started a business, importing
            spice and herbs. Things went well for us
65   until nineteen forty. Then the War came
            and the Dutch—(He turns the page.)
            defeat, followed by the arrival of the
            Germans. Then things got very bad for
            the Jews.'

70   (MR FRANK'S voice dies out as ANNE'S VOICE grows
            stronger.) **4**

ANNE   You could not do this and you could not do that.
            They forced father out of his business. We had
            to wear yellow stars. I had to turn in my bike. I
75   couldn't go to a Dutch school any more. I couldn't
            go to the cinema, or ride in an automobile, or even
            on a streetcar, and a million other things. But
            somehow we children still managed to have fun.
            Yesterday, father told me we were going into hiding.
80   Where, he wouldn't say. At five o'clock this morning
            mother woke me and told me to hurry and get
            dressed. I was to put on as many clothes as I could.
            It would look too suspicious if we walked along
            carrying suitcases. It wasn't until we were on our
85   way that I learned where we were going. Our hiding
            place was to be upstairs in the building where father
            used to have his business. Three other people were
            coming in with us—the Van Daans and their son
            Peter. Father knew the Van Daans but we had never
90   met them.

            (The sound of distant ships' sirens is heard.)

3 Why did the
Franks leave
Germany when
Hitler came to
power?

4 What is
happening on
stage here?

awkward
uncomfortable; not sure what to do or say

conspicuous
easily seen

indicate
to signal something with a movement or gesture

A replica of the bookcase that hid the door to the secret annex

5 Who does Mrs. Van Daan think has taken the Franks?

Scene Two
Early morning. July 1942.

The three members of the VAN DAAN *family are waiting for the* FRANKS *to arrive.* MR VAN DAAN *is smoking a cigarette and watching his wife with a nervous eye. His overcoat and suit are expensive and well-cut.* MRS VAN DAAN *is sitting on the couch. She is a pretty woman in her early forties and is clutching her possessions: a hat-box, a handbag and an attractive straw carry-all.* PETER VAN DAAN *is standing at the window in the room. He is a shy,* **awkward** *boy of sixteen. He wears a cap, a short overcoat, and long Dutch trousers, like 'plus fours'. All the* VAN DAANS *have the* **conspicuous** *yellow Star of David on the left breast of their clothing.*

MRS V.DAAN   Something's happened to them. I know it.

MR V.DAAN   Now, Kerli!

MRS V.DAAN   Mr. Frank said they'd be here at seven o'clock. He said . . .

MR V.DAAN   They have two miles to walk. You can't expect . . .

MRS V.DAAN   They've been picked up.

(The door below opens.)

That's what happened. They've been taken. **5**

*(*MR VAN DAAN **indicates** *that he hears someone coming.)*

MR V.DAAN   You see?

*(*MR FRANK *comes up the stairwell from below.)*

MR FRANK   Mrs. Van Daan, Mr. Van Daan. *(He shakes hands with them. He moves to* PETER *and shakes his hand.)* There were too many of the Green Police on the streets—we had to take the long way round.

dependable
trustworthy; able to be counted on or relied on

125

130

135

(MIEP, *not pregnant now,* MARGOT, MR KRALER, *and* MRS FRANK *come up the stairs.* MARGOT *is eighteen, beautiful, quiet and shy. She carries a leatherette hold-all and a large brown paper bag, which she puts on the table.* KRALER *is a Dutchman,* **dependable** *and kindly. He wears a hearing aid in his ear and carries two brief-cases.* MRS FRANK *is a young mother, gently bred and reserved. She, like* MR FRANK, *has a slight German accent. She carries a leatherette shopping bag and her handbag. We see the Star of David conspicuous on the* FRANKS' *clothing.* KRALER *acknowledges the* VAN DAANS, *moves to the shelves and checks their contents.* MIEP *empties her straw bag of the clothes it contains and piles them on the table.*)

MRS FRANK   Anne?

140

(ANNE FRANK *comes quickly up the stairs. She is thirteen, quick in her movements, interested in everything and mercurial in her emotions. She wears a cape, long wool socks and carries a school bag.*)

MR FRANK   My wife, Edith. Mr. and Mrs. Van Daan.

145

(MRS FRANK *shakes* MR VAN DAAN'S *hand, then hurries across to shake hands with* MRS VAN DAAN. *She then moves to the sink and inspects it.*)

Their son, Peter—my daughters, Margot and Anne. **6**

150

(ANNE *gives a polite little curtsy as she shakes* MR VAN DAAN'S *hand. She puts her bag on the left end of the table then immediately starts off on a tour of investigation of her new home, going upstairs to the attic room.*)

6 How many people will be living in the annex?

leisure

time when you are not working or busy with tasks

regulations

rules set by people in power to control how things are done

	KRALER	I'm sorry there is still so much confusion.
155	MR FRANK	Please. Don't think of it. After all, we'll have plenty of **leisure** to arrange everything ourselves.
	MIEP	*(indicating the sink cupboard)* We put the stores of food you sent in here. *(She crosses to the shelves.)* Your drugs are here—soap, linen, here.
	MRS FRANK	Thank you, Miep.
160	MIEP	I made up the beds—the way Mr. Frank and Mr. Kraler said. Forgive me. I have to hurry. I've got to go to the other side of town to get some ration books for you.
165	MRS V.DAAN	Ration books? If they see our names on ration books, they'll know we're here
	KRALER⎫ MIEP⎭	*(together)* There isn't anything . . . Don't worry. Your names won't be on them. *(As she hurries out.)* I'll be up later.

7 Who is helping the Franks hide?

	MR FRANK	Thank you, Miep. ▪7
170		*(MIEP exits down the stairwell.)*
	MRS FRANK	It's illegal, then, the ration books? We've never done anything illegal.
	MR FRANK	We won't be living exactly according to **regulations** here.
175	KRALER	This isn't the black market, Mrs. Frank. This is what we call the white market—helping all of the hundreds and hundreds who are hiding out in Amsterdam.
180		*(The carillon is heard playing the quarter hour before eight. KRALER looks at his watch. ANNE comes down from the attic, stops at the window and looks out through the curtains.)*
	ANNE	It's the Westertoren.

	KRALER	I must go. I must be out of here and downstairs in

185 | KRALER | I must go. I must be out of here and downstairs in the office before the workmen get here. Miep or I, or both of us, will be up each day to bring you food and news and find out what your needs are. Tomorrow I'll get you a better bolt for the door at the foot of the stairs. It needs a bolt that you can throw yourself and open only at our signal. *(To MR FRANK.)* Oh—you'll tell them about the noise?

190

MR FRANK | I'll tell them.

KRALER | Good-bye, then, for the moment. I'll come up again, after the workmen leave.

195 | MR FRANK | *(shaking* KRALER'S *hand)* Good-bye, Mr. Kraler.

MRS FRANK | *(shaking* KRALER'S *hand)* How can we thank you?

KRALER | I never thought I'd live to see the day when a man like Mr. Frank would have to go into hiding. When you think . . .

200

(KRALER breaks off and exits down the stairs.
MR FRANK follows him down the stairs and bolts the
door after him. In the **interval** *before he returns,*
PETER goes to MARGOT, gives a stiff bow and shakes
hands with her. ANNE watches, and as they complete
205 *their greeting, moves to PETER and holds out her*
hand. PETER does not see her and turns away.
MR FRANK comes up the stairs.)

MRS FRANK | What did he mean, about the noise?

MR FRANK | First, let's take off some of these clothes. [8]

210

(ANNE moves below the table, stands with her back
to the audience, removes her cape and beret and
puts them on the pile of clothes on the table. They
all start to take off **garment** *after garment. On each*
of their coats, sweaters, blouses, suits and dresses is
215 *another yellow Star of David. MR and MRS FRANK*
are under-dressed quite simply. The others wear
several things, sweaters, extra dresses, bathrobes,
aprons, etc. MRS FRANK takes off her gloves, carefully
folding them before putting them away.)

interval
a period of time between two dates or events

garment
an item of clothing

[8] Why do the Franks have so many clothes on?

220 **MR V.DAAN**   It's a wonder we weren't arrested, walking along the streets—Petronella with a fur coat in July—and that cat of Peter's crying all the way.

ANNE   *(removing a pair of panties)* A cat?

MRS FRANK   *(shocked)* Anne, please!

225 **ANNE**   It's all right. I've got on three more *(She removes two more pairs of panties. Finally, as they finish removing their surplus clothing, they settle down.)*

MR FRANK   Now. About the noise. While the men are in the building below, we must have complete quiet. Every
230   sound can be heard down there, not only in the workrooms, but in the offices, too. The men come about eight-thirty, and leave at about five-thirty. So, to be perfectly safe, from eight in the morning until six in the evening we must move only when it is
235   necessary and then in stockinged feet. We must not speak above a whisper. We must not run any water. We cannot use the sink, or even, forgive me, the WC. The pipes go down through the workrooms. It would be heard. No rubbish . . .

240   *(The sound of marching feet is heard.* MR FRANK, *followed by* ANNE, *peers out of the window. Satisfied that the marching feet are going away, he returns and continues.)*

No rubbish must ever be thrown out which might
245   reveal that someone is living here—not even a potato paring. We must burn everything in the stove at night. This is the way we must live until it is over, if we are to survive. **9**

9 What can't the Franks and Van Daans do from 8:00 to 6:00?

250   *(There is a pause.* MARGOT *accidentally drops the nightgown she is taking off.* PETER *jumps to pick it up for her.)*

MRS FRANK   Until it is over.

MR FRANK   After six we can move about—we can talk and laugh
and have our supper and read and play games—just
255 as we would at home. *(He looks at his watch.)* And
now I think it would be wise if we all went to our
rooms, and were settled before eight o'clock. Mrs.
Van Daan, you and your husband will go upstairs.
I regret that there's no place up there for Peter. But
260 he will be here, near us. This will be our common
room, where we'll meet to talk and eat and read, like
one family.

MRS V.DAAN   And where do you and Mrs. Frank sleep?

MR FRANK   This room is also our bedroom.

265 *(MRS VAN DAAN rises in protest.)*

MRS V.DAAN ⎫
MR V.DAAN ⎭   *(together)* That isn't right. We'll sleep here and you
take the room upstairs. It's your place.

MR FRANK   Please. I've thought this out for weeks. It's the best
arrangement. The only arrangement.

270 *(MR VAN DAAN starts to load his arms with the
clothes he and his wife have taken off and thrown
across the couch.)*

MRS V.DAAN   *(shaking* MR FRANK'S *hand)* Never, never can we
thank you. *(She moves to* MRS FRANK *and shakes her
275 hand.)* I don't know what would have happened to
us, if it hadn't been for Mr. Frank.

MR FRANK   You don't know how your husband helped me when
I came to this country—knowing no-one—not able
to speak the language. I can never repay him for
280 that. May I help you with your things? **10**

> **10** Why does Mr.
> Frank offer to
> help hide the
> Van Daans?

MR V.DAAN   No. No. *(He picks up the carton and moves towards
the attic stairs. To* MRS VAN DAAN*)* Come along,
liefje.

	MRS V.DAAN	You'll be all right, Peter? You're not afraid?
285	PETER	*(embarrassed)* Please, Mother. *(He picks up his gear. MRS FRANK goes to the head of the stairwell and stares thoughtfully down. MR and MRS VAN DAAN go upstairs.)*
290	MR FRANK	You, too, must have some rest, Edith. You didn't close your eyes last night. Nor you, Margot.
	ANNE	I slept, Father. Wasn't that funny? I knew it was the last night in my own bed, and yet I slept soundly.
295	MR FRANK	I'm glad, Anne. Now you'll be able to help me straighten things in here. *(To MRS FRANK and MARGOT.)* Come with me—you and Margot rest in this room for the time being.
	MRS FRANK	You're sure? I could help, really. And Anne hasn't had her milk.
300	MR FRANK	I'll give it to her. *(He crosses to the table and picks up the piles of clothes.)* Anne, Peter—it's best that you take off your shoes now, before you forget. *(He leads the way to the room, goes in and switches on the pendant light. MARGOT goes into the room. ANNE and PETER remove their shoes.)*
305	MRS FRANK	You're sure you're not tired, Anne?
	ANNE	I feel fine. I'm going to help father.
	MRS FRANK	Peter, I'm glad you are to be with us.
	PETER	Yes, Mrs. Frank.
310		*(MRS FRANK goes into the room and closes the door. During the following scene MR FRANK helps MARGOT to hang up clothes. PETER takes his cat out of its case.)*

	ANNE	What's your cat's name?
	PETER	'Mouschi'.
315	ANNE	Mouschi! Mouschi! Mouschi! *(She picks up the cat.)* I love cats. I have one—a darling little cat. But they made me leave her behind. I left some food and a note for the neighbors to take care of her—I'm going to miss her terribly. What is yours? A him or a her?
320	PETER	He's a tom. He doesn't like strangers. *(He takes the cat from* ANNE, *and puts it back in its carrier.)* **11**
	ANNE	Then I'll have to stop being a stranger, won't I? Is he fixed?
	PETER	Huh?
325	ANNE	Did you have him altered?
	PETER	No.
	ANNE	Oh, you ought to—to keep him from fighting. Where did you go to school?
	PETER	Jewish Secondary.
330	ANNE	But that's where Margot and I go. I never saw you around.
	PETER	I used to see you—sometimes.
	ANNE	You did?
335	PETER	In the school yard. You were always in the middle of a bunch of kids. *(He takes out a penknife from his pocket.)* **12**
	ANNE	Why didn't you ever come over?
	PETER	I'm sort of a lone wolf. *(He starts to rip off his Star of David.)*

11 How are Peter and his cat alike?

12 What do we know about Anne?

concentrate
to give all your attention to something

340   **ANNE**   What are you doing?

PETER   Taking it off.

ANNE   But you can't do that. *(She grabs his hands and stops him.)* They'll arrest you if you go out without your star.

345   **PETER**   *(pulling away)* Who's going out? *(He crosses to the stove, lifts the lid and throws the star into the stove.)* **13**

13 What does Peter realize that Anne doesn't quite understand?

ANNE   Why, of course. You're right. Of course we don't need them any more. *(She takes* PETER'S *knife and removes her star.* PETER *waits for her star to throw it away.)*

350

I wonder what our friends will think when we don't show up today?

PETER   I didn't have any dates with anyone.

355   **ANNE**   *(concentrating on her star)* Oh, I did. I had a date with Jopie this afternoon to go and play ping-pong at her house. Do you know Jopie de Waal?

PETER   No.

ANNE   Jopie's my best friend. I wonder what she'll think when she telephones and there's no answer?
360   Probably she'll go over to the house—I wonder what she'll think—we left everything as if we'd suddenly been called away—breakfast dishes in the sink—beds not made . . . *(As she pulls off her star, the cloth underneath shows clearly the colour and form of the
365   star.)* Look! It's still there. What're you going to do with yours?

PETER   Burn it. *(He moves to the stove and holds out his hand for* ANNE'S *star.* ANNE *starts to give the star to
370   PETER, but cannot.)*

ANNE   It's funny. I can't throw it away. I don't know why.

PETER   You can't throw . . . ? Something they branded you with? That they made you wear so they could spit on you?

375   ANNE   I know. I know. But after all, it is the Star of David, isn't it? **14**

(The VAN DAANS *have arranged their things, have put their clothes in the wardrobe and are sitting on the bed, fanning themselves.*)

380   PETER   Maybe it's different for a girl.

(ANNE *puts her star in her school bag.*)

MR FRANK   Forgive me, Peter. Now, let me see. We must find a bed for your cat. I'm glad that you brought your cat. Anne was feeling so badly about hers.

385   (He sees a small worn wash-tub and pulls it from the top shelf.)

Here we are. Will it be comfortable in that?

PETER   Thanks.

MR FRANK   And here is your room. But I warn you, Peter, you
390   can't grow any more. Not at inch, or you'll have to sleep with your feet out of the skylight. Are you hungry?

PETER   No.

MR FRANK   We have some bread and butter.

395   PETER   No, thank you.

MR FRANK   (with a friendly pat on PETER'S shoulder) You can have it for luncheon, then. And tonight we will have a real supper—our first supper together.

14 Would you have been able to burn something that was a symbol of your faith?

peculiar
strange; odd

15 How long does Anne think she will have to hide?

400	PETER	Thanks. Thanks. *(He goes into his room.* MR FRANK *closes the door after* PETER, *then sits and removes his shoes.)*
	MR FRANK	That's a nice boy, Peter.
	ANNE	He's awfully shy, isn't he?
	MR FRANK	You'll like him, I know.
405	ANNE	I certainly hope so, since he's the only boy I'm likely to see for months and months. **15**
	MR FRANK	Anne, there's a box there. Will you open it?
410		*(The sound of children playing is heard from the street below.* MR FRANK *goes to the sink and pours a glass of milk from the thermos bottle.)*
415	ANNE	You know the way I'm going to think of it here? I'm going to think of it as a boarding-house. A very **peculiar** Summer boarding-house, like the one that we . . . *(She breaks off as she looks in the box.)* Father! Father! My film stars. I was wondering where they were—and Queen Wilhelmina. How wonderful!
	MR FRANK	There's something more. Go on. Look further.
420		*(*ANNE *digs deeper into the box and brings out a velour-covered book. She examines it in delighted silence for a moment, then opens the cover slowly, and looks up at* MR FRANK *with shining eyes.)*
425	ANNE	A diary! *(She throws her arms around him.)* I've never had a diary. And I've always longed for one. *(She rushes to the table and looks for a pencil.)* Pencil, pencil, pencil, pencil. *(She darts across to the stair-well and starts down the stairs.)* I'm going down to the office to get a pencil.

MR FRANK   Anne! No! *(He strides to* ANNE *and catches her arm.*
430   MRS FRANK *aware of the sudden movement and*
sounds, sits up. After a moment she rises, goes to
the window and looks out, then returns and sits on
the bed.)

ANNE   *(startled)* But there's no-one in the building now.

435   MR FRANK   It doesn't matter. I don't want you ever to go beyond
that door.

ANNE   *(sobered)* Never? Not even at night time, when
everyone is gone? Or on Sundays? Can't I go down
to listen to the radio?

440   MR FRANK   Never. I am sorry, Anneke. It isn't safe. No, you
must never go beyond that door.

ANNE   I see. *(For the first time she realizes what 'going into*
hiding' means.) **16**

MR FRANK   It'll be hard, I know. But always remember this,
445   Anneke. There are no walls, there are no bolts,
no locks that anyone can put on your mind. Miep
will bring us books. We will read history, poetry,
mythology. *(He gives* ANNE *the glass of milk.)* Here's
your milk.

450   *(*MR FRANK *puts his arm about* ANNE, *and crosses*
with her to the couch, where they sit side by side.)

As a matter of fact, between us, Annie, being here
has certain advantages for you. For instance you
remember the battle you had with your mother the
455   other day on the subject of goloshes? You said you'd
rather die than wear goloshes. But in the end you
had to wear them. Well now, you see for as long as
we are here, you will never have to wear goloshes.
Isn't that good? And the coat that you inherited from
460   Margot—

*(*ANNE *makes a wry face.)*

—you won't have to wear that. And the piano. You
won't have to practice on the piano. I tell you, this is
going to be a fine life for you. **17**

16 What does "going into hiding" actually mean?

17 How is Mr. Frank trying to ease Anne's panic?

465   *(ANNE'S panic is gone. PETER appears in the doorway of his room, with a saucer in one hand and the cat in the other.)*

PETER   I—I—I thought I'd better get some water for Mouschi before . . .

470   **MR FRANK**   Of course.

                (The carillon begins its melody and strikes eight. As it does so, MR FRANK motions for PETER and ANNE to be quiet, tiptoes to the window in the rear wall and peers down. MR VAN DAAN rises and moves

475   *to the head of the attic stairs. MR FRANK puts his finger to his lips, indicating to ANNE and PETER that they must be silent, then steps down towards PETER indicating he can draw no water. PETER starts back to his room. ANNE rises and crosses below the table*

480   *to PETER. MR FRANK crosses quietly towards the girls' room. As PETER reaches the door of his room a board creaks under his foot. The three are frozen for a minute in fear. ANNE then continues over to PETER on tiptoe and pours some milk in the saucer. PETER*

485   *squats on the floor, putting the milk down before the cat and encouraging him to drink. MR FRANK crosses to them, gives ANNE his fountain pen, then crosses to the girls' room, goes inside, sits on the bed and puts a comforting arm around MRS FRANK. ANNE*

490   *squats for a moment beside PETER, watching the cat, then opens her diary and writes. All are silent and motionless, except MR VAN DAAN who returns to MRS VAN DAAN and fans her with a newspaper. The Westertoren finishes tolling the hour. As ANNE*

495   *begins to write, her voice is heard faintly at first, then with growing strength.)*

ANNE I expect I should be describing what it feels like to go into hiding. But I really don't know yet, myself. I only know it's funny never to be able to

500 go outdoors—never to breathe fresh air—never to run and shout and jump. It's the silence in the night that frightens me most. Every time I hear a creak in the house, or a step on the street outside, I'm sure they're coming for us. The days aren't so

505 bad. At least we know that Miep and Mr. Kraler are down there below us in the office. Our protectors, we call them. I asked father what would happen to them if the Nazis found out they were hiding us. Pim said that they would suffer the same fate that

510 we would. Imagine! They know this and yet when they come up here, they're always cheerful and gay as if there were nothing in the world to bother them. Friday, the twenty-first of August, nineteen forty-two. Today I'm going to tell you our general

515 news. Mother is unbearable. She insists on treating me like a baby, which I loathe. Otherwise things are going better. The weather is . . . **18**

18 Why is Anne amazed by Miep and Mr. Kraler?

THE CIRCUIT

by Francisco Jiménez

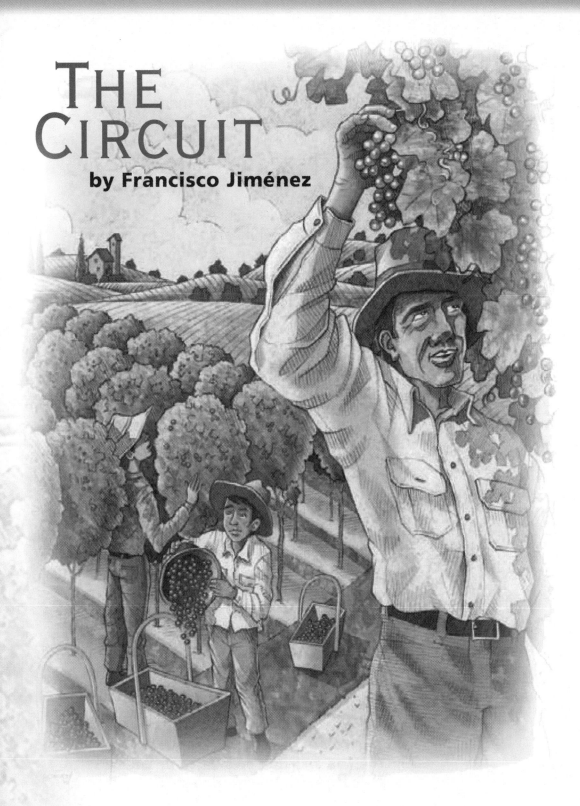

A family of migrant farmworkers finished picking the last of the strawberry crop. Now they are seeking work from a vineyard owner whose grapes are ready to harvest.

exchange

to trade; to give one thing for another

populated

lived in; filled with

At sunset we drove into a labor camp near Fresno.
5   Since Papá did not speak English, Mamá asked the
camp foreman if he needed any more workers. "We
don't need no more," said the foreman, scratching
his head. "Check with Sullivan down the road. Can't
miss him. He lives in a big white house with a fence
10 around it."

When we got there, Mamá walked up to the house.
She went through a white gate, past a row of rose
bushes, up the stairs to the front door. She rang the
doorbell. The porch light went on and a tall husky
15 man came out. They **exchanged** a few words. After
the man went in, Mamá clasped hands and hurried
back to the car. "We have work! Mr. Sullivan said we
can stay there the whole season," she said, gasping
and pointing to an old garage near the stables. **1**

1 Why is Mamá excited about an old garage?

20 The garage was worn out by the years. It had no
windows. The walls, eaten by termites, strained
to support the roof full of holes. The dirt floor,
populated by earthworms, looked like a gray
road map.

25 That night, by the light of a kerosene lamp, we
unpacked and cleaned our new home. Roberto
swept away the loose dirt, leaving the hard ground.
Papá plugged the holes in the walls with old
newspapers and tin can tops. Mamá fed my little
30 brothers and sisters. Papá and Roberto then brought
in the mattress and placed it on the far corner of the
garage. "Mamá, you and the little ones sleep on the
mattress. Roberto, Panchito, and I will sleep outside
under the trees," Papá said. **2**

2 What is the narrator's name?

35 Early next morning, Mr. Sullivan showed us where
his crop was, and after breakfast, Papá, Roberto,
and I headed for the vineyard to pick.

Around nine o'clock, the temperature had risen
to almost one hundred degrees. I was completely
40 soaked in sweat, and my mouth felt as if I had been

chewing on a handkerchief. I walked over to the end of the row, picked up the jug of water we had brought, and began drinking. "Don't drink too much; you'll get sick," Roberto shouted. No sooner
45 had he said that than I felt sick to my stomach. I dropped to my knees and let the jug roll off my hands. I remained **motionless** with my eyes glued on the hot sandy ground. All I could hear was the **drone** of insects. Slowly I began to recover. I poured
50 water over my face and neck and watched the black mud run down my arms and hit the ground.

I still felt a little dizzy when we took a break to eat lunch. It was past two o'clock and we sat underneath a large walnut tree that was on the side of the road.
55 While we ate, Papá jotted down the number of boxes we had picked. Roberto drew **designs** on the ground with a stick. Suddenly I noticed Papá's face turn pale as he looked down the road. "Here comes the school bus," he whispered loudly in alarm.
60 **Instinctively**, Roberto and I ran and hid in the vineyards. We did not want to get in trouble for not going to school. The yellow bus stopped in front of Mr. Sullivan's house. Two neatly dressed boys about my age got off. They carried books under their arms.
65 After they crossed the street, the bus drove away. Roberto and I came out from hiding and joined Papá. "*Tienen que tener cuidado*," he warned us. ▆3

After lunch, we went back to work. The sun kept beating down. The buzzing insects, the wet sweat,
70 and the hot dry dust made the afternoon seem to last forever. Finally the mountains around the valley reached out and swallowed the sun. Within an hour it was too dark to continue picking. The vines blanketed the grapes, making it difficult to
75 see the bunches. "*Vámonos*," said Papá, signaling to us that it was time to quit work. Papá then took out a pencil and began to figure out how much we had earned our first day. He wrote down numbers, crossed some out, wrote down some more. "*Quince*,"
80 he **murmured**. ▆4

motionless
still; not moving

drone
a low, humming noise

design
a pattern or drawing

instinctively
without thinking; in a natural or automatic way

murmur
to speak softly

▆3 Why didn't the boys go to school?

▆4 Why do they work from morning until it is too dark to see?

savor

to enjoy something deeply

5 Did they have a bathroom? How do you know?

When we arrived home, we took a cold shower underneath a waterhose. We then sat down to eat dinner around some wooden crates that served as a table. Mamá had cooked a special meal for us.
85 We had rice and tortillas with *"carne con chile,"* my favorite dish. **5**

The next morning I could hardly move. My body ached all over. I felt little control over my arms and legs. This feeling went on every morning for days,
90 until my muscles finally got used to the work.

It was Monday, the first week of November. The grape season was over and I could now go to school. I woke up early that morning and lay in bed, looking at the stars and **savoring** the thought of not going
95 to work and of starting sixth grade for the first time that year. Since I could not sleep, I decided to get up and join Papá and Roberto at breakfast. I sat at the table across from Roberto, but I kept my head down. I did not want to look up and face him. I knew he
100 was sad. He was not going to school today. He was not going tomorrow, or next week, or next month. He would not go until the cotton season was over, and that was sometime in February. I rubbed my hands together and watched the dry, acid-stained
105 skin fall to the floor in little rolls. **6**

6 Why do you think the narrator wasn't expected to pick cotton?

When Papá and Roberto left for work, I felt relief. I walked to the top of a small grade next to the shack and watched the *Carcachita* disappear in the distance in a cloud of dust.

110 Two hours later, around eight o'clock, I stood by the side of the road waiting for school bus number twenty. When it arrived I climbed in. No one noticed me. Everyone was busy either talking or yelling. I sat in an empty seat in the back.

115 When the bus stopped in front of the school, I felt very nervous. I looked out the bus window and saw boys and girls carrying books under their arms. I felt empty. I put my hands in my pants pockets and

walked to the principal's office. When I entered, I
120 heard a woman's voice say: "May I help you?" I was
startled. I had not heard English for months. For a
few seconds I remained speechless. I looked at the
lady who waited for an answer. My first instinct was
to answer her in Spanish, but I held back. Finally,
125 after struggling for English words, I managed to
tell her that I wanted to enroll in the sixth grade.
After answering many questions, I was led to the
classroom. **7**

Mr. Lema, the sixth grade teacher, greeted me and
130 assigned me to a desk. He then **introduced** me
to the class. I was so nervous and scared at that
moment when everyone's eyes were on me that
I wished I were with Papá and Roberto picking
cotton. After taking roll, Mr. Lema gave the class
135 the assignment for the first hour. "The first thing
we have to do this morning is finish reading the
story we began yesterday," he said **enthusiastically**.
He walked up to me, handed me an English book,
and asked me to read. "We are on page 125," he said
140 politely. When I heard this, I felt my blood rush to
my head; I felt dizzy. "Would you like to read?" he
asked hesitantly. I opened the book to page 125.
My mouth was dry. My eyes began to water. I could
not begin. "You can read later," Mr. Lema said
145 understandingly.

For the rest of the reading period, I kept getting
angrier and angrier with myself. I should have read,
I thought to myself. **8**

During recess, I went into the restroom and opened
150 my English book to page 125. I began to read in
a low voice, pretending I was in class. There were
many words I did not know. I closed the book and
headed back to the classroom.

introduce
to present one
person to another
person or to a
group

enthusiastically
with great energy
and excitement

7 Why was the
narrator
struggling with
his English?

8 Why was he
disappointed
with himself for
not reading?

Mr. Lema was sitting at his desk correcting papers.
155 When I entered he looked up at me and smiled. I
felt better. I walked up to him and asked if he could
help me with the new words. "Gladly," he said.

The rest of the month, I spent my lunch hours
working on English with Mr. Lema, my best friend
160 at school. **9**

9 What did the
narrator value
more than
making friends?

One Friday during lunch hour, Mr. Lema asked me
to take a walk with him to the music room. "Do you
like music?" he asked me as we entered the building.

"Yes, I like Mexican *corridos*," I answered. He then
165 picked up a trumpet, blew on it, and handed it to
me. The sound gave me goose bumps. I knew that
sound. I had heard it in many Mexican *corridos*.
"How would you like to learn to play it?" he asked.

He must have read my face, because before I could
170 answer, he added: "I'll teach you how to play it
during our lunch hours."

That day I could hardly wait to get home to tell Papá
and Mamá the great news. As I got off the bus, my
little brothers and sisters ran up to meet me. They
175 were yelling and screaming. I thought they were
happy to see me, but when I opened the door to our
shack, I saw that everything we owned was neatly
packed in cardboard boxes. **10**

10 Predict what
will happen
next.

from

The Autobiography of Malcolm X

with Alex Haley

Malcolm X was a Black Muslim minister, a militant, a social and political activist, and a hero to many. His journey toward activism began in prison, where he first learned to read with understanding and
5 *write with precision.*

It was because of my letters that I happened to stumble upon starting to **acquire** some kind of a homemade education. I became increasingly frustrated at not being able to express what I wanted
10 to convey in letters that I wrote, especially those to Mr. Elijah Muhammad. In the street, I had been the most articulate hustler out there—I had commanded attention when I said something. But now, trying to write simple English, I not only wasn't articulate, I
15 wasn't even **functional**. How would I sound writing in slang, the way I would say it, something such as "Look, daddy, let me pull your coat about cat, Elijah Muhammad—" **1**

Many who today hear me somewhere in person
20 or on television, or those who read something I've said, will think I went to school far beyond the eighth grade. This impression is due entirely to my prison studies. **2**

It had really begun back in the Charlestown Prison,
25 when Bimbi first made me feel **envy** of his stock of knowledge. Bimbi had always taken charge of any conversations he was in, and I had tried to emulate him. But every book I picked up had few sentences which didn't contain anywhere from one to nearly
30 all of the words that might as well

acquire
to gain; to earn; to come by

functional
in working order; able to do a task or job

envy
the feeling of wanting what someone else has

1 Why didn't Malcolm X want to write the way he spoke?

2 Where did Malcolm X get a homemade education?

have been in Chinese. When I just skipped those words, of course, I really ended up with little idea of what the book said. So I had come to the Norfolk Prison Colony still going through only book-reading
35 motions. Pretty soon, I would have quit even these motions, unless I had received the motivation that I did. [3]

3 Why didn't Malcolm X understand what he read?

I saw that the best thing I could do was get hold of a dictionary—to study, to learn some words. I was
40 lucky enough to reason also that I should try to improve my penmanship. It was sad. I couldn't even write in a straight line. It was both ideas together that moved me to request a dictionary along with some tablets and pencils from the Norfolk Prison
45 Colony school.

4 Malcolm X hoped to accomplish two things with his dictionary efforts. What were they?

I spent two days just riffling uncertainly through the dictionary's pages. I'd never realized so many words existed! I didn't know *which* words I needed to learn. Finally, just to start some kind of action,
50 I began copying.

In my slow, painstaking, ragged handwriting, I copied into my tablet everything printed on that first page, down to the punctuation marks.

I believe it took me a day. Then, aloud, I read back,
55 to myself, everything I'd written on the tablet. Over and over, aloud, to myself, I read my own handwriting. [4]

> **" Education is the passport to the future, for tomorrow belongs to those who prepare for it today. "**

I woke up the next morning, thinking about those words—immensely proud to realize that not
60 only had I written so much at one time, but I'd written words that I never knew were in the world. Moreover, with a little effort, I also could remember what many of these words meant. I reviewed the words whose meanings I didn't remember.
65 Funny thing, from the dictionary's first page right now, that *aardvark* springs to my mind. The dictionary had a picture of it, a long-tailed, long-

MASS STATE PRISON
22843

eared, burrowing African mammal, which lives off termites caught by sticking out its tongue as an
70 anteater does for ants.

I was so fascinated that I went on—I copied the dictionary's next page. And the same experience came when I studied that. With every succeeding page, I also learned of people and places and events
75 from history. Actually the dictionary is like a miniature encyclopedia. Finally the dictionary's A section had filled a whole tablet—and I went on into the B's. That was the way I started copying what **eventually** became the entire dictionary.
80 It went a lot faster after so much practice helped me to pick up handwriting speed. Between what I wrote in my tablet, and writing letters, during the rest of my time in prison I would guess I wrote a million words. **5**

85 I suppose it was **inevitable** that as my word base broadened, I could for the first time pick up a book and read and now begin to understand what the book was saying. Anyone who has read a great deal can imagine the new world that opened. Let me tell
90 you something: From then until I left that prison, in every free moment I had, if I was not reading in the library, I was reading on my bunk. You couldn't have gotten me out of books with a wedge. Between Mr. Muhammad's teachings, my **correspondence**,
95 my visitors—usually Ella and Reginald—and my reading of books, months passed without my even thinking about being imprisoned. In fact, up to then, I never had been so truly free in my life. **6**

The Norfolk Prison Colony's library was in the
100 school building. A variety of classes was taught there by instructors who came from such places as Harvard and Boston universities. The weekly **debates** between inmate teams were also held in the school building. You would be astonished

5 How would copying the dictionary help a person?

eventually
over time; in the end

inevitable
to be expected; hard to keep from happening

correspondence
written messages to and from other people

debate
a contest in which two sides argue the pros and cons of an issue

6 What newfound ability made Malcolm X feel truly free though he was in prison?

emphasis

the weight, value, or importance put on something

isolation

the state of being totally alone

7 How did inmates challenge the knowledge of one another?

8 What did the prison staff believe would happen to an inmate if he was interested in books?

> " My Alma mater was books, a good library . . . I could spend the rest of my life reading, just satisfying my curiosity. "

105 to know how worked up convict debaters and audiences would get over subjects like "Should Babies Be Fed Milk?" **7**

Available on the prison library's shelves were books on just about every general subject. Much of the big
110 private collection that Parkhurst had willed to the prison was still in crates and boxes in the back of the library—thousands of old books. Some of them looked ancient: covers faded, old-time parchment-looking binding. Parkhurst, I've mentioned, seemed
115 to have been principally interested in history and religion. He had the money and the special interest to have a lot of books that you wouldn't have in general circulation. Any college library would have been lucky to get that collection.

120 As you can imagine, especially in a prison where there was heavy **emphasis** on rehabilitation, an inmate was smiled upon if he demonstrated an unusually intense interest in books. There was a sizable number of well-read inmates, especially the
125 popular debaters. Some were said by many to be practically walking encyclopedias. They were almost celebrities. No university would ask any student to devour literature as I did when this new world opened to me, of being able to read and *understand*. **8**

130 I read more in my room than in the library itself. An inmate who was known to read a lot could check out more than the permitted maximum number of books. I preferred reading in the total **isolation** of my own room.

135 When I had progressed to really serious reading, every night at about 10:00 p.m. I would be outraged with the "lights out." It always seemed to catch me right in the middle of something engrossing.

Fortunately, right outside my door was a corridor
140 light that cast a glow into my room. The glow was
enough to read by, once my eyes **adjusted** to it.
So when "lights out" came, I could sit on the floor
where I could continue reading in that glow. **9**

At one-hour intervals the night guards paced past
145 every room. Each time I heard the approaching
footstep, I jumped into bed and feigned sleep. And
as soon as the guard passed, I got back out of bed
onto the floor area of that light-glow, where I would
read for another fifty-eight minutes—until the
150 guard approached again. That went on until three or
four every morning. Three or four hours of sleep a
night was enough for me. Often in the years in the
streets, I had slept less than that. **10**

adjust
to get used to
something

9 What did
Malcolm X
choose to do
instead of sleep?

10 Malcolm X was
used to very
little sleep. Tell
the difference
between his
reasons for
staying up while
on the streets
and while in
prison. Which
reason was
more beneficial?

from

Breaking Night by Liz Murray

By the time I was almost five years old, we had become a functional, government-dependent family of four. The first of the month, the day Ma's stipend from welfare was due, held all the ritual and
5 celebration of Christmas morning. Our collective **anticipation** of the money filled the apartment with a kind of electricity, guaranteeing that Ma and Daddy would be agreeable and upbeat for at least twenty-four hours each month. It was my parents'
10 one **consistency**. **1**

The government gave the few hundred dollars monthly to those who, for one reason or another, were unable to work for a living—although I often saw our able-bodied neighbors crowded beside the
15 mailboxes, eagerly watching as they were stuffed with the thin, blue envelopes. Ma, who was legally blind due to a degenerative eye disease she'd had since birth, happened to be one of SSI's legitimate recipients. I know, because I went with her the day
20 she interviewed to **qualify**. **2**

The woman behind the desk told her that she was so blind that if she ever drove a car, she would "probably end the life of every living thing in her path."

25 Then she shook Ma's hand and congratulated her both for qualifying and for her ability to successfully cross the street.

"Sign right here. You can expect your checks on the first of every month."

30 And we did. In fact, there was nothing our family looked forward to more than Ma's check. The mailman's arrival had a domino effect, setting the whole day, and our treasured ritual, in motion. It was my job to lean my head out of my bedroom
35 window, which faced the front, and to call out any sighting of the mailman to Ma and Daddy.

anticipation
a feeling of excitement about something that is about to happen

consistency
something done in the same way, time after time

qualify
to show that you have the right to do or have something

1 Why was the first of the month like a holiday?

2 Why did they receive a welfare check?

invaluable

extremely useful or precious and hard to replace

3 What is Ma like?

4 Who is the "planner" in the family?

"Lizzy, let me know when you see *any* sign of him. Remember, look *left*."

40 If Ma could know a few minutes earlier that he was coming, she could grab her welfare ID out of the junk drawer, snatch her check from the mailbox, and be the first in line at the check-cashing store. The role I played in those days became an **invaluable** part of the routine.

45 Elbows jutting behind me, I would clutch the rusted window guard and extend my neck as far as possible into the sun, over and over again throughout the morning. The task gave me a sense of importance. When I saw the blue uniform appear over the hill—
50 an urban Santa Claus pushing his matching cart—I could not wait to announce him. In the meantime, I'd listen to the sound of my parents waiting.

Ma in her oversize worry chair, picking out yellow stuffing. **3**

55 "Damn. Damn. He's dragging his ass."

Daddy going over the details of their plans a hundred times, pacing, weaving circles in the air as though to somehow shorten the feel of his wait.

"Okay, Jeanie, we're going to stop off to buy coke,
60 then we take care of the electric bill with Con Edison. Then we can get a half pound of bologna for the kids. And I need money for tokens." **4**

The moment I spotted the mailman, I could tell them the very second I knew, or I could wait just a
65 little longer. It was the difference between having their attention and giving it away—relinquishing the one moment when I was as significant as they were, as necessary as the mailman or even the money itself. But I could never hold back; the moment I saw
70 him round the corner I'd shout, "He's coming! I see him! He's coming!" Then we could all move on to the next stage of our day.

❀   ❀   ❀

Behind the gaudy glass storefront of the check-cashing place, there was something for everyone.
75 Children gravitated to the twenty-five-cent machines, a row of clear boxes on metal poles with toys jumbled inside. They waited impatiently for quarters to free the plastic spider on a ring, the man who expanded to ten times his size in water,
80 or the wash-away tattoos of butterflies, comic book heroes, or pink and red hearts. Tacked up high near the register were lottery tickets for stray men with gambling **ailments** or hopeful women who allotted just a few of the family's dollars to the allure of
85 a lucky break. Often these ladies dramatically waved the sign of the cross over themselves before scratching away with a loose dime or penny. But for many, even the smallest item was completely unaffordable until their turn in line. **5**

90 Women made up that endless line; women clutching the monthly bills, women frowning, women with children. Their men (if present at all) stood off to the side, leaning coolly on the metal walls. Either they came in with the women but stood back,
95 waiting for the check to be cashed, or they arrived beforehand, anticipating the routine, sure to shake down their wives or girlfriends for a **portion**. The women would fend them off to the best of their ability, giving up what they had to and making the
100 most of what was left. Lisa and I became so used to the chaos that we hardly looked up at the adults **clamoring** with one another. **6**

Lisa lingered by the quarter machines, captivated by the glittery stickers. I stayed close to our parents,
105 who were different from the other adults in that they functioned as a team, having arrived in pursuit of a shared goal. I was a participant in their giddiness, eager to make their excitement my own.

ailment
a sickness or something that causes pain and discomfort

portion
one part of a greater whole

clamor
to demand something in a noisy or angry way

5 How would this life seem to a five-year-old child?

6 Why do you think it was mostly women in line?

reassuring

comforting; causing you to feel less worried

elaborate

very complex; having many parts

7 Why did Ma need Lizzy at home and at the check-cashing store?

8 Where are they now? Why are they not in line anymore?

If I could break the joy of check day down into small segments, then nothing topped the time Ma and I spent together in line. As she waited for her turn at the counter, again I was her helper. In these urgent moments, full of anticipation, Ma relied on me most. It was my moment to shine, and I always rose to the occasion. **7**

"Eight more ahead of us, Ma. Seven. Don't worry, the cashier's moving fast."

Her smile as I delivered the progress report belonged to me. Calling out the numbers in a **reassuring** tone determined the amount of attention she paid me. I would have traded the rest of check day for ten more people in line ahead of us, because for this guaranteed amount of time, she wasn't going anywhere. I wouldn't have to worry about Ma's habit of leaving us in the middle of things.

Once, the four of us walked over to Loews Paradise Theater on the Grand Concourse to see a discounted showing of *Alice in Wonderland*. Daddy explained on the walk over that the Concourse used to be an area of luxury, a strip of **elaborate** architecture that attracted the wealthy. But all I could see as we walked were vast, dirty brick buildings with the occasional tarnished cherubs or gargoyles over doorways, chipped and cracked but still hanging on. We sat down in a nearly empty theater. **8**

Ma didn't stay until the end. It's not that she didn't try; she got up once, twice, three times for a "smoke." Then she got up for a final time and didn't come back. When we returned home that evening, the record player was spinning a woman's sad, throaty singing. Ma was taking a pull off her cigarette and studying her own slender, naked body in the full-length mirror.

145 "Where were you guys?" she asked naturally, and I wondered if I might have imagined that she'd come with us at all.

But in the check line, she wasn't going anywhere. As much as she fidgeted, Ma wouldn't leave without the 150 money. So I took the opportunity to hold her hand and to ask her questions about herself when she was my age. **9**

"I don't know, Lizzy. I was bad when I was a kid. I stole things and cut school. How many more people 155 in front of us, pumpkin?"

Each time I faced her, Ma motioned toward the cashier, urging me to keep an eye out. Holding her attention was tricky, a balancing act between slipping in questions and showing that I was on top 160 of things. I always assured her that we were almost there; privately, I wished she'd have to wait as long as possible, longer than anyone else.

"I don't know, Lizzy. You're a nicer kid, you never cried when you were a baby. You just made this 165 noise like *eh, eh*. It was the cutest thing, almost polite. Lisa would scream her head off and smash everything, rip up my magazines, but you never cried. I worried you were retarded, but they said you were all right. You were always a good kid. How 170 many more people, pumpkin?" **10**

Even if I was told and retold the same stories, I never tired of asking.

"What was my first word?"

"'Mommy.' You handed me your bottle and said 175 'Mommy,' like you were telling me to fill 'er up. You were a riot."

"How old was I?"

"Ten months."

9 Why did Lizzy enjoy the time with Ma in the check line more than at the theater?

10 What is Lizzy like?

euphoric

feeling great happiness and excitement; overjoyed

11 Why didn't Ma answer Lizzy's last question?

"How long have we lived in our house?"

180 "Years."

"How many?"

"Lizzy, move over, my turn's coming." **11**

At home, we split off into two rooms: the living room for us kids, and next to it, the kitchen for Ma 185 and Daddy. Unlike most times, on that first day of the month, food was abundant. Lisa and I dined on Happy Meals in front of the black-and-white TV, to the sound of spoons clanking on the nearby table, chairs being pulled in—and those elongated 190 moments of silence when we knew what they were concentrating on. Daddy had to do it for Ma because with her bad eyesight she could never find a vein. **12**

12 What were Lizzy's parents doing in the kitchen?

At last, the four of us enjoyed the second-best part 195 of the day. We sat together, all spread around the living room, facing the flickering TV. Outside, the ice cream truck rattled its loop of tinny music and children gathered, scrambled, gathered, and scrambled again in a game of tag.

200 The four of us together. French-fry grease on my fingertips. Lisa chewing on a cheeseburger. Ma and Daddy, twitching and shifting just behind us, **euphoric**. **13**

13 How much of the check do you think is left after the first day?

From Homeless to Harvard

outcome
a result or the way something ends

The winter evening is cold and windy with crisp-looking stars shining over Bronx, New York. Liz Murray, just 12 years
5 old, doesn't want to go home because her parents are doing drugs again. She is walking the streets, alone, headed for the home of a friend. She knocks
10 on an apartment door, hoping to spend the night on the sofa in her friend's apartment. Hopefully, her friend's parents won't mind. Maybe she'll go
15 home to check on her mother in the morning, or maybe she'll go to school. **1**

What could the future hold for a child who lives like this?
20 Could a person whose life began in a background of parental drug addiction and poverty hope to be educated at a famous university and
25 become a public success? That **outcome** is unlikely, but Liz Murray made it possible.

1 Why doesn't Liz want to go home?

Liz Murray inspires the audience at a speaking engagement.

Born into Poverty

Liz Murray was born into a life of poverty and addiction in the Bronx in 1980. An eye disease soon left her mom legally blind. As a result of her disability, she received welfare from the government and relied on Liz to take care of her and "be her eyes." Liz was forced to do things such as watch for the mailman on the first of every month and stand in line at the check-cashing store with the other welfare recipients— while other kids her age were playing innocent games of tag and hide and seek. Once the check was cashed, her drug-addicted parents used the money for drugs and began the cycle of neglect and mistreatment of their children.

Liz remembers eating well on the first of each month. However, during the rest of the month, her parents used their support to feed their drug addictions instead of their children. Some months, after spending their welfare check on drugs, her parents only had $30 left to feed Liz and her sister. **2**

When Liz was growing up, she lived in filthy conditions. Because of this, Liz was unbathed, wore unclean clothing, and often had lice. Liz was aware of the smell she gave off and the unwelcome stares from kids at school. The shame of this caused Liz to hate school and plead to stay home. Often, her mother agreed. She loved her parents and felt fortunate that they loved her back. **3**

Death Brings Realization

Eventually, her parents separated. Liz's older sister, Lisa, went to live with their mom and her new boyfriend. Liz stayed with her father because she didn't want him to be alone. When Liz was 11, her mother was **diagnosed** with HIV and died five years later.

While her mother grew more sick, Liz's father moved to a shelter for the homeless. Liz was sent to a group home, but **conditions** at the home were so bad that she didn't stay long. Living on

---

diagnose
to find out and name what is wrong with someone or something

conditions
all the things in the surroundings that affect how a person acts or feels

2 Liz's parents sacrificed the well-being of their children for what?

3 Why did Liz miss school?

Liz's mother (top) and Liz with her dad (bottom)

alternative
different from other things of its kind

motivated
focused on reaching one or more goals

apply
to ask for something in writing or by filling out a form

4 How did Liz's life dramatically change at age 16?

5 How did Liz determine to improve her life?

6 What kind of high school did Liz attend? How long did it take her to graduate?

7 How was Liz able to go to an expensive school like Harvard?

the streets of New York, she
95 found food in garbage bins
and shelter in friends' homes
or on subway trains. **4**

After her mother's death,
Liz suddenly realized that
100 she was truly on her own.
Her mother had said many
times, "Someday life will
get better." But Liz realized
her mother died before she
105 could fix anything, so Liz
resolved to change her life
for the better before it was
too late. She began to think
seriously about her own life.
110 She wondered if she could
rise out of her background
of poverty and improve her
life with education. This idea
pushed her forward. **5**

Getting an Education

115 At 17, Liz heard about
alternative high schools.
She researched different
schools and finally found
one that would accept her.
120 Because she was intelligent
and **motivated** and had
taught herself to read, Liz
did well in school despite her
lack of previous schooling.
125 She determined to graduate
in two years instead of the
usual four. Because of her
willingness to study often,
anywhere she could—school
130 hallways, libraries, stairwells
in apartment buildings—she
did it.

During this time, she was
still homeless, sleeping out
135 on the streets sometimes
and working at odd jobs to
earn money. At school, her
teachers encouraged her.
She began to believe in
140 herself, but she never let
anyone know how she was
living. Then, something
happened that set the course
of her life. **6**

145 A teacher chose her and a
few other students to visit
Boston, Massachusetts. While
there, she visited Harvard
University, a respected Ivy
150 League university known for
academic excellence. As she
stood gazing at the campus,
her teacher told her that it
was possible for her to go
155 to school at Harvard, and
she believed him. Liz would
later write in her memoir,
Breaking Night, that it was
a good thing he didn't tell
160 her how hard it was to get
accepted to this university.
Then, she heard about a *New
York Times* scholarship for
needy students and **applied**
165 for it. Applicants had to
write an essay describing any
hardships they had overcome
to achieve academic success.
Liz was one of six students
170 who received the scholarship.
She applied and was accepted
to Harvard. **7**

Liz enrolled at Harvard in the fall of 2000 and completed several semesters of academic study. Then, in 2003, her father became sick with AIDS, and she returned to New York to take care of him. **8**

A New Direction

Despite what appeared to be a setback in New York, Liz continued her education at Columbia University. The unexpected changes in her life also brought many exciting **opportunities**. The *New York Times* published a story about her scholarship, then the television show "20/20" told her story, and Oprah Winfrey interviewed her. Also in 2003, a television movie was made about her life. **9**

Liz's father died in 2006, having finally overcome his drug addiction. Liz returned to Harvard in May 2008 to complete her degree. She realized that her story might have the power to help others. But, even better, her experiences and her knowledge might allow her to create **strategies** to help people cope with hardships. People might use these ways to move beyond their hardships to a meaningful life. **10**

Today, Liz has a company. Through workshops, she **lectures** to groups throughout the country, encouraging others to rise to their own dreams. Her sister also graduated from college and is a teacher. Whatever their dreams are, whatever background they come from, however hard they need to work, Liz Murray gives people **inspiration** to change their lives. **11**

NEW YORK TIMES BESTSELLER

"A white-knuckle account of survival... full of heart and deeply moving"
—THE NEW YORK TIMES BOOK REVIEW (EDITORS' CHOICE)

Breaking Night

A Memoir of Forgiveness, Survival, and My Journey from Homeless to Harvard

LIZ MURRAY

Murray's memoir was published in 2010.

opportunity
a chance to do something you want to do

strategy
a plan for doing something over time

lecture
to give an organized talk in public

inspiration
energy to do something new or creative

8 Why did Liz have to leave Harvard?

9 Why did Liz become a subject of the media?

10 What did Liz's father do before he died that would have made Liz proud?

11 Why do you think Liz is interested in helping others?

The Symbol of Freedom

Nelson Mandela's lifelong fight for the cause of
freedom in South Africa is a tale of inspiration and
determination; it is a tale of struggle. During his
27 years in prison, he became a powerful symbol
5 of resistance to the racial **discrimination** that has
plagued South Africa, and he emerged as the first
black president of South Africa in 1994. **1**

South Africa's landscape and environment have been
described as the most enticing in the world. South
10 Africa has a mild climate, similar to that of the
San Francisco Bay. The land is fertile with plentiful
mineral **resources**. In fact, South African mines are
world leaders in the production of diamonds, gold,
and platinum. These qualities combined to make
15 South Africa attractive to European powers in the
17th, 18th, and 19th centuries.

South Africa had much to offer European powers
looking for natural resources and economic gain.
The land was colonized by the Dutch in the 1600s.
20 During the following century, England became
interested in the land and eventually defeated the
Dutch. South Africa remained a colony of England
until 1961. **2**

discrimination

the act of treating
some people worse
than others for
unfair reasons

resources

things that can
be sold to create
wealth

1 Nelson Mandela
was South
Africa's first
what?

2 Who ruled
South Africa
until 1961?

invent

to make up or think of

access

to find a way into; to gain entry to

impose

to force upon; to burden with

3 What were apartheid laws designed to do?

4 What happened to people who protested apartheid laws?

Apartheid

25 The political parties in control of the country consisted primarily of white men of European ancestry. These groups **invented** apartheid as a means to control the 30 economy and the people. *Apartheid* is a Dutch word that means "separateness." Apartheid laws were aimed to keep the white, European 35 minority in power. The laws discriminated against the black people of African ancestry, who made up more than 70 percent of the nation's 40 population, as well as people of mixed race and Asian descent. **3**

These laws touched every aspect of social life. 45 Nonwhites could not go to white schools or hospitals or visit white beaches. They could not vote and were segregated from many jobs. 50 To **access** designated white areas, all black Africans were required to carry "pass books" containing fingerprints, a photo, and 55 personal information. Black Africans were forced to live in specific areas on the outskirts of South Africa and needed passports to enter the 60 rest of the country. They were treated as visiting foreigners in their own country.

The penalties **imposed** on those who protested 65 against the discrimination were severe. Thousands of individuals were tortured and killed. Those who were tried in court were typically 70 sentenced to death, exile, or life in prison—like Nelson Mandela. **4**

Apartheid and the People of South Africa		
	Blacks	**Whites**
Population	19 million	4.5 million
Land allocation	13%	87%
Annual expenditures on education per pupil	$45	$696
Teacher/pupil ratio	1/60	1/22

Disproportionate Treatment circa 1978. Source: Moraine Park Technical College

Apartheid sign in English and Afrikaans; South African pass book

Mandela burning his pass book

A Means to an End

When Mandela was 12 years old, his father died of lung disease, causing his life to abruptly change. He was adopted by a tribal chief. He lived in a palace and learned African history from elder chiefs who visited. He learned how the African people had lived in relative peace until the coming of the Europeans. According to the elders, the people of South Africa had lived as brothers, but the white man shattered this fellowship. While the black man shared his land, air, and water with the white man, the white man took all of these things for himself.

At age 16, Mandela heard a tribal leader speak with great sadness about the future of young men in South Africa. The tribal leader explained that because the land was controlled by white men, the young black men would struggle to earn a living and never have the power to **govern** themselves. This speech profoundly **impacted** Mandela and set the course for his life of activism.

After years of performing well at various schools, Mandela enrolled in law school, where he met people of all races and backgrounds. He was exposed to liberal and Africanist thought in addition to racism and discrimination. This experience served to further fuel his passion for politics. In 1944, he joined the African National Congress to become a voice for those who didn't have one. **5**

Mandela Challenges the Apartheid Government

As more and more laws were passed to limit the progress of black South Africans, the ANC staged a campaign against apartheid laws that was structured around the theory of **passive** resistance. Mandela opened a law practice and campaigned against apartheid. Soon after, Mandela was charged with high treason, but the charges were eventually dropped. Mandela continued his important mission. The resistance to apartheid grew stronger, as did the commitment by the government to maintain white rule.

Tension with the government continued to grow. It peaked in 1960 when 69 black people were shot dead by police. The government declared a state of emergency and banned the ANC. In response, the ANC abandoned its policy of non-violence, and Mandela helped lead the armed struggle for freedom. **6**

govern
to rule; to direct

impact
to have an effect on

passive
not taking action; letting something happen to you

5 What organization did Mandela join? What kind of organization was this?

Top: *Entrance to the high-security prison at Robben Island, South Africa, now a national and World Heritage Site*

Bottom: *The inside of Mandela's prison cell as it was when he was imprisoned in 1964*

6 What policy did the ANC abandon in 1960? Why?

harmony

friendly agreement;
the working
together of all parts

transform

to change into
something new

7 For what ideal
was Mandela
prepared to die?
What was his
actual sentence?

8 What landmark
event took place
in South Africa
in 1994?

9 Mandela was
the symbol of
what?

Imprisonment

After playing a minor role in
a workers' strike and illegally
155 leaving the country in 1961,
Mandela began a five-year
prison sentence. During
that time, Mandela and
other members of the ANC
160 were tried for plotting to
overthrow the government by
violence. Mandela defended
himself during his trial with
words about democracy,
165 freedom, and equality. "I
have cherished the ideal of a
democratic and free society
in which all persons live
together in **harmony** and
170 with equal opportunities,"
he said. "It is an ideal for
which I hope to live and to
see realized. But if needs be,
it is an ideal for which I am
175 prepared to die." The verdict
was life in prison. **7**

Apartheid Ends

Mandela's fight did not end.
During his years in prison,
he became an international
180 symbol of resistance to
apartheid. In 1990, the
South African government
responded to international
pressure and released
185 Mandela. Talks of
transforming the old-style
government of South Africa to
a new multiracial democracy
began. In 1994, for the first
190 time in South Africa's history,
all races voted in democratic
elections, and Mandela was
elected president. **8**

Nelson Mandela struggled
195 to end apartheid in South
Africa. He led the charge,
became the face of resistance,
and shared the hopes and
dreams of many; he was the
200 symbol of freedom. Jailed
for 27 years, he emerged to
become the country's first
black president and play a
leading role in the drive for
205 human rights across the
world. **9**

Mandela supporters await the verdict at the Rivonia Trial.

I Am Prepared to Die

An abridged version of Nelson Mandela's speech "I Am Prepared to Die," April 20, 1964, from the opening of the Rivonia Trial

I am the first accused. I am a convicted prisoner
5 serving five years for leaving the country without a
permit and for inciting people to go on strike at the
end of May 1961.

At the outset, I want to say that the suggestion that
the struggle in South Africa is under the influence
10 of foreigners or communists is wholly incorrect. I
have done whatever I did because of my experience
in South Africa and my own proudly felt African
background.

contribution
something given in support of an effort or cause

exploitation
the act of using someone for your own selfish gain

defy
to boldly resist; to challenge

In my youth, I listened to the elders of my tribe telling stories of wars fought by our ancestors in defense of the fatherland. I hoped then that life might offer me the opportunity to serve my people and make my own humble **contribution** to their freedom struggle.

Some of the things so far told to the court are true and some are untrue. I do not, however, deny that I planned sabotage. I did not plan it in a spirit of recklessness, nor because I love violence. I planned it as a result of a calm assessment of the political situation that had arisen after many years of tyranny, **exploitation**, and oppression of my people by the whites.

I admit that I was one of the persons who helped to form Umkhonto we Sizwe. I deny that Umkhonto was responsible for a number of acts which have been charged in the indictment against us. We felt that without sabotage there would be no way open to the African people to succeed in their struggle against white supremacy. All lawful modes of expressing opposition had been closed by legislation, and we were placed in a position in which we had either to accept permanent inferiority or to **defy** the government. We chose to defy the government. **1**

1 What does Mandela admit he helped to plan? What reasons does he give for this?

We first broke the law in a way which avoided violence; when this form was legislated against, and the government resorted to a show of force to crush opposition, only then did we decide to answer violence with violence. But the violence we chose was not terrorism. We who formed Umkhonto were all members of the African National Congress and had behind us the ANC tradition of non-violence.

The African National Congress was formed in 1912 to defend the rights of the African people, which had been seriously curtailed. For 37 years—that is, until 1949—it adhered strictly to a constitutional struggle. It put forward demands and resolutions;

it sent delegations to the government in the belief that African grievances could be settled through peaceful discussion. But white governments
55 remained unmoved, and the rights of Africans became less instead of becoming greater.

suspend
to put off or do away with

policy
a rule; a way of doing things

The founding members of the ANC, originally known as the South African Native National Congress (SANNC)

Even after 1949, the ANC remained determined to avoid violence. At this time, however, a decision was taken to protest against apartheid by peaceful, but
60 unlawful, demonstrations. More than 8,500 people went to jail. Yet there was not a single instance of violence. I and nineteen colleagues were convicted, but our sentences were **suspended** mainly because the judge found that discipline and non-violence
65 had been stressed throughout. **2**

2 The ANC was determined not to use what?

During the defiance campaign, the Public Safety Act and the Criminal Law Amendment Act were passed. These provided harsher penalties for offenses against the laws. Despite this, the protests
70 continued and the ANC adhered to its **policy** of non-violence.

In 1956, 156 leading members of the Congress Alliance, including myself, were arrested. When the court gave judgment some five years later, it found
75 that the ANC did not have a policy of violence. We were acquitted.

massive

huge; on a very large scale

In 1960, there was the shooting at Sharpeville, which resulted in the declaration of the ANC as unlawful.* My colleagues and I, after careful
80 consideration, decided that we would not obey this decree. The African people were not part of the government and did not make the laws by which they were governed. We believed the words of the Universal Declaration of Human Rights, that "the
85 will of the people shall be the basis of authority of the government." The ANC refused to dissolve but instead went underground. **3**

3 What did the government declare the ANC to be? How did the ANC respond?

The government held a referendum which led to the establishment of the republic. Africans, who
90 constituted approximately 70% of the population, were not entitled to vote. I undertook to be responsible for organizing the national stay-at-home called to coincide with the declaration of the republic. The stay-at-home was to be a peaceful
95 demonstration. Careful instructions were given to avoid any recourse to violence.

The government's answer was to introduce new and harsher laws, to mobilize its armed forces, and to send armed vehicles into the townships in a
100 **massive** show of force. The government had decided to rule by force alone, and this decision was a milestone on the road to Umkhonto. **4**

4 What was the government's answer to the stay-at-home strike organized by Mandela?

What were we, the leaders of our people, to do? We had to continue the fight. Anything else would have
105 been surrender. Our problem was not whether to fight, but was how to continue the fight.

By this time, violence had become a feature of the South African political scene. There had been violence in 1957 when the women of Zeerust
110 were ordered to carry passes; there was violence in 1958 with the enforcement of cattle culling in Sekhukhuneland; there was violence in 1959 when the people of Cato Manor protested against pass raids; there was violence in 1960 when the
115 government attempted to impose Bantu authorities in Pondoland. Each disturbance pointed to the growth among Africans of the belief that violence

Protesters run for safety after police open fire in the Sharpeville Massacre.

was the only way out. A government which uses
force to maintain its rule teaches the oppressed to
120 use force to oppose it.

I came to the conclusion that as violence was
inevitable, it would be unrealistic to continue
preaching peace and non-violence. This conclusion
was not easily arrived at. It was only when all
125 channels of peaceful protest had been barred that
the decision was made to embark on violent forms
of struggle. I can only say that I felt morally obliged
to do what I did. **5**

Four forms of violence are possible. There is
130 sabotage, there is guerrilla warfare, there is
terrorism, and there is open revolution. We chose to
adopt the first. Sabotage did not involve loss of life,
and it offered the best hope for future race relations.

5 Why did
Mandela stop
preaching peace
and non-
violence?

prospect

a possibility that something will happen soon

6 Why did the ANC decide that sabotage was the form of violence they should use?

7 What seemed inevitable, or likely to happen? How did Mandela's group prepare for this?

135 The initial plan was based on a careful analysis of the political and economic situation of our country. We believed that South Africa depended to a large extent on foreign capital. We felt that planned destruction of power plants, and interference with rail and telephone communications, would scare
140 away capital from the country, thus compelling the voters of the country to reconsider their position. The selection of targets is proof of this policy. Had we intended to attack life, we would have selected targets where people congregated and not empty
145 buildings and power stations. **6**

The whites failed to respond by suggesting change; they responded to our call by suggesting the laager. In contrast, the response of the Africans was one of encouragement. Suddenly, there was hope again.
150 People began to speculate on how soon freedom would be obtained.

But we in Umkhonto weighed the white response with anxiety. The lines were being drawn. The whites and blacks were moving into separate camps,
155 and the **prospect**s of avoiding a civil war were made less. The white newspapers carried reports that sabotage would be punished by death.

We felt it our duty to make preparations to use force in order to defend ourselves against force.
160 We decided, therefore, to make provision for the possibility of guerrilla warfare. All whites undergo compulsory military training, but no such training was given to Africans. It was in our view essential to build up a nucleus of trained men who would be
165 able to provide the leadership if guerrilla warfare started. **7**

At this stage, the ANC decided that I should attend the Conference of the Pan-African Freedom Movement, which was to be held 1962. After the
170 conference, I would take a tour of the African states with a view to whether facilities were available for the training of soldiers. My tour was successful.

Wherever I went, I met sympathy for our cause and promises of help. All Africa was united against the
175 stand of white South Africa.

I started to make a study of the art of war and revolution and, while abroad, underwent a course in military training. If there was to be guerrilla warfare, I wanted to be able to fight with my people. On my
180 return, I found that there had been little alteration in the political scene save that the threat of a death penalty for sabotage had now become a fact. **8**

Another of the allegations made by the state is that the aims and objects of the ANC and the
185 Communist Party are the same. The allegation is false. The creed of the ANC is, and always has been, the creed of freedom and fulfillment for the African people in their own land. The most important document ever adopted by the ANC is
190 the Freedom Charter. It is by no means a blueprint for a socialist state. It calls for redistribution, but not nationalization, of land; it provides for nationalization of mines, banks, and monopoly industry because big monopolies are owned by
195 one race only, and without such nationalization, racial domination would be perpetuated. Under the Freedom Charter, nationalization would take place in an economy based on private enterprise. The realization of the Freedom Charter would open up
200 fresh fields for a prosperous African population.

As far as the Communist Party is concerned, and if I understand its policy correctly, it stands for the establishment of a state based on the principles of Marxism. The Communist Party's main aim was to
205 remove the capitalists and to replace them with a working-class government. The Communist Party sought to emphasize class distinctions, while the ANC seeks to harmonize them. This is a vital distinction. **9**

8 What did Mandela learn during his tour of the African states? What did he learn on his return home?

9 How is the ANC different from the Communist Party? (Remember, *harmony* means "all parts working together".)

The ANC Freedom Charter of 1955 laid the groundwork for change.

— 60 —

legacy

something passed down from earlier people or times

During my lifetime
this struggle of the Afri...
against White domination,
Black domination.   I have
democratic and free soci...
together in harmony and wi...
is an ideal which I hope ...
But if needs be, it is an
pared to die.

10 Why did the ANC choose to work with the Communist Party? Give two reasons.

Certainty of
unpredictable
consistently
freedom
political
Amandla
Mul...

11 Why do Mandela and his colleagues think some form of socialism— redistribution of wealth—is needed?

210 It is true that there has often been close cooperation between the ANC and the Communist Party. But cooperation is merely proof of a common goal—in this case, the removal of white supremacy—and is not proof of a complete community of interests.

215 The history of the world is full of similar examples. Perhaps the most striking is the cooperation between Great Britain, the United States, and the Soviet Union in the fight against Hitler. Nobody but Hitler would have dared to suggest that such cooperation

220 turned Churchill or Roosevelt into communists.

What is more, for many decades communists were the only political group in South Africa prepared to treat Africans as human beings and their equals; who were prepared to eat with us, talk with us, and

225 work with us. They were the only group prepared to work with the Africans for the attainment of political rights. **10**

Because of this, many Africans today tend to equate freedom with communism. They are supported

230 in this belief by a legislature which brands all exponents of democratic government and African freedom as communists and banned many of them under the Suppression of Communism Act. Although I have never been a member of the

235 Communist Party, I myself have been convicted under that act.

I have always regarded myself, in the first place, as an African patriot. Today, I am attracted by the idea of a classless society, an attraction which springs

240 in part from my admiration of the structure of early African societies. The land belonged to the tribe. There were no rich or poor, and there was no exploitation.

I and many leaders of the new independent states

245 accept the need for some form of socialism to enable our people to catch up with the advanced countries of this world and to overcome their **legacy** of extreme poverty. But this does not mean we are Marxists. **11**

250 Our fight is against real and not imaginary
hardships or, to use the language of the state
prosecutor, "so-called hardships." Basically, we fight
against two features of African life in South Africa:
poverty and lack of human dignity. We do not need
255 communists to teach us about these things.

South Africa is the richest country in Africa. But it
is a land of remarkable contrasts. The whites enjoy
the highest standard of living, while Africans live
in poverty and misery. The complaint of Africans,
260 however, is not only that they are poor and the
whites are rich, but that the laws are designed to
preserve this situation. **12**

There are two ways to break out of poverty. The
first is by formal education, and the second is by the
265 worker acquiring a greater skill at his work and thus
higher wages. As far as Africans are concerned,
both these avenues of advancement are deliberately
curtailed by legislation.

The government has always sought to **hamper**
270 Africans in their search for education. There is
compulsory education for all white children at
virtually no cost to their parents. But approximately
40% of African children between seven and fourteen
do not attend school. For those who do, the
275 standards are vastly different from those afforded
to white children.

The other main obstacle to the advancement of the
African is the industrial color bar under which all
the better jobs of industry are reserved for whites.
280 Moreover, Africans in the unskilled and semi-
skilled occupations are not allowed to form trade
unions. This means that they are denied the right of
collective bargaining permitted to white workers. **13**

hamper
to make it hard for someone to do something

12 What is the main complaint of black Africans?

"There are two ways to break out of poverty. The first is by formal education, and the second is by the worker acquiring a greater skill at his work and thus higher wages."

13 How does the African government hamper blacks' opportunities for advancement?

– 60 –

irrelevant

unrelated; beside
the point

During my lifetime

this struggle of the African

against White domination,

Black domination.   I have

democratic and free societ

together in harmony and wi

is an ideal which I hope

But if needs be, it is a

pared to die.

285 The government answers its critics by saying
that Africans in South Africa are better off than
inhabitants of other countries in Africa. Even if this
statement is true, it is **irrelevant**. Our complaint is
not that we are poor by comparison with people in
other countries, but that we are poor by comparison
290 with the white people in our own country, and that
we are prevented by legislation from altering this
imbalance.

The lack of human dignity experienced by Africans
is the direct result of the policy of white supremacy.
295 White supremacy implies black inferiority.
Legislation designed to preserve white supremacy
entrenches this notion. Menial tasks in South
Africa are invariably performed by Africans. When
anything has to be carried or cleaned, the white
300 man will look around for an African to do it for him.
Because of this sort of attitude, whites tend to regard
Africans as a separate breed. They do not look upon
them as people with families of their own; they do
not realize that we fall in love, that we want to be
305 with our wives and children, that we want to earn
enough money to support our families properly. **14**

14 How do whites
view black
Africans? Why?

Poverty and the breakdown of family have
secondary effects. Children wander the streets
because they have no schools to go to, or no
310 parents at home to see that they go, because both
parents, if there be two, have to work to keep the
family alive. This leads to a breakdown in moral
standards, to an alarming rise in illegitimacy, and
to violence. Not a day goes by without somebody
315 being stabbed or assaulted. And violence is carried
out of the townships into the white living areas.
People are afraid to walk the streets after dark.
Housebreakings and robberies are increasing,
despite the fact that the death sentence can now be
320 imposed for such offences. Death sentences cannot
cure the festering sore. **15**

15 What are some
secondary
effects of
poverty?

The only cure is to alter the conditions under which
Africans are forced to live. Africans want to be paid
a living wage. Africans want to perform work which
325 they are capable of doing. We want to be allowed

to own land. We want to be part of the general population and not confined to ghettoes. We want to be allowed out after eleven o'clock at night and not to be confined to our rooms like children. We
330 want to be allowed to travel in our own country. We want security and a stake in society.

Above all, we want equal political rights because without them, our disabilities will be permanent. I know this sounds revolutionary to the whites in
335 this country because the majority of voters will be Africans. This makes the white man fear democracy.

Nelson Mandela addresses the All in Africa Conference in Pietermaritzburg, 1961.

But this fear cannot be allowed to stand in the way of the only solution which will guarantee racial harmony and freedom for all. It is not true
340 that the enfranchisement of all will result in racial domination. Political division, based on color, is entirely artificial. When it disappears, so will the domination of one color group by another. The ANC has spent half a century fighting against racialism.
345 When it triumphs, it will not change that policy. **16**

16 What do black South Africans want, above all? Why do white South Africans fear this?

- 60 -

Our struggle is a national one. It is a struggle of the African people, inspired by our own suffering and our own experience. It is a struggle for the right to live. During my lifetime, I have dedicated 350 myself to this struggle. I have fought against white domination, and I have fought against black domination. I have cherished the ideal of a democratic and free society in which all persons live together in harmony and with equal opportunities. 355 It is an ideal for which I hope to live and to see realized. But if needs be, it is an ideal for which I am prepared to die. **17**

17 For what is Nelson Mandela prepared to die?

> **"Your long walk to freedom has ended in a physical sense. Our own journey continues. We have to continue working to build the kind of society you worked tirelessly to construct."**
>
> **Jacob Zuma, South African President at Mandela's funeral**

Madiba (Nelson Mandela's clan name) died at his home in Johannesburg on December 5, 2013. Representatives from all over the world gathered to celebrate his life and legacy.

Unit 1

Word	Meaning

Unit 2

Word	Meaning

Unit 3

Word	Meaning

Unit 4

Word	Meaning

Unit 5

Word	Meaning

Unit 6

Word	Meaning

Six Traits of Writing: Basic

	Ideas and Development	Organization	Voice and Audience Awareness	Word Choice	Sentence Fluency	Language Conventions
4	Focuses on the topic. Main idea (topic sentence) is clear and well supported with details and elaboration (examples, evidence, and explanations).	Topic sentence clearly states main idea. Ideas are clear and logically organized. Contains concluding sentence.	The words have a strong sense of person and purpose. Brings topic to life.	Words are specific to the content, accurate, and vivid. Word choice enhances meaning and the reader's enjoyment.	Writes complete sentences and varies sentence structure.	There are no grammar errors. There are few or no errors in spelling, capitalization, or punctuation.
3	Mostly focuses on the topic. Sentences supporting the main idea (topic sentence) may be general rather than detailed and specific.	Topic sentence states main idea. Organization mostly clear and logical. May contain concluding sentence.	The words have some sense of person and purpose.	Words are correctly used but may be somewhat general and unspecific.	Writes complete sentences and attempts to use expanded sentences.	There are no major grammar errors. There are few errors in spelling, capitalization, or punctuation.
2	Main idea (topic sentence) is unclear and/or lacks sufficient support.	Structure may not be entirely clear or logical. Paragraph may seem more like a list and/or be hard to follow.	The words have little sense of person and purpose.	Words may be used inaccurately or repetitively.	Writes mostly simple and/or awkwardly constructed sentences. May include some run-ons and fragments.	There are a few grammar errors. There are a few errors in spelling, capitalization, or punctuation.
1	Does not address prompt and/or lacks a topic sentence. Supporting details are absent or do not relate to topic.	No evident structure. Lack of organization seriously interferes with meaning.	The words have no sense of person or purpose. No sense of audience.	Extremely limited range of words. Restricted vocabulary impedes message.	Numerous run-ons and/or fragments interfere with meaning.	There are many grammar and/or spelling errors. There are many errors in capitalization and punctuation.

Six Traits of Writing: Expository

	Ideas and Development	Organization	Voice and Audience Awareness	Word Choice	Sentence Fluency	Language Conventions
4	The thesis is very clear and well focused. Supporting details make the paper very easy to understand and interesting.	Ideas are very clearly organized. All parts of the essay (introduction, the body, and conclusion) work together to support the thesis.	The writer's voice is distinctive and very well chosen. They create pictures in the reader's mind.	Words are used correctly and are very well chosen. They create pictures in the reader's mind.	Sentences have an easy flow and rhythm. Transitions are very smooth.	There are no grammar errors. There are few or no errors in spelling, capitalization, or punctuation.
3	The thesis is clear. Supporting details make the paper easy to understand.	Ideas are clearly organized. The paper includes all parts of an essay (introduction, body, and conclusion).	The writer's voice is natural and shows an interest in the topic. The writer knows who his or her audience is.	Words are used correctly. Some words may be a bit general.	Sentences are formed correctly and are varied in structure. Transitions are clear.	There are no major grammar errors. There are few errors in spelling, capitalization, or punctuation.
2	The thesis is not clear. The ideas are somewhat developed, but there are only a few details.	Ideas are fairly well organized. The paper includes all parts of an essay (introduction, body, and conclusion), may be vague.	The writer's voice is natural, but the writer is not fully engaged in the topic. At times, the writer's viewpoint may be vague.	Words are used correctly. A few words are too general. Some words are repeated.	Sentences are formed correctly, although they may be similar in structure. Most transitions are clear.	There are a few grammar errors. There are a few errors in spelling, capitalization, or punctuation.
1	The thesis of the paper is unclear or missing. The paper is poorly developed and/or confusing.	Ideas are not clearly organized. The paper may be missing an introduction or a conclusion.	The writer seems uninterested in the topic and unaware of his or her audience.	Most words are used incorrectly, or many are too general or frequently repeated.	The sentences do not flow well and lack structure. They are short and choppy or long and confusing.	There are many grammar and/or spelling errors. There are many errors in capitalization and punctuation.

Six Traits of Writing: Fiction

	Ideas and Development	Organization	Voice and Audience Awareness	Word Choice	Sentence Fluency	Language Conventions
4	Clear plot events, as well as a readily identifiable conflict/problem and setting. The climax and resolution are clear. Rich details and sensory description make characters come to life. No irrelevant material.	Beginning grabs reader's attention. Logically sequenced plot. Story transitions link events. Conclusion caps off story and does not leave the reader hanging.	Strong sense of person and purpose behind the words. Brings story to life.	Words are specific, accurate, and vivid. Word choice enhances meaning and reader's enjoyment.	Writes complete sentences with varied sentence patterns and beginnings.	There are no major grammar errors. There are few errors in spelling, capitalization, or punctuation.
3	Identifiable plot events. Conflict/problem may not be entirely clear. The climax or resolution may not be clear. Some details/sensory description. Characters present but may not be fully developed. Setting may be missing. Limited irrelevant material.	Beginning interests reader. Plot somewhat logically sequenced but may lack one story element such as climax or satisfying conclusion. Story transitions link some events.	Some sense of person and purpose behind the words.	Words are correctly used but may be somewhat general and unspecific.	Writes complete sentences with some expansion. Limited variety.	There are a few grammar errors. There are a few errors in spelling, capitalization, or punctuation.
2	Limited plot and/or the conflict/problem is not clear. The setting, climax, and/or resolution may not be apparent. There are insufficient details and description. Characterization is weak. Too repetitious or too much irrelevant material.	Beginning does not capture reader's interest. Plot underdeveloped and two or more story elements (setting, initiating event, climax, resolution) missing. Story transitions missing.	Little sense of person and purpose behind the words.	Word choice limited. Words may be used inaccurately or repetitively.	Writes mostly simple and/or awkwardly constructed sentences. May include some run-ons and fragments.	There are many grammar or spelling errors. There are quite a few errors in capitalization and punctuation.
1	Does not address the prompt or the plot, conflict/problem are not discernible. Description, details, and characterization are missing.	Text has no evident structure. Lack of organization seriously interferes with meaning.	No sense of person or purpose behind the words.	Extremely limited range of words. Restricted vocabulary impedes message.	Numerous run-ons and/or sentence fragments interfere with meaning.	There are many spelling and grammar errors. There are many errors in capitalization and punctuation.

Six Traits of Writing: Persuasion

	Ideas and Development	Organization	Voice and Audience Awareness	Word Choice	Sentence Fluency	Language Conventions
4	Clearly states a position on the issue. Fully develops main ideas with evidence, examples, and explanations that are compelling. No irrelevant information.	Introduction clearly states position. Ideas logically sequenced. Transition sentences link ideas. Conclusion ties essay together and gives reader something to think about. Follows required format.	Strong sense of person and purpose behind the words. Brings issue to life.	Words are specific, accurate, and vivid. Word choice enhances meaning and reader's enjoyment.	Writes complete sentences with varied sentence patterns and beginnings.	There are no major grammar errors. There are few errors in spelling, capitalization, or punctuation.
3	States a position on the issue. Develops main ideas adequately with some evidence, examples, and explanations. Limited required format.	Introduction states position. Ideas mostly logically sequenced. Some linkage among ideas. Conclusion ties essay together. Follows required format.	Some sense of person and purpose behind the words. Sense of commitment to the issue. Text may be too casual for the purpose.	Words are correctly used with some expansion. Limited variety.	Writes complete sentences with some errors in spelling, capitalization, or punctuation.	There are a few grammar errors. There are a few errors in spelling, capitalization and punctuation.
2	Does not state a clear position on the issue and/or does not support main ideas with sufficient evidence, examples, and explanations. May be too repetitious or too much irrelevant information.	Introduction may not state a position. Ideas not logically sequenced. Transition sentences missing. Conclusion may be missing. Does not follow required format.	Little sense of person and purpose behind the words. Very little engagement with reader. Text may be too casual for the purpose.	Word choice limited. Words may be used inaccurately or repetitively.	Writes mostly simple and/or awkwardly constructed sentences. May include some run-ons and fragments.	There are many grammar or spelling errors. There are quite a few errors in capitalization and punctuation.
1	Does not address the prompt or does not develop a position. Elaboration lacking or unrelated to the issue.	Text has no evident structure. Lack of organization seriously interferes with meaning.	No sense of person or purpose behind the words. No sense of audience.	Extremely limited range of words. Restricted vocabulary impedes message.	Numerous run-ons and/or sentence fragments interfere with meaning.	There are many spelling and grammar errors. There are many errors in capitalization and punctuation.

Six Traits of Writing: Literary Analysis

	Ideas and Development	Organization	Voice and Audience Awareness	Word Choice	Sentence Fluency	Language Conventions
4	States thesis clearly. Develops main ideas fully with elaborations. Direct quotations from text support ideas. All information pertinent to thesis.	Introduction contains thesis statement and cites title, author of work. Ideas logically sequenced. Transition sentences link ideas. Conclusion offers some evaluation of the work.	Strong sense of person and purpose behind the words. Brings topic to life.	Words are specific, accurate, and vivid. Word choice enhances meaning and reader's enjoyment.	Writes complete sentences with varied sentence patterns and beginnings.	There are no major grammar errors. There are few errors in spelling, capitalization, or punctuation.
3	States thesis clearly. Develops main ideas with some elaboration. May lack direct quotations from text to support ideas. Limited amount of irrelevant information.	Introduction contains thesis statement and cites title, author of work. Ideas mostly logically sequenced. Some linkage of main ideas. Formulaic conclusion may not offer evaluation of the work.	Some sense of person and purpose behind the words. Sense of commitment to the topic. Text may be too casual for purpose.	Words are correctly used but may be somewhat general and unspecific.	Writes complete sentences with some expansion. Limited variety.	There are a few grammar errors. There are a few errors in spelling, capitalization, or punctuation.
2	Does not state thesis clearly and/or minimal development of main ideas. No direct quotations to support ideas. Too repetitious or too much irrelevant information.	Introduction may not have clear thesis. Ideas not logically sequenced. Transitions may be missing. May lack conclusion, or conclusion is formulaic with no evaluation of the work.	Little sense of person and purpose behind the words. Very little engagement with the reader. Text may be too casual for purpose.	Word choice limited. Words may be used inaccurately or repetitively.	Writes mostly simple and/or awkwardly constructed sentences. May include some run-ons and fragments.	There are many grammar or spelling errors. There are quite a few errors in capitalization and punctuation.
1	Does not address the prompt or does not develop a thesis. Elaboration lacking or unrelated to a thesis.	No evident structure. Lack of organization seriously interferes with meaning.	No sense of person or purpose behind the words. No sense of audience.	Extremely limited range of words. Restricted vocabulary impedes message.	Numerous run-ons and/or sentence fragments interfere with meaning.	There are many spelling and grammar errors. There are many errors in capitalization and punctuation.

Copyright Acknowledgements

Holes
From HOLES © 1998 by Louis Sachar. Reprinted by permission of Farrar, Straus, and Giroux, LLC. All rights reserved.

"Thank You, M'am"
From SHORT STORIES by Langston Hughes. Copyright © 1996 by Ramona Bass and Arnold Rampersad. Reprinted by permission of Hill and Wang, a division of Farrar, Straus and Giroux, LLC.

"If I Were in Charge of The World"
Reprinted with the permission of Atheneum Books for Young Readers, an imprint of Simon & Schuster Children's Publishing Division from IF I WERE IN CHARGE OF THE WORLD AND OTHER WORRIES by Judith Viorst. Text copyright © 1981 Judith Viorst.

"We Real Cool"
From *Selected Poems*. Copyright © 1963 by Gwendolyn Brooks. Reprinted by consent of Brooks Permissions.

The Outsiders
From THE OUTSIDERS by S.E. Hinton, copyright © 1967 by S.E. Hinton. Used by permission of Viking Children's Books, a division of Penguin Group (USA) Inc.

From *The Play of The Diary of Anne Frank*
Copyright © 1956, renewed by Albert Hackett, David Huntoon & Frances Neuwirth in 1986. Used by permission of Flora Roberts, Inc.

The Diary of a Young Girl
From THE DIARY OF A YOUNG GIRL by Anne Frank with an Introduction by Eleanor Roosevelt. Copyright © 1967 by Doubleday, a division of Random House, Inc. Used by permission of Doubleday, a division of Random House, Inc. Any third party use of this material, outside of this publication, is prohibited. Interested parties must apply directly to Random House, Inc. for permission.

"The Circuit"
From *The Circuit: Stories from the Life of a Migrant Child* by Francisco Jiménez. © Francisco Jiménez. Reprinted by permission of the author.

From *The Autobiography of Malcolm X*
"Saved" from THE AUTOBIOGRAPHY OF MALCOLM X by Malcolm X as told to Alex Haley, copyright © 1964 by Alex Haley and Malcolm X. Copyright © 1965 by Alex Haley and Betty Shabazz. Used by permission of Random House, an imprint of The Random House Publishing Group, a division of Random House LLC. All rights reserved.

From *Breaking Night*
From *Breaking Night: A memoir of Forgiveness, Survival, and My Journey from Homeless to Harvard* by Liz Murray. Copyright © 2010 by Liz Murray. By permission of Hachette Book Group, Inc. All rights reserved.

"I Am Prepared to Die"
Abridged version of Nelson Mandela's Speech "An Ideal for Which I am Prepared to Die," April 20, 1964, from the dock at the opening of the Rivonia Trial.

Photo and Illustration Credits

1, 3–6: ©basictextures.com. 5: ©istockphoto.com/APCortizasJr. 6: (lizard) ©Clipart.com, (author) ©Matthew C. Wright. Jacket cover from HOLES © 1998 by Louis Sachar. Reprinted by permission of Farrar, Straus, and Giroux, LLC. All rights reserved. 17, 19: ©istockphoto.com/Nathan Fabro. 19: (helix) ©istockphoto.com/Luis M. Molina. (DNA) ©Wikimedia Commons/Public Domain/ParinoidMarvin. (kit) ©123rf.com/Dani Simmonds. 20: ©istockphoto.com/Ploter. 24: *top.* ©istockphoto.com/Elkor. *middle.* ©Wikimedia Commons/Public Domain/Cindamuse. *bottom.* ©istockphoto.com/Nancy Catherine Walker. 41: *top.* ©Associated Press. *bottom.* ©Public Domain/Griffith J. Davis. (map) ©Public Domain/Gaylord Watson, 1891. 57, 59: ©Masterfile. 61: ©AP Photo/Richard Drew. ©Associated Press. 74, 75, 79, 80, 81, 86 Licensed By: Warner Bros. Entertainment Inc. All Rights Reserved. 85: *top.* ©istockphoto.com/Aldo Murillo. *middle.* ©istockphoto.com/Aldo Murillo. *bottom.* ©istockphoto.com/mura. 99, 112: ©Dan Kacvinski/ The Jewish Journal. 101: (signature) ©Public Domain. (Anne) ©Getty/Anne Frank Fonds-Basel/Anne Frank House. 101–117: (diary detail and cover) Permission from the Anne Frank Museum. 102: ©Wikimedia Commons/Massimo Catarinella. 104: ©Wikimedia Commons/Bungle. 118: © Bettmann/CORBIS. (theatre) ©istockphoto.com/helenecanada. (scripts) ©istockphoto.com/DNY59. 145, 147–152: ©Dean Hollingsworth. 153: (cardboard) ©stock.xchng/renacuaje. (author as a boy) ©Copyright by Francisco Jiménez. Reproduced with author's permission. Jacket covers from *Breaking Through, Mas alla de mi,* and *The Circuit* by Francisco Jiménez. Copyright ©HMH Books for Young Readers. Reprinted by permission of Houghton Mifflin Harcourt Publishing Company. All rights reserved. 158: *left.* ©istockphoto.com/Robert Churchill. *middle.* ©istockphoto.com/4thegrapes. *right.* ©istockphoto.com/snapphoto. 167, 173: ©Jason Nahrung/Flickr (Creative Commons). 169: ©Associated Press. 171: ©cara.savelli@state.ma.us/Cara Savelli. 189, 210, 212, 214–215: ©istockphoto.com/meshaphoto. 193: (candy machine) ©istockphoto.com/slobo. (spider rings) ©istockphoto.com/sdominick. 194: ©Wikimedia Commons/Jim Henderson. 196: (ice cream truck) ©Wikimedia Commons/Rob Sinclair. (tv) ©istockphoto.com/wdstock. (fries) ©istockphoto.com/ vsurkov. 212: Permission granted from Duke University. 213: (mother) Courtesy of Liz Murray. (father) ©AP Photo/Bebeto Matthews. 215: Jacket cover from BREAKING NIGHT: A memoir of Forgiveness, Survival, and My Journey from Homeless to Harvard by Liz Murray. Copyright © 2010 by Liz Murray. By permission of Hachette Book Group, Inc. All rights reserved. 229, 231, 252: ©Wikimedia Commons/Htonl. 231: (flag) ©Wikimedia Commons/Public Domain. ©istockphoto.com/Georgia Court. ©Wikimedia Commons/jalo. ©istockphoto.com/stuz01. ©Wikimedia Commons/Public Domain. ©istockphoto.com/Joesboy. 232: (sign) ©Wikimedia Commons/Public Domain. (burning passbook) ©Eli Weinberg and Mayibuye Archive. 233: *top.* ©istockphoto.com/ BassanK. *bottom.* ©Wikimedia Commons/Witstinkhout. 234: ©Getty Images/Jurgen Schadeberg. 255: *top.* ©Bailey's African History Archives, Photograph by Alf Kumalo. (signature and young Mandela) ©Wikimedia Commons/Public Domain. 255–266: ©Jurgen Schadeberg. 259: ©Bailey's African History Archives, Photograph by Ian Berry. 265: ©Bailey's African History Archives, Photograph by Drum Photographer. 266: AP Photo/Bernat Armangue.